Natalya Ryabinska

UKRAINE'S POST-COMMUNIST MASS MEDIA

Between Capture and Commercialization

With a foreword by Marta Dyczok

ibidem-Verlag
Stuttgart

Bibliografische Information der Deutschen Nationalbibliothek
Die Deutsche Nationalbibliothek verzeichnet diese Publikation in der Deutschen Nationalbibliografie; detaillierte bibliografische Daten sind im Internet über http://dnb.d-nb.de abrufbar.

Bibliographic information published by the Deutsche Nationalbibliothek
Die Deutsche Nationalbibliothek lists this publication in the Deutsche Nationalbibliografie; detailed bibliographic data are available in the Internet at http://dnb.d-nb.de.

Cover picture: © Maryna Turowska, Cover of Ukrainian Week Magazine, 9 August 2012. Reprint with kind permission.

∞

Gedruckt auf alterungsbeständigem, säurefreien Papier
Printed on acid-free paper

ISSN: 1614-3515

ISBN-13: 978-3-8382-1011-7

© *ibidem*-Verlag
Stuttgart 2017

Alle Rechte vorbehalten

Das Werk einschließlich aller seiner Teile ist urheberrechtlich geschützt. Jede Verwertung außerhalb der engen Grenzen des Urheberrechtsgesetzes ist ohne Zustimmung des Verlages unzulässig und strafbar. Dies gilt insbesondere für Vervielfältigungen, Übersetzungen, Mikroverfilmungen und elektronische Speicherformen sowie die Einspeicherung und Verarbeitung in elektronischen Systemen.

All rights part of this publication may be reproduced, stored in or introduced into a retrieval system, or transmitted, in any form, or by any means (electronical, mechanical, photocopying, recording or otherwise) without the prior written permission of the publisher. Any person who does any unauthorized act in relation to this publication may be liable to criminal prosecution and civil claims for damages.

Printed in the EU

Soviet and Post-Soviet Politics and Society (SPPS) Vol. 162
ISSN 1614-3515

General Editor: Andreas Umland,
Institute for Euro-Atlantic Cooperation, Kyiv, umland@stanfordalumni.org

Commissioning Editor: Max Jakob Horstmann,
London, mjh@ibidem.eu

EDITORIAL COMMITTEE*

DOMESTIC & COMPARATIVE POLITICS
Prof. **Ellen Bos**, *Andrássy University of Budapest*
Dr. **Ingmar Bredies**, *FH Bund, Brühl*
Dr. **Andrey Kazantsev**, *MGIMO (U) MID RF, Moscow*
Prof. **Heiko Pleines**, *University of Bremen*
Prof. **Richard Sakwa**, *University of Kent at Canterbury*
Dr. **Sarah Whitmore**, *Oxford Brookes University*
Dr. **Harald Wydra**, *University of Cambridge*
SOCIETY, CLASS & ETHNICITY
Col. **David Glantz**, *"Journal of Slavic Military Studies"*
Dr. **Marlène Laruelle**, *George Washington University*
Dr. **Stephen Shulman**, *Southern Illinois University*
Prof. **Stefan Troebst**, *University of Leipzig*
POLITICAL ECONOMY & PUBLIC POLICY
Prof. em. **Marshall Goldman**, *Wellesley College, Mass.*
Dr. **Andreas Goldthau**, *Central European University*
Dr. **Robert Kravchuk**, *University of North Carolina*
Dr. **David Lane**, *University of Cambridge*
Dr. **Carol Leonard**, *Higher School of Economics, Moscow*
Dr. **Maria Popova**, *McGill University, Montreal*

FOREIGN POLICY & INTERNATIONAL AFFAIRS
Dr. **Peter Duncan**, *University College London*
Prof. **Andreas Heinemann-Grüder**, *University of Bonn*
Dr. **Taras Kuzio**, *Johns Hopkins University*
Prof. **Gerhard Mangott**, *University of Innsbruck*
Dr. **Diana Schmidt-Pfister**, *University of Konstanz*
Dr. **Lisbeth Tarlow**, *Harvard University, Cambridge*
Dr. **Christian Wipperfürth**, *N-Ost Network, Berlin*
Dr. **William Zimmerman**, *University of Michigan*
HISTORY, CULTURE & THOUGHT
Dr. **Catherine Andreyev**, *University of Oxford*
Prof. **Mark Bassin**, *Södertörn University*
Prof. **Karsten Brüggemann**, *Tallinn University*
Dr. **Alexander Etkind**, *University of Cambridge*
Dr. **Gasan Gusejnov**, *Moscow State University*
Prof. em. **Walter Laqueur**, *Georgetown University*
Prof. **Leonid Luks**, *Catholic University of Eichstaett*
Dr. **Olga Malinova**, *Russian Academy of Sciences*
Prof. **Andrei Rogatchevski**, *University of Tromsø*
Dr. **Mark Tauger**, *West Virginia University*

ADVISORY BOARD*

Prof. **Dominique Arel**, *University of Ottawa*
Prof. **Jörg Baberowski**, *Humboldt University of Berlin*
Prof. **Margarita Balmaceda**, *Seton Hall University*
Dr. **John Barber**, *University of Cambridge*
Prof. **Timm Beichelt**, *European University Viadrina*
Dr. **Katrin Boeckh**, *University of Munich*
Prof. em. **Archie Brown**, *University of Oxford*
Dr. **Vyacheslav Bryukhovetsky**, *Kyiv-Mohyla Academy*
Prof. **Timothy Colton**, *Harvard University, Cambridge*
Prof. **Paul D'Anieri**, *University of Florida*
Dr. **Heike Dörrenbächer**, *Friedrich Naumann Foundation*
Dr. **John Dunlop**, *Hoover Institution, Stanford, California*
Dr. **Sabine Fischer**, *SWP, Berlin*
Dr. **Geir Flikke**, *NUPI, Oslo*
Prof. **David Galbreath**, *University of Aberdeen*
Prof. **Alexander Galkin**, *Russian Academy of Sciences*
Prof. **Frank Golczewski**, *University of Hamburg*
Dr. **Nikolas Gvosdev**, *Naval War College, Newport, RI*
Prof. **Mark von Hagen**, *Arizona State University*
Dr. **Guido Hausmann**, *University of Munich*
Prof. **Dale Herspring**, *Kansas State University*
Dr. **Stefani Hoffman**, *Hebrew University of Jerusalem*
Prof. **Mikhail Ilyin**, *MGIMO (U) MID RF, Moscow*
Prof. **Vladimir Kantor**, *Higher School of Economics*
Dr. **Ivan Katchanovski**, *University of Ottawa*
Prof. em. **Andrzej Korbonski**, *University of California*
Dr. **Iris Kempe**, *"Caucasus Analytical Digest"*
Prof. **Herbert Küpper**, *Institut für Ostrecht Regensburg*
Dr. **Rainer Lindner**, *CEEER, Berlin*
Dr. **Vladimir Malakhov**, *Russian Academy of Sciences*

Dr. **Luke March**, *University of Edinburgh*
Prof. **Michael McFaul**, *Stanford University, Palo Alto*
Prof. **Birgit Menzel**, *University of Mainz-Germersheim*
Prof. **Valery Mikhailenko**, *The Urals State University*
Prof. **Emil Pain**, *Higher School of Economics, Moscow*
Dr. **Oleg Podvintsev**, *Russian Academy of Sciences*
Prof. **Olga Popova**, *St. Petersburg State University*
Dr. **Alex Pravda**, *University of Oxford*
Dr. **Erik van Ree**, *University of Amsterdam*
Dr. **Joachim Rogall**, *Robert Bosch Foundation Stuttgart*
Prof. **Peter Rutland**, *Wesleyan University, Middletown*
Prof. **Marat Salikov**, *The Urals State Law Academy*
Dr. **Gwendolyn Sasse**, *University of Oxford*
Prof. **Jutta Scherrer**, *EHESS, Paris*
Prof. **Robert Service**, *University of Oxford*
Mr. **James Sherr**, *RIIA Chatham House London*
Dr. **Oxana Shevel**, *Tufts University, Medford*
Prof. **Eberhard Schneider**, *University of Siegen*
Prof. **Olexander Shnyrkov**, *Shevchenko University, Kyiv*
Prof. **Hans-Henning Schröder**, *SWP, Berlin*
Prof. **Yuri Shapoval**, *Ukrainian Academy of Sciences*
Prof. **Viktor Shnirelman**, *Russian Academy of Sciences*
Dr. **Lisa Sundstrom**, *University of British Columbia*
Dr. **Philip Walters**, *"Religion, State and Society", Oxford*
Dr. **Zenon Wasyliw**, *Ithaca College, New York State*
Dr. **Lucan Way**, *University of Toronto*
Dr. **Markus Wehner**, *"Frankfurter Allgemeine Zeitung"*
Dr. **Andrew Wilson**, *University College London*
Prof. **Jan Zielonka**, *University of Oxford*
Prof. **Andrei Zorin**, *University of Oxford*

* While the Editorial Committee and Advisory Board support the General Editor in the choice and improvement of manuscripts for publication, responsibility for remaining errors and misinterpretations in the series' volumes lies with the books' authors.

Soviet and Post-Soviet Politics and Society (SPPS)
ISSN 1614-3515

Founded in 2004 and refereed since 2007, SPPS makes available affordable English-, German-, and Russian-language studies on the history of the countries of the former Soviet bloc from the late Tsarist period to today. It publishes between 5 and 20 volumes per year and focuses on issues in transitions to and from democracy such as economic crisis, identity formation, civil society development, and constitutional reform in CEE and the NIS. SPPS also aims to highlight so far understudied themes in East European studies such as right-wing radicalism, religious life, higher education, or human rights protection. The authors and titles of all previously published volumes are listed at the end of this book. For a full description of the series and reviews of its books, see

www.ibidem-verlag.de/red/spps.

Editorial correspondence & manuscripts should be sent to: Dr. Andreas Umland, c/o DAAD, German Embassy, vul. Bohdana Khmelnitskoho 25, UA-01901 Kyiv, Ukraine. e-mail: umland@stanfordalumni.org

Business correspondence & review copy requests should be sent to: *ibidem* Press, Leuschnerstr. 40, 30457 Hannover, Germany; tel.: +49 511 2622200; fax: +49 511 2622201; spps@ibidem.eu.

Authors, reviewers, referees, and editors for (as well as all other persons sympathetic to) SPPS are invited to join its networks at
www.facebook.com/group.php?gid=52638198614
www.linkedin.com/groups?about=&gid=103012
www.xing.com/net/spps-ibidem-verlag/

Recent Volumes

154 *Abel Polese*
Limits of a Post-Soviet State
How Informality Replaces, Renegotiates, and Reshapes Governance in Contemporary Ukraine
With a foreword by Colin Williams
ISBN 978-3-8382-0845-9

155 *Mikhail Suslov (ed.)*
Digital Orthodoxy in the Post-Soviet World
The Russian Orthodox Church and Web 2.0
With a foreword by Father Cyril Hovorum
ISBN 978-3-8382-0871-8

156 *Leonid Luks*
Zwei „Sonderwege"? Russisch-deutsche Parallelen und Kontraste (1917-2014)
Vergleichende Essays
ISBN 978-3-8382-0823-7

157 *Vladimir V. Karacharovskiy, Ovsey I. Shkaratan, Gordey A. Yastrebov*
Towards a New Russian Work Culture
Can Western Companies and Expatriates Change Russian Society?
With a foreword by Elena N. Danilova
Translated by Julia Kazantseva
ISBN 978-3-8382-0902-9

158 *Edmund Griffiths*
Aleksandr Prokhanov and Post-Soviet Esotericism
ISBN 978-3-8382-0903-6

159 *Timm Beichelt, Susann Worschech (eds.)*
Transnational Ukraine?
Networks and Ties that Influence(d) Contemporary Ukraine
ISBN 978-3-8382-0944-9

160 *Mieste Hotopp-Riecke*
Die Tataren der Krim zwischen Assimilation und Selbstbehauptung
Der Aufbau des krimtatarischen Bildungswesens nach Deportation und Heimkehr (1990-2005)
Mit einem Vorwort von Swetlana Czerwonnaja
ISBN 978-3-89821-940-2

161 *Olga Bertelsen (ed.)*
Revolution and War in Contemporary Ukraine
The Challenge of Change
ISBN 978-3-8382-1016-2

Contents

Foreword 7
Acknowledgement 9
Introduction 11

Chapter 1
Media and politics in the 'gray zone' between democracy and authoritarianism: an interdisciplinary approach 23

    1.1. If not 'transition' then what? State capture and formation of a disabling environment for democratization 25
        1.1.1. State capture 25
        1.1.2. Bad habits from the past? 28
        1.1.3. Informal institutions 32
        1.1.4. Informal institutions and state building in transitional societies 34

    1.2 The case of Ukraine 39
        1.2.1. Ukraine's oligarchic system 39
        1.2.2. The role of informal rules 43
        1.2.3. A trajectory of institutional change in Ukraine in 1994–2013 45
        1.2.4. Institutional void, flawed formal rules, and the supremacy of informal institutions 50

Chapter 2
Media capture in post-communist Ukraine 55

    2.1. Media capture in Ukraine: actors, methods, and effects ... 59
        2.1.1. Who are the captors of private media in Ukraine? 59
        2.1.2. How does media capture affect Ukrainian media content? 70
        2.1.3. What methods do media captors use? 75

2.2. Disabling environment: media regulators and media law . 82
    2.2.1. Regulatory and monitoring bodies 82
    2.2.2. Media-related laws 88

Chapter 3
The media market and ownership, and economic dimension of media capture in Ukraine 95

3.1. The Ukrainian media market 95
    3.1.1. Size and wealth 95
    3.1.2. Dependence on political advertising 97
    3.1.3. Unfinished privatization 98
    3.1.4. Foreign investments 101
    3.1.5. The Russian factor 105

3.2. The dark side of media privatization and commercialization in Ukraine 108
    3.2.1. Oligarchic media ownership 108
    3.2.2. Concentration of media ownership and its nature in Ukraine 112
    3.2.3. Implications of oligarchic media ownership 116
    3.2.4. Market-driven tabloidization or 'political yellowing'? 119

Conclusion: New obstacles to media reform in post-communist Ukraine 127

Bibliography 137

Name index 165

Subject index 171

Foreword

Twenty five years after Ukraine became independent, there were still very few scholarly studies about contemporary Ukraine's mass media. This book is a welcome contribution to the field. Thoroughly researched, Ryabinska provides the reader with an account of what has been happening in Ukraine's media landscape, and a convincing explanation why the country continues to face challenges in this sphere and remains described as 'partly free' by international organizations.

She draws on the theoretical literature of comparative politics and regime change studies and presents an original argument. This discussion seems important for post-communist media research since the role of cultural legacies in media transformations is often overestimated there at the expense of analysis of structural obstacles to democratization which could arise or be purposely maintained in some post-communist countries in the period after the fall of communism, which (nota bene) has lasted about 25 years already. Her explanation is that Ukraine's media has been captured by political and commercial forces as part of the larger process of state capture that continues to plague the country.

One of the key structural issues is ownership. Scholars have long argued that who owns the media matters (Bagdikian, Herman and Chomsky, McChesney, Schiller) since this determines editorial policy, and, to a large degree, content. Corporate media owners rarely have the public interest as their main goal, and this is also true in Ukraine. However, in Ukraine media ownership patterns have suffered from non-transparency, and Ukraine's corporate media owners have many other businesses that are their main sources of profit. Researching and documenting the holdings these large corporate actors (who are sometimes referred to as oligarchs) is challenging, though not impossible. Ryabinska did this by drawing on available sources, previous publications (Dovzhenko, Dutsyk, Dyczok, Ligachova), and expert interviews, which she used to trace the patterns of media ownership in Ukraine, and describe how this continues to pose an obstacle to the goal of freedom of speech. Furthermore, she places Ukraine in the broader, comparative context of other countries which had experienced communism.

In my own work (2014) I demonstrated how in numerous ways Ukraine's media system is following global trends as it faces the same challenges as other countries do: a rapidly changing international environment, a globalized economy, as well as cultural and media convergence patterns. Ryabinska shifts the focus and argues that the trajectories of post-communist state- and institution-building do have relevance in Ukraine, and other east European states, and they largely affect as the media systems themselves, and their responses to various challenges.

Both approaches highlight the need for a comprehensive, comparative perspective for media analysis, since neither countries nor their media systems exist in vacuums, separate from political, economic, social, and international forces. Ryabinska's study provides a detailed examination of all of these factors. An important feature of her analysis is that she does not view the state as a unitary actor, but explores the different dimensions and interplay between formal and informal institutions and practices. How a sophisticated array of legislation protecting media freedom and journalists' rights has not safeguarded either, since laws are selectively enforced, and often used as a punitive tool rather than how they were intended. How media ownership is integrally connected to political and other economic interests, and the implications of this. An innovative way of examining the classic tension between structure and agency.

Marta Dyczok,
August 2016

Acknowledgement

I am grateful to my host institution, Collegium Civitas, for supporting my research in its final stage. I also gratefully acknowledge the role of the Central European University in Budapest in the rise and development of the ideas herein presented. It was the post-graduate course *Ukrainian media change in Central-Eastern European Perspective*, which I developed in the framework of its Curriculum Resource Center grant, that gave initial impetus to this research. Of particular value was the access to the Central European University library provided to me within this grant and other projects.

I also wish to express my gratitude to Ihor Balynskyi, Otar Dovzhenko, Diana Dutsyk, Zurab Alasania, Vahtang Kipiani, Ihor Roskladai, Victoria Siumar, and many other Ukrainian media scholars, journalists, and critics whose knowledge of the Ukrainian media system—as well as expertise on its formal and informal regulation—were highly helpful and stimulating for my research.

Several people read all or part of the manuscript version of this book and offered significant criticisms and suggestions. I am especially thankful to Volodymyr Kulyk, Marta Dyczok, and Serhiy Kudelia, whose valuable comments did much to make this book better. I am also grateful to participants of the Conference "'Braking' News: Censorship, Media and Ukraine" at Harriman Institute, Columbia University in 2013, the Central and East European Communication and Media Conferences in 2013, 2014, and 2015—as well as other academic symposia where I presented portions of this study. I would especially like to note a thoughtful discussion at Danyliw Annual Research Seminar in contemporary Ukrainian Studies at the University of Ottawa in 2012, and express thanks to Dominique Arel, Paul D'Anieri, and Alexandra Hrycak who read my paper and made many valuable comments. Of course, all responsibility for any remaining shortcomings and errors is mine alone.

For permission to reproduce a caricature by Maryna Turovska on the cover of this book I am thankful to the Chief Editor of the *Ukrainian Week* magazine, Dmytro Krapyvenko.

I am also deeply thankful to Philip Earl Steele for proofreading the book.

Natalya Ryabinska,
October 2016

Introduction

This book is an attempt to contribute to the analysis of the reasons behind the slow progress of media democratization in the democratic 'laggards' of post-communist Europe and Eurasia by focusing on the case of Ukraine.[1] Since 1989, some former communist countries (outside of the Soviet Union) have demonstrated remarkable success in achieving a degree of freedom in their media. Others—for example, Albania, Macedonia, Serbia, as well as most of the former Soviet republics—fell behind other European states, thereby revealing the persistence of the old divides between communist and non-communist Europe. Ukraine finds itself in the second category, with its media demonstrating comparatively modest progress toward establishing independence and assuring pluralism since the end of Soviet communism: indeed, Ukraine has even experienced several antidemocratic backlashes.[2] Why do the Ukrainian media still remain only 'partly free' while the citizens of Poland, the Czech Republic, and the Baltic states have enjoyed a 'free' media since the mid-1990s? Why, despite the adoption of media laws corresponding to European standards and the establishment of private ownership in the media, are the Ukrainian press and broadcasting still far from independent?

---

1   The earlier versions of some parts of this book previously appeared in the form of articles: chapter 2 is based on "Media Capture in Post-Communist Ukraine: Actors, Methods and Conditions" (*Problems of Post-Communism*, 61, no. 2 [2014] © M. E. Sharpe), and elements of Chapter 3 are based upon "The Media Market and Media Ownership in Post-Communist Ukraine: Impact on Media Independence and Pluralism" (*Problems of Post-Communism*, 58, no. 6 [2011] © M. E. Sharpe).
2   According to Freedom House's annual assessments of the freedom of the press, Ukrainian media remained 'partly free' since 1993, with only exceptions in 2003, when Ukraine appeared in a 'non-free' group and in 2014. Its press freedom scores significantly deteriorated in early 2000s during the second presidency of Leonid Kuchma and after 2010 when Yanukovych succeeded Yushchenko as president, reaching an extremely low point during the EuroMaidan protests in late 2013 early 2014, when harassment and violence against journalists dramatically increased as they covered the EuroMaidan events.

These questions and the idea for this book arose in 2010–2011 when in the framework of the Central European University's Curriculum Resource Center grant I developed an academic course entitled "Ukrainian media change in Central-Eastern European perspective" and delivered it to PhD students of the Kyiv-Mohyla School of Journalism in Kyiv, Ukraine. Together with my students I was then comparing the state of Ukrainian media with the advancements in the media systems of Central-Eastern Europe (CEE) at the moment when Ukraine witnessed a grave setback for democracy under the presidency of Viktor Yanukovych. We were also searching for answers as to the causes of the slow progress of media democratization in Ukraine. Having finished this study in 2016, I am convinced that the question I was asking and the answers I subsequently found (as based upon analysis of Ukraine's media change between the start of Ukraine's transformations in the early 1990s and the end of Yanukovych's regime in 2013) have by no means lost their relevance. Even after the 'Revolution of Dignity' in late 2013–early 2014, which led to Yanukovych's fleeing the country and the formation of a new pro-Western government in Kyiv, Ukrainian citizens continue to witness phenomena which had become usual for the Ukrainian media landscape over the previous two decades—namely: 'media wars' between oligarchs,[3] instrumental use of the media by politicians and government officials, and politicized media ownership. This makes me assume that at least some of the mechanisms for constraining the media's independence as described in this book are still at work—and, moreover, that there still

---

[3] *Oligarchs* are big businesspeople who are able to influence the politics of a country for their own benefit owing to their assets (Matuszak 2012). In post-communist studies the term is used mostly with respect to the politics and media in the non-Baltic former Soviet republics where 'oligarch' often assumes the meaning 'owner of the media' because those countries' richest businessmen often own, in addition to their industrial and financial empires, media campaigns, as well (see Mommsen 2012; Puglisi 2003, 2008; Åslund 2005; Pleines 2012). However, in recent years the term 'oligarch' has also started to appear in studies of the media systems in young CEE democracies, such as the Czech Republic, Bulgaria, and Latvia (Stetka 2012, 2015).

persist far too intense links between the country's media, politics, and economy. Which is to say that this study can help understand not only the recent history of Ukraine's media transformation, but also the ongoing events in Ukrainian media, politics, and society.

This study examines the media system in a country that is not fully democratic. Ukraine, similarly as with certain other countries of post-communist Europe and Eurasia is often categorized as a 'hybrid regime' that combines elements of democracy and authoritarianism (Berglund and Ekman 2013; Pleines 2012).[4] The post-communist development of these countries, especially in the case of the non-Baltic former Soviet states, strongly differs from that of the successful new democracies of Central-Eastern Europe. This is usually explained in reference to the distinct initial conditions under which the former began their transformations—in particular, their longer and/or more severe experience of communism (cf. Ekiert 2012).[5] The studies of media systems in the former Soviet republics, which (to date) have failed to carry out a democratic transformation of their media systems, are not numerous as compared to

---

[4] According to Sten Berglund and Joakim Ekman (Berglund and Ekman 2013), in 2011 in post-communist Europe and Eurasia there were 12 democracies, 7 autocracies, and 10 hybrid regimes. The latter group included five former Soviet states: Armenia, Georgia, Kyrgyzstan, Moldova, and Ukraine.

[5] The post-communist transformations of media systems in Central-Eastern Europe, especially in the countries which are the members or candidate members of the European Union, often become a subject of international research projects of a comparative character, as well as single-country studies (for recent contributions to this literature, consider: Zielonka 2015a; Dobek-Ostrowska and Głowacki 2015, 2011; Downey and Mihelj 2012; Gross and Jakubowicz 2012a; Jakubowicz 2012, 2011; Dobek-Ostrowska et al. 2010). Compared to them, the studies of media change in former Soviet Union are far less numerous, most of them focusing on the case of Russia (last years publications include: Capello 2015; Becker 2014; Oates 2013; de Smaele 2012; Roudakova 2012; Vartanova 2012; Kiriya and Degtereva 2010; Pasti 2010; Rosenholm et al. 2010). As for the research of the Ukrainian media system, they are few and include Dyczok 2006, 2009, 2015; Kulyk 2010, 2011, 2013, 2014; Szostek 2014a, 2014b; Ryabinska 2014, 2011; Dutsyk 2010; Belyakov 2009; Khabiuk 2009; Krasnoboka and Brants 2006; Krasnoboka and Semetko 2006; Nikolayenko 2004; Riabchuk 2001.

the research of more successful cases of media reform in the advanced new European democracies. Of course, the primary exception here is Russia, whose deteriorating media freedom has become a subject of relatively numerous studies. Thus, my book aims to contribute to this literature by concentrating on the media system in Ukraine, the second biggest country in the former Soviet Union (FSU), and whose media developments in different moments of its post-communist transformation more than once raised hopes as big as the subsequent disappointments.

This study focuses on the relationships between media, politics, and the market. Politics and the market are surely not the only driving forces of media systems. In particular, some authors (Gross 2002, 2008; Coman and Gross 2012; Vartanova 2012) claim that culture, especially the heritage of the communist past, plays a central role in the transformation of post-communist media systems. An important role is assigned also to new communication technologies, which are believed by many to have a significant democratizing potential for transitional societies and their mass media (Krasnoboka and Brants 2006; Krasnoboka and Semetko 2006; Salovaara-Moring 2012).

This work however builds on scholarship that presumes the centrality of politics-media relationships for media change in societies undergoing transformation (Downing 1996; Sparks and Reading 1998; Sparks 2000) and presumes that power relationships are at the core of understanding their media dynamics. Additionally, because the Ukrainian case seems to provide strong evidence for these studies' assumption about the close interrelationship between political and economic power, also with regard to the mass media (see e.g., Åslund 2005; Dyczok 2009; Puglisi 2003; Matuszak 2012), special attention in this book is also paid to Ukraine's media market and ownership.[6]

---

[6] The book deals predominantly with internal factors of media change in Ukraine and does not concentrate on the impact of external forces on Ukrainian media

Differently from works which concentrate upon the cultural heritage of the past as the main obstacle to successful media democratization—or those that believe it is chiefly political culture and, more broadly, politics, not the economy, that determines media change in countries like Ukraine—this study takes another stance. First, it focuses not on the inherited obstacles to media democratization, but on the environment for media independence which was shaped in Ukraine after the fall of communism and over the more than two decades of the country's uneasy transformation. Second, my study pays attention not to cultural factors, but rather to media-related structures and institutions and, what is especially important, to the way they were built in post-communist Ukraine. In this book I argue that during the last two decades certain new obstacles to media independence have appeared in Ukraine, ones which effectively hamper media democratization. They include the telltale structure of media ownership, with the news media being concentrated in the hands of politically engaged business tycoons; the fuzzy and contradictory legislation in the media realm; and the informal institutions of political interference in the media. My second thesis is that these barriers were formed by the mutual influence and interdependence of both political and market forces.

The study of media systems in the post-communist countries lagging behind the democratic frontrunners like Poland or Estonia often appears to be a challenging enterprise because of problems of a theoretical nature. This is especially true for the non-Baltic post-Soviet countries: a number of works on their media change start from problematizing the theoretical tools available in media studies (see e.g., Becker 2004, Oates 2007, de Smaele 1999, 2005,

---

in the sense that it never offers an exhaustive analysis on the issue, which deserves to be addressed in a separate study (a convincing argument about the significance of the external forces for media transformations in former Soviet bloc was recently developed by Hallin and Mancini 2012b). Yet this issue is touched upon in Chapter 3, where a discussion of Ukrainian media market and the factors impacting its development touches upon, among others, the issue of competition from Russian media companies Ukrainian media businesses have to face.

Koltsova 2001, 2006; Dyczok 2006; Dyczok and Gaman-Golutvina 2009), and in some cases even questioning their explanatory power regarding media systems in former Soviet republics (Koltsova 2006). Indeed, as some advocates of de-Westernizing media studies point out, one of the disadvantages of the above tools with regard to the study of non-Western (including post-communist) media systems is that they are embedded in the experiences of Western democracies and therefore have limited capacity to explain media systems and media change in societies which are not (fully) democratic (Hallin and Mancini 2012b; Koltsova 2006; Curran and Park 2000b; Sparks and Reading 1998).[7]

Today, in the mid-2010s, the problem of the relevance of media-studies conceptual tools for the study of the media in some of the former communist countries in Europe and Eurasia seems even more acute. These days, when more than two decades have passed since the end of communism, it is evident that the process of post-communist transformation is more complex than the mere movement from authoritarianism (or totalitarianism) to democracy, and that some of the countries which departed from the communist system appear to be stuck in transition or even to have reached a state of equilibrium short of being a full-fledged democracy (Ekiert 2012). Indeed, if we take the former Soviet Union, only three countries (Estonia, Lithuania, Latvia) of the 15 former Soviet republics can today be classified as stable democracies; another seven are clear-cut autocracies (Berglund and Ekman 2013).[8] The other five, including Ukraine, are categorized as hybrid regimes, and, despite this 'mixture' of democracy and authoritarianism that might seem to

---

[7] It is worth mentioning here that the thesis about inadequacy (or limited adequacy) of Western media theories for the study of post-communist media was put forward not exclusively with regard to media systems in democratic 'laggards' or 'hybrids,' but also to other countries in the region (see Zielonka 2015b; Lauk 2015).

[8] In this fragment I base my remarks upon the operationalization of political regimes proposed by Jonas Linde and Joakim Ekman (Linde and Ekman 2011).

be rather unstable, for at least four of them (Armenia, Georgia, Moldova, Ukraine) it has been a quasi-permanent option for more than two decades already (Berglund and Ekman 2013). In Central-Eastern Europe the picture is also far from idyllic: five of its countries are hybrid regimes (Berglund and Ekman 2013),[9] and some of the remaining group (for example Romania, Bulgaria or Serbia) though being qualified as democracies are experiencing noticeable problems with press freedom and are consistently ranked as 'partly free' in Freedom House's Press Freedom Index (see Freedom House 2010–2014). This means that post-communist media studies, which are, as mentioned above, using conceptual tools rooted predominantly in democratic media research may need to expand their theoretical toolkit by including analytical instruments able to explain and investigate media change in countries with protracted or/and problematic media reform,[10] and, possibly, also refine some of already used analytical categories. Being mindful of this need, I pay special attention in this book to the discussion of its analytical framework which is presented principally in Chapter 1.

In recent years in the framework of post-communist media studies there have appeared several valuable works contributing to the development of theoretical instruments adequate to the study of the media in democratic 'laggards' or 'hybrids' (see, in particular, Zielonka 2015a; Dobek-Ostrowska and Głowacki 2015; Gross and Jakubowicz 2012a; Downey and Mihelj 2012). Of great value are

---

9 They are: Albania, Bosnia Herzegovina, Macedonia, Montenegro, and Kosovo (Berglund and Ekman 2013).
10 These theoretical tools could also be useful for the study of the media in countries usually scoring higher in indicators of democracy and media freedom. In the last decade one could observe a wave of "posttransitional and postaccession backlash" (Rupnik 2007), which was manifested, among others, in more or less durable reduction of media autonomy even in such advanced new democracies as Czech Republic, Hungary or Poland. Commenting on some of these instances, Vaclav Stetka (2012) pointed at the emergence in some of these countries of the patterns of media-politics-business relations resembling the ones which are widespread in the societies eastward to CEE. This suggests that the research tools designed to explain the state of affairs with the media in democratic 'laggards' may contribute to understanding some media-related processes even in the most advanced democracies of post-communist Europe.

also the theoretical findings in the studies of media in transitional democracies around the globe, especially Hallin and Mancini (2012a) and Voltmer (2013). Among the most important contributions from the perspective of the present study is Alina Mungiu-Pippidi's model of three diverging paths of media evolution in post-communist countries, of which only one is the movement to a full-fledged market economy and democracy; with the accompanying notion of *media capture*, introduced to explain the path where the media persist in an intermediate state between autonomy and open censorship, being indirectly controlled either by governments or by vested interests strongly tied to politics (Mungiu-Pippidi 2008). Highly instructive are also Katrin Voltmer's works (Voltmer 2008; 2012) where she unpacks and problematizes received understandings of such concepts as 'the media market' and 'the role of the state vis-à-vis the media' in light of the research into the media in new democracies.

Much more systematic efforts on creating the conceptual tools for analysis of the transformation of social institutions in the post-communist countries with trajectories of change deviating from the success story of the advanced new CEE democracies have been carried out not within the framework of media studies, but in comparative politics and democratization studies (Voltmer 2008, 23–24). These areas of political science, which (different from media studies) have a long tradition of tackling the challenges of analyzing transitional societies, have developed over the past decades rather advanced conceptual and research instruments for the study of societies like Ukraine's (see e.g., Carothers 2002; Diamond 2002; Levitsky and Way 2002; Helmke and Levitsky 2004, 2006; O'Donnell 1994; King 2001; Grzymala-Busse 2008).

Significantly, in political science the awareness of the plurality of possible trajectories of post-communist development in the former Soviet bloc arose much earlier and resulted in much more comprehensive research than in media studies. For example, already in 2002 Thomas Carothers called the attention of both academics and practitioners to the limited analytic capacity of the so-called 'transition paradigm,' which presupposed that the development of any country moving away from dictatorial rule could be considered as a transition toward democracy, and this transition in addition proceeded in a unidirectional or linear fashion (Carothers 2002). Carothers pointed out that some 'transitional' countries (including those in post-communist Europe and Eurasia) could substantially deviate from the transition 'path.' There was no obligation to move forward along the paths to democracy, as they could also go backward or stagnate: moreover, quite a lot of them have demonstrated very limited progress in democratization, but instead seemed to occupy a 'politically gray zone' between democracy and authoritarianism, and this has proved to be a rather persistent and stable condition. Quite logically, in the last decade we have witnessed the rise of a number of studies within the framework of political science aimed at explaining the character, inner logic, and viability of 'gray zone' regimes, including those in the region of the former Soviet Union, among them Ukraine (see e.g., Way 2004; Darden 2002; D'Anieri 2007; Meyer 2008; Grzymala-Busse 2008; Hale 2010; Kudelia 2012; Gel'man 2004, 2012; Fisun 2007, 2012).

This study draws on some of the above-outlined theoretical developments both in media studies and political science, paying particular attention to integration of the theoretical tools of comparative politics and regime change studies into the study of media change in the democratic 'laggards' of post-communist Europe and Eurasia. Discussion of these tools with respect to the study of the transformation of media systems in countries like Ukraine is provided in Chapter 1. That chapter also briefly outlines Ukraine's post-communist transformations and gives a general picture of the political-economic and institutional context within which Ukraine's media system operates.

Chapter 2 and 3 focus respectively on the political and economic aspects of the media transformation in Ukraine. Chapter 2 examines media-politics relationships in the country, and gives an account of how political control over the media is achieved in post-communist Ukraine where formal structures and regulations seem to be designed to prevent the state and political interests from interfering in media independence. The chapter operates with the concept of media capture which allows us to introduce into the analysis of politics-media relations the dimension of corruption, which, as Mungiu-Pippidi has convincingly demonstrated in Mungiu-Pippidi (2008, 2012), should necessarily be taken into account in the studies of the media in non-consolidated democracies, especially those affected by so-called systemic corruption (or state capture), which is the case for Ukraine.

Chapter 3 examines what 'media market' and 'media ownership' mean in the Ukrainian context (as compared to the contexts of certain other post-communist countries) and what are the obstacles to formation of a strong and developed media market in the country. It highlights the importance of economic and market development for the rise of independent and sustainable media, but simultaneously shows that the market in Ukraine is significantly influenced by political concerns that distort the market logic. The chapter traces how privatization of the state-run media and the rise of commercial media, which are commonly expected in accordance with democratic media theories to lead to a free press, paradoxically contributed to the rise of new barriers to media autonomy and pluralism.

This study is based upon a wide array of sources. They include, first, academic studies of the media and democratization in Ukraine and other FSU countries, as well as new Central-Eastern European democracies, especially those with 'partly free' media. An important source is also that of the reports by Ukrainian and international organizations monitoring developments in Ukrainian politics, society, economy and the media. With regard to the media themselves, I widely drew on information by Ukrainian and international media watchdogs, in particular the Institute of Mass Information in Kyiv, Telekrytyka, the Kyiv Media Law Institute, the Academy of Ukrainian Press (AUP), Internews-Ukraine, Reporters Without Borders, the International Research and Exchanges Board, International Media Support, Freedom House, Article XIX. Beyond this, I also consulted the data concerning regulatory and legal frameworks of the media in Ukraine, including the media laws and regulations themselves as well as their analysis by legal scholars and human rights or/and media freedom organizations. Last but not the least, an important source for this book was also that of daily media-related news, interviews, and discussions from specialist online publications focused on organizational and professional aspects of news making, mass media, and journalism in Ukraine (e.g., Mediasapiens, Telekrytyka, Media Business, Mediananny). Together with the cases of journalistic investigations into media ownership, in-house censorship in Ukrainian editorial offices published in Ukraine's independent media, along with information from Ukrainian media watchdogs, these publications have given me an opportunity to look behind the scenes of formal rules and structures in the media realm in Ukraine, and catch a glimpse of the informal practices in media-politics relationships that are otherwise barely accessible to outsiders.

Though this study concentrates on the case of a single country, in no way does it support a uniqueness claim, or the idea about the uniqueness of Ukrainian media system and its post-communist transformation. From the very start of this research it was evident that the Ukrainian case is not exceptional and the developments in the Ukrainian media system are similar to those in other societies in post-communist Europe and Eurasia. For example, Chapter 3 in this book concludes that there are significant commonalities between the development of the media market in Ukraine and south European post-communist countries (Albania, Bulgaria, Macedonia, Montenegro, Romania, Serbia). There are also essential similarities between the Ukrainian media's changes and those of other FSU countries, in particular Russia. One should bear in mind, however, that the Russian case shows similarity with the Ukrainian one predominantly in the first decade of transformation, up to the early 2000s, when, after the strengthening of presidential power during the first term of Vladimir Putin's presidency, Russia decisively shifted towards authoritarianism, whereas Ukraine remained in the group of semi-democratic/semi-authoritarian societies. In any case, being aware of the aforementioned commonalities, this study explores the Ukrainian media change through the prism of the transformations in other former Soviet bloc countries, and operates with concepts and categories established by general theories and comparative analysis.

Chapter 1
Media and politics in the 'gray zone' between democracy and authoritarianism: an interdisciplinary approach

What theoretical tools are available for analysing media systems in emerging democracies? This study has chosen to use ideas from comparative politics and regime change studies to examine media and politics in the former Soviet republics, with a focus on Ukraine.

As underlined in the Introduction, the theoretical instruments which media studies have at their disposal are mostly rooted in democratic media research: therefore, they are of limited applicability to the study of media in societies which are not (fully) democratic. This is especially true for the non-Baltic former Soviet republics, none of which is classified today as a stable democracy (Berglund and Ekman 2013). Compared to media studies, comparative politics and regime change studies are conceptually much more well-established with regard to the societies which, like Ukraine, remain in-between democracy and authoritarianism. Moreover, because the media and politics are far from being separated in the former Soviet countries, the study of media transformations in these countries, as some critical voices within post-communist media studies do point out, should be approached not within a single-discipline, but as an interdisciplinary task (Krasnoboka 2009, see also: Sparks and Reading 1998, 21; Downing 1996, 26–27).[11]

This book takes as its point of departure the idea that the dynamic of media systems in developing democracies is more complex than a linear model of democratic transition, and is by no

---

[11] Media and politics are linked not only in former Soviet countries, but also in many other places around the world, including established democracies (see, for ex., Hallin and Mancini 2004; 2012). However, in the emerging democracies, especially those 'stuck in transition' the relationship is in some ways different and more complex, which is what this study is about.

means unidirectional (Voltmer 2012, 233; Mungiu-Pippidi 2008, 90–91). As Carothers sees it, the 'transitional societies' shifting away from dictatorial or authoritarian rule do not necessarily move towards democracy. Instead they often settle into foggy equilibria, a 'gray zone' between authoritarianism and democracy, which is not an exceptional or temporary condition, but "a state of normality for many societies" (Carothers 2002). This 'state of normality' has become a subject of numerous studies within sub-disciplines of political science in the last few decades (see e.g., Diamond 2002; O'Donnell 1994; King 2001; Levitsky and Way 2002; Helmke and Levitsky 2004, 2006; Grzymala-Busse 2008). Importantly, new analytical frameworks were developed which have allowed political scientists to move beyond the transition paradigm in the study of 'in-between' countries.

This study draws on these ideas, builds on them, and presents a new perspective. It argues that the role of cultural legacies in media transformations in post-communist states is often overestimated at the expense of an analysis of structural and institutional obstacles to democratization. These structural obstacles arose (or were purposely preserved) in some post-communist countries in the period after the fall of communism, which (nota bene) has lasted about 25 years already.

The purpose of this chapter is twofold. First, it introduces certain theoretical frameworks developed within political science for the study of societies in-between authoritarianism and democracy. It addresses the issue of obstacles to democratization in the in-between societies presented within these frameworks, including the barriers which are relevant to press freedom. Particular attention is paid to discussion of emergent *vs.* inherited impediments to democratization.

The second aim of this chapter is to describe the wider environment within which the media are functioning in post-communist Ukraine, because, as Hallin and Mancini astutely noted, one cannot understand the news media without understanding the nature of the state, the pattern of relations between economic and political interests, as well as certain other elements of social structure. (Hallin and Mancini 2004, 8). The second part of the chapter is therefore devoted to a general analysis of this environment as well as to the process of its development in the transformational period. It especially focuses on the trajectory of Ukraine's institution building, specifically on its agents, internal logic and tendencies, and, finally, on general characteristics of the resulting institutional environment (including both formal structures and informal institutions) from the point of view of its potential influence on democratic transformations in general, and media reform in particular. The timespan considered in this chapter as well as in the whole study is 1994–2013; it encompasses the periods of the presidency of Leonid Kuchma (1994–2005), Viktor Yushchenko (2005–2010), and Viktor Yanukovych (2010–2014). It does not start from the beginning of Ukraine's transformation in 1991, because, as will be shown later, it was during president Kuchma's time in office that the basic institutional and market structures preventing Ukraine from consolidating media freedom were principally shaped.

1.1. If not 'transition' then what? State capture and formation of a disabling environment for democratization

1.1.1. State capture

When talking about the problems of democratization in the 'gray zone' societies, political scientists often raise the issue of an informal order that coexists in these societies alongside the rules and institutions of the market and democracy, but often interferes with their maintenance and consolidation. This informal order is sometimes defined as corruption (Holmes 2006): not in the sense of petty corruption, which exists everywhere to some degree, but of high-level, or systemic corruption (sometimes defined also as state capture), under which the state falls into the hands of incumbent elites who "capture private benefits from the public offices they hold" (Grzymala-Busse 2008).

When looking at the annual reports from Freedom House one can see that the issue of corruption is indeed important for the study of post-communist transformations in CEE and FSU in general: what is more, it is also highly relevant for an explanation of the problems with democratic media reform in these countries. Indeed, media freedom scores correlate strongly with corruption scores in these countries.[12] In former Soviet republics (Moldova, Russia, Georgia, Ukraine) and in most Balkan states (Albania, Macedonia, Serbia, Croatia, Bulgaria, Romania), the level of corruption is higher than in the advanced new democracies of Central Eastern Europe like Poland, the Czech Republic, and Hungary. Freedom House also ranks the first group of countries as partly free or unfree in its report on media freedom.

In Ukraine, the problem of corruption has been rather significant during the last two decades.[13] Some researchers even assume that corruption in Ukraine is not just a systemic anomaly, but that it forms an integral part of the system of the state's functioning (Darden 2002, 2008; D'Anieri 2007). The concept often used in regime change and democratization studies to analyze and comprehend the high-level corruption in Ukraine and other former Soviet states after the fall of communism, is *state capture*.

The concept of *state capture* is used in the literature mainly in reference to "the elite extraction of state resources for private gain" (Grzymala-Busse 2008; Hellman 1998; Hellman and Kauffmann 2001; Karklins 2005; Bennich-Björkman 2009). State capture

---

12 For more on this, see Freedom House 2012. Corruption scores are measured by Freedom House within its Nations in Transit project. The assumption that there is a link between the degree of media freedom and corruption levels is tested in World Bank 2000, Mungiu-Pippidi 2008, and elsewhere.

13 In 2014 it was ranked 142nd out of 176 states in the Transparency International Corruption Perception Index. During the last decade, the Ukraine's corruption rate as assessed by Freedom House's Nations in Transit project, oscillated between 5.75 and 6.25 close to the poorest possible level, and never raised higher than 5,75 (the rating is based on a scale of 1 to 7, with 1 representing the highest and 7 the lowest level of democratic progress).

in a post-communist condition designates the situation in which the post-communist state has not succeeded in becoming an autonomous actor towards interest groups or vested interests (Mungiu-Pippidi 2008). The agents of state capture can be, first, outside interests (predominantly, economic actors, such as oligarchs, big business groups) able to bend state laws, policies, and regulations to their (mainly financial) benefit through corrupt transactions with public officers and politicians (Hellman 1998), and second, the agents within the state, such as dominant parties, factions, high-ranking officials and other state actors, which appropriate the state by way of controlling public resources (such as budgetary funds, administrative resources, state mineral resources etc.) and using them and public office itself for their own economic or/and political gain (Grzymala-Busse 2008).

According to Mungiu-Pippidi, an integral component of state capture is media capture, i.e., the situation in which the media have not managed to gain an autonomous position in society, but rather are controlled "either directly by governments or by vested interests networked with politics" (Mungiu-Pippidi 2008, 91). The actors or interest groups that capture the media use them to gain political influence and advance their own political and economic interests. For example, in Romania, as Mungiu-Pippidi illustrated in her study in 2008, politically engaged businessmen used the media they captured to promote their protégés to government posts and discredit political opponents, as well as to advance their pocket political parties in elections (Mungiu-Pippidi 2008). As far as the government is concerned, it seeks to capture the media for the purpose of securing itself electoral support (Mungiu-Pippidi 2008).

Importantly, state capture is described in the literature not as a temporary state, a short-term deviation on the road to competitive democracy, but as a rather permanent condition (see e.g., Hellman 1998, Karklins 2002). Joel Hellman (1998) the author of a seminal work *Winners Take All: The Politics of Partial Reform in Postcommunist Transitions*, supposes that the countries addressed in academic studies as 'laggards' in the post-communist transitions fall into a 'partial reform trap' because of the interests of some powerful economic/political actors. Hellman points out that the start of economic reforms generates extraordinary short-term gains for a relatively narrow group of economic and political actors, namely those in a position to take advantage of a range of market distortions associated with partial economic reforms. These actors are interested, as Hellman assumes, in preserving the distortions of the initial reforms which are for them the sources of considerable rents and which would be eliminated in case of advancing reform. They do their best to block completion of the reform process, not least by influencing the formation of laws, regulations, decrees and other government policies in their countries. Their interests supported by the considerable resources cumulated by them during the initial reforms serve in effect to freeze the economy and society in partial reform equilibrium.

1.1.2. Bad habits from the past?

Trying to explain the phenomenon of state capture and its causes in post-communist countries, some authors advance the argument of historical heritage (Karklins 2002, 2005; Mungiu-Pippidi 2012). For example, Karklins (2002) commenting on the situation in former Soviet countries, draws attention to elite continuity in most of them; she argues that the old *nomenklatura* elite survived the change of regimes and continued to hold power, reproducing the Soviet-time collusive power networks and the bad habits of the past based on subordination of the interests of public office to private interests. In her turn, Mungiu-Pippidi (2012) supposes that it is a particular culture resulting from a society's previous history which creates conducive conditions for state capture. This is the culture where the public and the private spheres are not clearly delimited and individuals are not treated equally by the state as the norm of *universalism* dictates: instead *particularism* prevails in the relationships between the state and particular citizens or groups. The way they are treated depends on their distance from power holders. The outcome of this lack of private/public divide and a culture of privilege, is, on the one hand, that power holders treat the state as their private property and do not hesitate to use it for private gain; on the other, that average citizens, instead of trying to prevent civil servants from receiving private gain from their public service, struggle to enter the privileged group (or at least its close surrounding) and thus to gain an access to the illegal advantages it enjoys (Mungiu-Pippidi 2005). In this way cultural norms and attitudes inherited from communist (and, as some authors claim, also pre-communist) times contribute to the rule under which elite groups 'privatize' the state.

It is exactly the cultural-legacy argument, quite common in the comparative politics' explanations of democratization problems in post-communist Europe (see e.g., Sandholtz and Rein 2005; Sztompka 2000; Inglehart 2000), which is popular also in the in post-communist media studies' debate around partial and uncertain media reforms in some former communist countries. For example, in her recent publication Elena Vartanova (2012) argues that one of the key determinants of the Russian media model responsible for its uniqueness compared to the Western media models is the 'statist mentality' based on the belief in the regulatory/decisive role of the state (or state agencies). Ioana Coman and Peter Gross (2012, 468), referring to the Romanian case, claim that widespread corruption in and surrounding the country's media is an effect of its 'permanence of the past,' which has sedimented in Romanian culture in the form of such traditional values and behavior patterns as reliance on acquaintances and connections as well as an "inclination to always seek to evade rules, regulations, and laws if it is in one's personal interest."

The cultural-legacy explanation of the problems of post-communist developments has, however, its critics among the scholars of post-communist transformations in comparative politics. For example, Vladimir Gel'man (2003) warns that the legacy-of-the-past reasoning regarding the post-Soviet transformations poses the danger of falling into a closed logic of explanation: that is, while post-Soviet countries cannot achieve democracy because of their "wrong' culture, there is little chance of the 'right' culture emerging because of the absence of democracy. Besides, Gel'man considers that it would be problematic to explain, using the culturalist argument, a different progress of reforms in different fields of national life (Gel'man 2012). I would assume that the same is true for applying the legacy-of-the-past reasoning for explaining the cases of uneven transformation in one particular field over different time intervals. For example, it would be difficult to explain, using the culturalist approach, the zigzag trajectory of change of the media system in Ukraine after the break of communism. Not only was it characterized by as much as two democratic setbacks in 2003–2004 and 2014, but at least one of these 'downs' in the degree of media independence (which occurred soon before the Orange Revolution) was in addition followed by a sharp 'up,' or improvement of the country's media freedom record after the Orange government came to power in 2005.[14] Bearing in mind that cultural phenomena (such as norms, traditions, and habits) are characterized by considerable inertia, the factor of cultural legacy cannot account for such an uneven, abruptly changing path of institutional transformation.

The above does not mean, however, that the cultural-legacy arguments should be abandoned altogether in explanation of post-communist transformations.[15] It rather shows their limitations. One of them, which is important for the present discussion, is that while

---

14 After being categorized by Freedom House's Press Freedom survey as 'partly free' for more than ten years after the Ukraine's independence in 1991, the country was downgraded to 'non-free' category under Leonid Kuchma's regime in 2003, then increased its score to a 'partly free' level already in 2005 (after the Orange Revolution). In 2005–2013 it again perpetuated in 'partly free' state just to appear in the 'not free' group in 2014 (during the rule of Viktor Yanukovych). After the several months lasting public protests in late 2013–early 2014 which resulted in the change of government in Ukraine, the country experienced significant positive developments in the realm of media freedom. However, its Freedom of the Press score remained low in 2014–2016, which to some extend was a consequence of restrictions to press freedom and violence against journalists in the areas of Donetsk and Luhansk occupied by Russia-backed separatists.

15 Not occasionally, Vladimir Gel'man, whose critique of the 'legacy of the past' reasoning was quoted above, has recently named the historical-cultural legacy explanation among several mutually complementary approaches to the difficulties of post-Soviet transitions (Gel'man 2012, 298).

concentrating on the obstacles for democratic reforms shaped under the communist rule, the legacy-of-the-past approach overlooks the democracy-disabling structures and institutions which appeared as soon as in the transformational period. The developments in comparative politics discussed later in this study help to shed light on these recently appeared or/and steadily reproduced barriers and thereby help us obtain a more comprehensive account for the problems of democratic change in post-communist Europe.

The debate around state capture in transformational societies itself gives some keys for understanding these barriers. The studies of state capture in post-communist Europe and other parts of the world show that appropriation of state institutions by private interests usually not only prevents the former from proper functioning, but also contributes to the development of a surrounding that disables accomplishment of economic and political reforms.

For example, the World Bank (2000) study of corruption and state capture in Central-Eastern Europe and the former Soviet Union demonstrated that the transitional countries' early choices about the structure of political institutions and the nature of economic policies may vary, not least because of different legacies of the past, but these choices then determine different paths of their transition, and the extent of state capture in a country is both a product of such a transition path and a driving force for further developments (World Bank 2000). As Grzymala-Busse (2008, 668) pointedly noted, "state capture and state formation go hand in hand." Indeed, as the studies on state capture evidence, the elites which appropriate the state, influence the formation of laws to their own advantage, and, more generally, construct institutions and structures which help them preserve their privileged positions, and simultaneously reduce the chances for furthering democratic reforms. For example, the rulers which capture the state can purposefully weaken the institutions of audit or regulatory agencies and in such a way enhance their own ability to control these agencies as well as to use them selectively against political opponents (Grzymala-Busse 2008). They can also build specific institutions to serve their extractive goals, as well as construct the respective rules and durable practices of redistribution, budgeting, and authority (Grzymala-Busse 2008).

1.1.3. Informal institutions

An important concept used in political science to analyze the inner workings of the political regimes where state institutions are captured by private interests, and to understand the particular barriers (old and new) for these countries' democratic transformation in various realms is a concept of informal institutions.[16] *Informal institutions* are "socially shared rules, usually unwritten, that are created, communicated, and enforced outside of officially sanctioned channels" (Helmke and Levitsky 2004, 727). Scholars of informal institutions argue that though formal institutional frameworks introduced in a number of transitional countries are quite democratic, political behavior within many of them often deviates from a *formal* content of their constitutions and laws, and conforms instead to *informal* rules. According to some researchers (see e.g., Gallina and Hayoz 2011; Gel'man 2003), in some cases the formal rules (constitutions, laws and other regulations) modeled on democratic West European

---

[16] The concept was used, for instance, for the study of the transformations in the post-communist countries of Europe and Eurasia (see, for ex., Meyer 2008; Grzymala-Busse 2010; Rupnik and Zielonka 2013; Paneyakh 2003; Gel'man 2003, 2004; Hale 2011; Darden 2002). Applied toward investigation of post-Soviet republics, in particular their politics (Zimmer 2008; Gel'man 2003, 2012; Sharafutdinova 2010), institutional change (Kudelia 2012), and economy (Paneyakh 2003, Ledeneva 1998; Ledeneva and Shekshnia 2011), it significantly enriched our understanding of the nature and inner workings of post-Soviet gray-zone regimes.
It also recently appeared in media studies. Several tentative attempts were made to use it for describing the state of affairs with the media beyond the world of advanced democracies. In particular, Elena Vartanova (2012), addressing the developments in Russia after the break of the Communism, pointed out that "the Russian state has mostly exerted informal pressure on the media" (Vartanova 2012, 135). Duncan McCargo (2012) has noted that to explain the conduct and performance of the media in the countries in-between democracy and authoritarianism one should take into consideration that the informal (in terms of markets, parallelism, partisanship and censorship) proliferates here.

templates serve only as a *façade* covering informal institutions which in their turn significantly deviate from democratic principles.

Though it is generally agreed that informal institutions may have different, not obligatory detrimental consequences for democracy, (see e.g., Helmke and Levitsky 2004, Grzymala-Busse 2010, Ledeneva 2009), many studies suggest that in much of developing and post-communist world informal rules and practices undermine the democratic process, erode emergent formal rules and delay the consolidation of democratic institutions (O'Donnell 1996; Lauth 2000, Böröcz 2000). In these countries informal 'rules of the game' which coexist with new democratic, market, and state institutions often dominate; they do not only replace or subvert many of the newly established formal rules, but also cause negative social effects. Clientelism, patronage, personalistic awarding of jobs and contracts as well as selective enforcement of the formal law are only some of the many examples of informal institutions which are justly criticized in many new democracies around the world, including Latin America (O'Donnell 1996; Helmke and Levitsky 2006), Central Asia (Collins 2006), Central-Eastern Europe, and the former Soviet Union (Meyer 2008).

Scholars of informal institutions in newly democratized countries often assume that they are rooted in previous regimes. In former Soviet countries pervasive informality is supposed to be inherited from the communist past. As Ledeneva puts it, "the Soviet regime was penetrated by widely spread informal practices, depended on it, and allowed them to compensate for its own rigidity." (Ledeneva 2009, 261). Significant feature of this regime was informal *nomenklatura* networks operating to redistribute wealth in favor of their members, who subordinated the interests of their posts to personal and particular interests (Karklins 2002). Part of the members of the communist-time acquisitive *nomenklatura* networks survived the institutional change and remained in power. This was characteristic especially for such countries as the former Soviet Republics or some Balkan states where anticommunist opposition was not so strong as for example in Poland and Hungary and true circulation of elites did not take place (see e.g., Kryshtanovskaya and White 1996; Ganev 2007). The communist *nomenklatura* cadres not only brought the acquisitive informal networks back into the politics and economy of newly born independent post-communist states, but also introduced in their workings the old-regimes informal practices and rules such as *blat* and *krugovaya poruka* in Russia and other post-Soviet countries (Ledeneva 2006; 2009).[17]

However, as the growing body of research demonstrates (Gel'man 2012; Helmke and Levitsky 2004; Ledeneva 2009; Paneyakh 2003), historical legacy is just one among several reasons of the rise and pervasiveness of informal institutions in transitional societies. Indeed, as Gretchen Helmke and Steven Levitsky point out (Helmke and Levitsky 2004), informal institutions are not just historical givens. Neither are they static, but can be modified, adapted, disappear or emerge (Helmke and Levitsky 2004; see also Ledeneva 2009; Gel'man 2004). For example, Alena Ledeneva and Stanislav Shekshnia (2011) as well as Ella Paneyakh (2003) have described a variety of new informal institutions and practices which were invented in post-communist Russia around regulation of economic activity of private entrepreneurs.

1.1.4. Informal institutions and state building in transitional societies

For the present study especially valuable are the works which analyze not only the origin of informal institutions in societies under transformation, but also the reasons why they persist and continue to dominate over the formal rules long after the introduction of new formal frameworks. This is characteristic, for example, for many

---

[17] *Blat* is "the use of personal networks for obtaining goods and services in short supply and for circumventing formal procedures" (Ledeneva 2009, 257); *krugovaya poruka* is a pattern of collective (ir)responsibility, co-dependence and mutual concealment characteristic for Russia and some other post-Soviet countries; in the last two decades it has turned into "the ubiquitous form by which bureaucrats collude with other bureaucrats to skirt the law, high rollers arrange and then conceal their illicit deals" (Legvold 2009, 206).

post-Soviet societies; for example, as the studies of post-communist change in Russia and Ukraine demonstrate, in both countries informal rules still triumph over formal ones in many realms of public life despite the fact that more than two decades have passed since the introduction of new democratic institutions (Gel'man 2012; Zimmer 2008; Kudelia 2012; Robinson 2013).

Looking for explanations for such a state of affairs, some researchers assume that the dominance of informal institutions in transitional societies may negatively impact the process of building a democratic state (Grzymala-Busse and Luong 2002). One of its negative effects, according to O'Donnell (1996), is little horizontal accountability in transitional societies: in many of them the executive, O'Donnell argues, makes strenuous, often successful efforts to erode whatever horizontal accountability does exist. This concerns primarily the judiciary as well as other agencies of control endowed with legally defined authority to sanction unlawful or otherwise inappropriate actions by other state agents. In many newly democratized countries these agencies, O'Donnell shows, are deliberately weakened by the executive or even reduced to passivity.

Lack of horizontal accountability is highly detrimental to the institutionalization of democratic institutions. As O'Donnell (1996) assumes, the way individuals performing public roles, especially high-ranking officials, exercise their authority, depends not only, or even mostly on whether they are personally guided by the orientations on the public good. Rather, it depends largely on "institutional arrangements of control and accountability and on expectations built around these arrangements, which furnish incentives (including the threat of severe sanctions and public discredit) for that kind of behavior" (O'Donnell 1996, 7; see also O'Donnell 1998). Correspondingly, an inefficiency or weakness of the agencies of horizontal accountability reduces the chances that these institutional arrangements will work as they are supposed to, and gives therefore a space for particularistic and self-interested behavior of state agents.

Speaking about hindrances to advancement of the democratic reforms which appeared in transitional societies in the process of post-communist transformations, several scholars raise the question of the bad quality of formal rules, assuming that this is an imperfection of newly adopted formal rules that causes the emergence of informal institutions (Ledeneva 2009; Paneyakh 2003). Yet another researchers show that the gaps in formal regulations are exploited by self-interested elites: they mine legal loopholes, capitalize on poor specifications of formal institutions, and substitute the latter with informal institutions which allow them to advance their private interests at the expense of the public good. For example, according to Gel'man's investigation (2004), the Russian law on freedom of speech adopted in the early 1990s never took into account property rights in the media, and this deficiency was exploited by oligarchs to redistribute control over the media in their own favor.

Importantly, an entangled and contradictory legal framework itself is considered by some authors to be an outcome of deliberate actions. For example, Gel'man (2012) points out that electoral laws in Russia have a number of omissions and loopholes; they also give large discretion to electoral commissions (formed by local governments), which together create one-sided preferences to incumbents. He concludes that as a result of the purposeful actions of the agents who affected the 'rules of the game' in Russia in transformational period, fuzzy legality penetrated major regulations related to electoral campaigns, party financing, and the media. This opened a door for selective implementation of these laws and the resolution of disputes among electoral contenders in favor of pro-government parties and candidates. Kerstin Zimmer (2008), basing her work on the study of Ukrainian transformations, shows that formal rules (in particular, laws) are designed in Ukraine so as to necessitate the application of informal practices, but this is not a result of ignorance or transformation frictions. On the contrary, an insufficient legal framework is designed purposely to create uncertainty and to serve as an instrument to exercise control and power.

Gel'man (2012) considers the self-interest of institution builders to be one of the main reasons for a stable dominance of informal institutions in Russia and some other post-Soviet countries. Along with certain other researchers (Zimmer 2008), he assumes that as a rule formal institutions are distorted by rent-seeking interest groups, the early 'winners' of post-communist reforms. They use their bargaining power to influence the formation of laws to their own advantage and, more generally, to create structures and institutions which would help them preserve their privileged positions (Gel'man 2004, 2012). Besides, the 'flexible' institutional framework they diligently construct is intended to minimize formal constraints on government and other institutions, and to open thus various (informal) opportunities for the use of political power for private ends (Zimmer 2008).

An important issue which throws additional light on the resilience of informal institutions is the one concerning their enforcement. Definitions presume that *informal institutions* are "socially shared rules," which are "enforced outside of officially sanctioned channels" (Helmke and Levitsky 2004, 725), and which are "widely recognized and taught as such" (Grzymala-Busse 2010). However, that they are 'socially shared' and 'widely recognized' does not mean that informal institutions are followed (only) for the reason that individuals and the society approve them. As Grzymala-Busse (2010) rightly notes, informal institutions are complied with not necessarily voluntarily, but may be as well enforced through coercion. Recent studies of post-Soviet realities provide the examples supporting this assumption. For instance, Ledeneva basing on Russian experience asserts that selective use of the law or even use of the law for extralegal purposes may serve as ammunition to punish noncompliance with informal rules. As Ledeneva puts it, "the violation of unwritten rules can result in the enforcement of written ones" (Ledeneva 2006, 13).

The widespread informality in post-Soviet countries has not only a political, but also an economic dimension. According to Gulnaz Sharafutdinova (2010), the analysis of informal institutions in

Russia and some other post-Soviet countries is limited, if political sphere is investigated without taking into account that political power is fused with the economic one in this part of the world. She argues that the informal institutions that emerged in post-communist Russia are not simply the heritage of corruption, or the *blat* prevalent under the Soviet system. Their understanding is problematic unless we take into account the results of both political and economic reforms (especially the process of privatization) which together created new incentive structures that conditioned the behavior of post-communist elites in various realms.

Intermediary conclusions

To sum up the above theoretical discussion, the concepts of *state capture* and *informal institutions* are the theoretical instruments that can sensitize media researchers engaged in analysis of post-communist media transformations to the peculiar surrounding in which the media categorized in international ratings as 'partly free' exist. Specific interplay of politics and the economy, to explain which the concept of state capture was developed, as well as institutional frameworks (often informal) crafted by the early winners of post-communist reforms to promote their particular economic cum political interests rather than to advance the public good, create significant barriers for promotion of democratic reforms. These barriers usually include, among others matters, fuzzy and contradictory legislation in the realms principally important for distribution of power and resources (in particular, the laws regulating elections, party financing, and the media), as well as weak agencies of horizontal accountability, especially the judiciary and other controlling state agencies. The control over these agencies by the ruling elites not only reduces the constraints on self-serving informal politics of the latter (among others, also in the media realm), but also contributes to persistence of informal regulation in various areas of public life, including the media.

1.2 The case of Ukraine

How does the above theory relate to Ukraine's post-communist transformations and Ukrainian media?

In the comparative studies of corruption Ukraine is categorized as a country where the degree of state capture by powerful vested interests is particularly high. The World Bank and the European Bank for Reconstruction and Development (ERBD) assess Ukraine as a 'high-capture country' with one of the biggest degrees of state capture among the 21 transition countries of Eastern Europe and the former Soviet Union (World Bank 2000; EBRD 1999; see also World Bank 2011). Starting from the late 1990s, Ukraine was classed as a country trapped in a partial reform equilibrium (Åslund et al. 2001; Puglisi 2003), and even after the promising Orange Revolution in 2004 the country's authorities avoided costly institutional reforms that would have harmed particularistic interests, but could have strengthened state capacity and promoted democratic consolidation (Kudelia 2011).

1.2.1. Ukraine's oligarchic system

An important role in Ukrainian politics and economy is played by so-called oligarchs, or well-connected big businessmen. Publications on political transformations and regime change in Ukraine describe the Ukrainian political system as an oligarchic one with state institutions 'privatized' (or captured) by economic-political elites who use them as a means of supporting, generating, and maximizing their own economic profits (Matuszak 2012; see also: Åslund 2005, 2015; Puglisi 2003, 2008; Pleines 2012; Sirutavičius 2006). In fact, politics and the economy are closely intertwined in Ukraine. In the 2014 Crony Capitalism Index ranking calculated by *The Economist* Ukraine was scored 4-th, which means that it belongs to the countries where politically connected businessmen are most likely to prosper (The Economist 2014).

Oligarchs appeared in Ukraine in the mid-1990s, under the first term in office of president Leonid Kuchma, in the process of so-called *nomenklatura* privatization (Puglisi 2003; Sherr 2007).[18] Very quickly they became owners of the most profitable industrial enterprises, as well as the main media assets in Ukraine, including nationwide TV channels with the largest coverage (Åslund 2005; Matuszak 2012). The oligarchs and oligarchic groups (named also *clans*)[19] are mainly interested in the accumulation of assets, profitable activities, and new markets; and they have to maintain close connections with politics to go on enjoying access to oligarchic rents and secure their properties in the conditions of weakness of rule of law characteristic to Ukraine. This is achieved via the clans' cooperation with and mutual support of patrons in politics as well as via direct assimilation of oligarchs or other members of oligarchic clans into political activity (Pleines 2012; Åslund 2015).[20] According to Anders Åslund, before the Orange Revolution 300 out of the 450 deputies in the Ukrainian Parliament were dollar millionaires (Åslund 2005, 7–8), and after the elections of 2012 the Parliament still remained a club of millionaires, which was quite strange for a country where the per-capita GDP was less than $4,000 (Åslund 2014, October 1). Oligarchs also happened to hold government office: for example, Petro Poroshenko (who is the Ukrainian president at the time of writing) started his career it state administration back in 2005, when he became a secretary of the National Security and Defence Council under the Orange government. The developments in Ukraine in early 2014, when the government decided to appoint some oligarchs as governors of Eastern regions in the situation of

---

18 This thesis was disputed recently by the economist Oleh Havrylyshyn (2015, 35), who suggested that it was under Kravchuk's presidency, in 1992–1994 that "the embryonic evolution of the oligarchic class" occurred in Ukraine. He argues that the cause for the oligarch formation in the early 1990s was the "intentional delay" in reforms led by the government of the former communist Kravchuk. Havrylyshyn, however, never denies that the oligarchs "were nurtured and matured" in the years of president Kuchma's tenure in office.
19 Recent detailed information on the Ukraine's oligarchic clans can be found in Matuszak (2012).
20 Analysis of the oligarchs' engagement in and impact on Ukraine's politics can be found in: D'Anieri (2007), Matuszak (2012).

deep political-economic crisis caused by the unrest of armed separatists supported by Russia in Eastern Ukraine, showed once more how significant is the role of oligarchs in Ukraine's politics.

According to Åslund (2015), the oligarchic system is harmful for Ukraine's economic and market development.[21] Monopolization of the country's key economic sectors by oligarchic clans deforms the market and constrains competition. The oligarchs are not interested in free and fair competition in Ukraine; therefore they use their economic and political power to erect entry barriers that protect their advantaged positions on respective markets. This, in its turn, contributes to a very unfavorable investment climate in Ukraine and a low level of foreign investments in the country's economy. It also prevents the development of small and medium business (and, correspondingly, the growth of the middle class): for whereas big business lobbies for solutions which are favorable to itself, small and medium enterprises have to confront risks and the instability of the market on their own (Matuszak 2012). Besides, the oligarchs' influence on Ukrainian politics spawns the fact that the government in many cases is guided by the interests of big businessmen instead of the interests of the country; this leads to multi-billion losses in the Ukrainian state budget, which additionally weakens Ukraine's economy and markets (Matuszak 2012, 5; see also Wolowski 2008, 43–45). Additionally, this impedes the reforms essential for the country's economic development: especially in the sectors where the oligarchs have a strong interest, the reforms have little chances to be advanced (see e.g., Matuszak 2012, 76–77).

Also, though various scholars point out some positive effects of oligarchs on Ukraine's politics (in particular, the competition between oligarchic clans is supposed to contribute to a certain form of pluralism in political life and the media (Wolowski 2008, 40; Matuszak 2012, 79), the overall impact of big business on politics in Ukraine is commonly assessed as negative. First, the oligarchs, who are the winners of partial economic reforms, seek to stall the

---

21 Quite similarly the impact of oligarchs on Ukraine's economic development is assessed in: Wolowski (2008) and Robinson (2013).

country in a partial reform equilibrium in which winners take all (Matuszak 2012; see also: D'Anieri 2007; Wolowski 2008). They therefore use their impact on politics to prevent the deepening of the country's economic and political liberalization. Second, the misuse of public revenues for private purposes deplete Ukraine of vital resources that would otherwise be employed to strengthen the state's capacity necessary for building a legal-rational bureaucracy and strengthening of the rule of law (Puglisi 2003).

It would be wrong however to state that oligarchs are the only agents who impact the political transformations and institutional change in Ukraine. The other important group of players (inside Ukraine) are surely power-holders of the day, especially those who represent the executive branch of authority.[22] The political system in Ukraine has an executive nature (D'Anieri 2007), therefore control over the executive branch of power is important for the elites seeking for extraction of political rents (Kudelia 2013). As many scholars of the Ukrainian transformations show, in the conditions of weak civil society (which after the mass protests in 2013–2014 seems to have become a notable player in Ukraine's politics) and a fragmented party system the two types of actors (namely, the rent-seeking big businessmen and state bureaucracy) are the main agents having enough power or/and resources to impact political decision-making and shape institutions and structures of the state in the first two decades of the transformations (Fisun 2012; Zimmer 2008; Fritz 2007). As mentioned earlier, the two types of actors are closely intertwined or at least closely cooperate. Therefore some authors even consider that the two have become "one and the same," and therefore "the distinction is perhaps unimportant" (D'Anieri 2007, Ch. 3; see also: Holmes 2006, 308). However, this study supports the line of argument that the interests of the govern-

---

[22] As stated in Introduction, this work never focuses on the external factors of Ukraine's media transformations. One exception is Chapter 3 where the factor of competition with the powerful presence of neighbouring (Russian) media market is concerned.

ment and those of particular business magnates or economic-political interest groups do not always coincide in Ukraine (Fisun 2012), and therefore they should be approached as separate entities, at least analytically.

1.2.2. The role of informal rules

To explain the essence and workings of Ukraine's political system after the fall of communism, political scientists more and more often resort to the concept of informal institutions. The new institutional framework which was shaped in Ukraine back in 1990s is described as one in which "informal (patrimonial) and formal (bureaucratic) logic of action coexist" (Fisun 2007, 2012; Zimmer 2008; Hale 2011; Malygina 2010). By this it is meant that formally codified democratic rules (constitution, laws, and other formal regulations) do matter in Ukraine, however these rules are not enforced in a consistent and equitable way, and their circumvention is as usual as compliance with them. Whereas formal rules are often disregarded, actors extensively rely on informal (patron-client) networks and personal dependencies, as well as informal institutions (for example, clientelism, patronage, and rent-seeking) as the main guiding principles of action (Fisun 2012). The latter informal institutions are called 'subversive' by some scholars of Ukraine's transformation (Fritz 2007), to highlight their detrimental effect on democratization and the establishment of the rule of law and good governance.

The exercise of political power which corresponds to the above institutional framework is sometimes defined in political science as 'neo-patrimonial,' which combines the two types of political domination described in Weber's *Economy and Society* (1978): the patrimonial and the legal-rational. In the neo-patrimonial system, the ruling groups regard society as their own private domain, and the fulfillment of public functions as a legitimate means to their own personal enrichment (Bratton 2011). Electoral contestation in a neo-patrimonial system is an elite affair where powerful groups compete over state control (Bratton and van de Walle 1994); appropriation of state institutions and extraction of state-generated rents are the main incentives of political competition (Zimmer 2008).

According to Fisun (2012), Puglisi (2003), Zimmer (2008), van Zon (2001) and Malygina (2010), Ukraine had developed into a neo-patrimonial state already under the rule of the country's second president Leonid Kuchma. Fisun (2012) defines the main features of post-Soviet neo-patrimonialism that is characteristic, as he thinks, to many post-Soviet countries, including Ukraine, as:

1. The formation of a stratum of rent-seeking political businessmen and/or neo-patrimonial bureaucrats who use a combination of *élan*, politics, and property in order to achieve economic goals.
2. A more or less private appropriation of governmental administrative resources, primarily coercive and aimed at the fiscal functions of the state, and which are used largely to defeat any political opposition and eliminate economic competitors.
3. The crucial role of informal patron-client networks for the structuring of political and economic processes.

Fisun (2012), as well as some other scholars of Ukrainian transformations (Zimmer 2008; Kudelia 2012; Malygina 2010), argue that Ukraine remained a neo-patrimonial state for most of the period of its post-communist transformation. Even the Orange Revolution, which was initially accepted by many Ukrainian and international scholars as a start of true democratization in the country (see, for example, Hale 2006; Kuzio 2005; McFaul 2005), did not principally change this state of affairs (Fisun 2007, 2012; Malygina 2010; Zimmer 2008). Kudelia (2010) adds to this that informal norms which guided the elite's behavior in the political realm from the rule of president Leonid Kuchma to that of president Yanukovych, are:

1. Coercion or the use of law-enforcement agencies for political purposes.[23]
2. Rent-seeking or the use of public resources for private financial gains.
3. Patronage or exchange of public sector employment for political loyalty.

1.2.3. A trajectory of institutional change in Ukraine in 1994–2013

According to Kudelia (2012), the whole period of Ukrainian post-communist transformation was characterized by a continuous supremacy of informal rules and norms in the regulation of elite relations within the state and with various non-state groups as well as an absence of any progress in building the fundamental institutions of the state. Importantly, as he assumes, there were the actions (or sometimes inactions) of the ruling elites competing for power and resources that regularly hampered and undermined the construction of a strong institutional basis of democracy in the country (Kudelia 2012). Let us take a short look at the trajectory of Ukraine's institutional change in 1994–2013, starting from the presidency of Leonid Kuchma. As mentioned earlier, his time in office was associated with the formation of the stratum of oligarchs who, together with self-interested state bureaucrats and politicians were keen to appropriate the state and use/shape its institutions in accordance with their private purposes.

Leonid Kuchma's presidency was marked by the centralization of executive authority and its concentration in the hands of the president. As mentioned before, Ukrainian political system is characterised by an excessive weight of the executive agencies, therefore the executive is the largest source of rent-seeking opportunities in Ukraine (Kudelia 2013). The Ukrainian Constitution adopted in

---

23 Some authors (D'Anieri 2007; Darden 2002; Way 2004) mention also other state agencies which are used as an instrument of political pressure in Ukraine, namely tax authorities, the licensing inspectorate, the government control commission, as well as other state agencies of control and oversight.

1996 expanded the formal powers of the presidency, which gave the President considerable control over law enforcement, administration of various regulations from building and fire codes to taxes, as well as over government jobs. The latter now included the power to nominate or dismiss the Prime Minister, appoint or dismiss members of cabinet and other executive agencies, as well as to make appointments and nominations in the judicial branch, central bank, and a number of other agencies (D'Anieri 2007). Kuchma did not, however, use his extended formal power to conduct speedy reforms in Ukraine and establish the dominance of formal institutions and rules. He exploited it instead to accumulate informal power (D'Anieri 2007; Hale 2010), which he could use along with his formal prerogatives to fight political opponents and maintain his power. For example, the control over law enforcement and controlling state agencies were widely used by Kuchma and his cabinet for harassment of the opposition and independent media (Way 2004), a most prominent case of which was the brutal murder of oppositional journalist Georgi Gongadze.

According to Kudelia (2012), during the years of his presidency Leonid Kuchma managed to reinforce the dominance of informal norms. In particular, he established a relatively centralized control over the distribution of rents. He also turned patronage, or the exchange of public sector employment for political loyalty, into one of his main levers of control over the bureaucratic hierarchy (see e.g., D'Anieri 2007). Simultaneously, as Kudelia (2012) points out, Kuchma prevented the development of strong formal institutions. For example, he consistently blocked any initiative that would introduce independent oversight agencies or autonomous centers of power. He also resisted any civil service reform that would make bureaucratic recruitment more transparent and less politicized (Kudelia 2012).

The Orange Revolution in 2004, which was caused not least by the public outrage at rampant corruption and the discontent of the social groups excluded from the process of the redistribution of national wealth brought an end to Kuchma's authoritarian turn in

Ukraine. Viktor Yushchenko's victory in the presidential elections of 2004 led to a certain democratization of political life, an increase in political pluralism, and improvement in the quality of elections. A significant benefit of the Orange Revolution was also greater media freedom. However, Yushchenko did not manage to fight corruption and sever the ties between the politics and the big business, as he and his political allies promised during the Orange Revolution. As Kudelia puts it, the new country's leadership happened to be unwilling to give up on the informal practices of their predecessors (Kudelia 2012). Not incidentally, Ukraine consistently received low scores on the quality of democratic governance and high corruption scores under the Orange rule, which indirectly proves that informal institutions remained a highly significant instrument regulating the country's political-economic realm (see e.g., Freedom House 2005–2009; Transparency International 2009).

The democratization of political life under Yushchenko's presidency was not an effect of the reforms promised by the leaders of the Orange Revolution, but rather a consequence of constitutional amendments they had to compromise over with the former Ukrainian leadership in order to gain power (Malygina 2010; Fisun 2012).[24] Ukraine's constitutional reform of 2004, which entered into force in 2006, curbed presidential power and shifted much of the powers to the prime minister. These constitutional changes led to decentralization of the executive authority and the rise of at least two competing power centers (that of the president and that of the prime minister) instead of the previously existing single one, and this in turn caused greater political pluralism, not least because oligarchs began to support different centers of authority, and, correspondingly, different political forces (Pleines 2010, as quoted in Malygina 2010). Because control over the executive branch and the

---

24 The constitutional reform backed by outgoing president Kuchma was supported by Viktor Yushchenko during Orange Revolution in 2004 in order to reach political compromise with the acting authorities, which tried to commit electoral fraud in favor of his rival Viktor Yanukovych. The support of the reform helped Yushchenko to win the presidency in the elections of 2004.

respective formal and informal power were now divided between the president and prime minister, neither had the same ability that Kuchma did to use government and administrative resources for electoral purposes (D'Anieri 2007). The same concerns the state's control over the media. As Hale (2009) justly commented it on, "Media and business now knew that if they ran afoul of one patron, they could always find political cover under the other." This helps understand why after the Orange Revolution Ukraine's press freedom scores improved considerably.

Despite some evident democratic achievements of the Orange Revolution, the exercise of political power in Ukraine did not undergo substantial change under the 'Orange' government (Fisun 2011; Hale 2009). According to Fisun, in 2004–2009 the nature of the Ukrainian political system remained, as in the pre-Orange period, oriented not towards the production of 'the public good,' but towards rent extraction. Similar to their predecessors, the 'Orange' authorities enjoyed patronage opportunities and maintained rent-seeking schemes (Kudelia and Kuzio 2015). They also systematically used the judiciary (which continued to be far from independent, like in Kuchma times) as an instrument of elite power struggles (Kudelia 2012; Malygina 2010). Characteristically, no one among those suspected of corruption during the Kuchma regime was ever charged or convicted under the Orange rule (Puglisi 2008).

Similar to Leonid Kuchma and his allies, the Orange rulers prevented the judiciary from becoming an independent check on executive power and used it as an instrument of political struggle. According to Trochev (2010), under Yushchenko the courts became even more vulnerable to political interference than they were under Kuchma. Yushchenko fired unfavorable judges on numerous occasions, he also used the SBU (the Security Service of Ukraine) to discredit them (see e.g., Wolowski 2008; Malygina 2010). The instrumentalization of courts during the political crisis-2007, when Yushchenko issued a decree to dismiss three judges of the Constitutional Court in order to influence the Court's decision about constitutionality of his decision to dissolve Parliament, or the developments around reprivatization and redistribution of property (see e.g., Wolowski 2008) led to the discrediting of Ukrainian courts and continued to hurt judicial independence in the country (Wolowski 2008; Popova 2010). The same effect arose from the President's pressure on the court during his second attempt to schedule an early parliamentary election in 2008, and so did some other events (Hale 2009, 4; Popova 2010, 23).

Being engaged in an incessant fight for power and resources between themselves, the Ukraine's two centers of power—the president and the prime minister—rather did not care about strengthening the institutional foundations of democracy. This especially concerned the improvement of horizontal accountability between government branches and the advancement of the rule of law, which received little support from the political decision-makers in post-Orange Ukraine (Kudelia 2012; Popova 2014). As a result, as Kudelia (2012) pointedly notes, the Ukraine's democratization under Yushchenko became an ephemeral and easily reversible achievement.

It is probably the lack of basic changes in Ukraine's institutional arrangement in post-Orange period that explains why the country's media independence, despite its significant advancement after 2004, continued to raise the concern of domestic and international media watchdogs: during the whole period of Viktor Yushchenko's presidency the Ukrainian media remained only 'partly free' in the Freedom House's index of media freedom (Freedom House 2005–2010). Nota bene, some of Ukraine's press freedom scores, after they swiftly improved immediately after the Orange Revolution, noticeably slid down in the last years of president Yushchenko's rule (see e.g., MSI-Ukraine 2008–2009, REF-Ukraine 2007). The experts evaluating the condition of mass media in Ukraine pointed out a growing instrumentalization of the country's news outlets (both the state owned and the commercial ones) for political purposes in this period (MSI-Ukraine 2008–2009).

Yushchenko's successor as president in 2010, Viktor Yanukovych, his former rival in the elections of 2004, quickly reversed the constitutional reform of 2004 and restored Kuchma's 1996 super-presidential constitution. Under his presidency Ukraine returned to presidential, monopolistic control over the political sphere, including both the formal and the informal power levers. The country experienced a steep democratic decline, including deterioration of its democratic institutions (which was reflected in Ukraine's significant worsening in Freedom House indices), erosion of civil liberties, and curbs on press freedom. Under Yanukovych the trend toward the use of the courts to achieve political goals, which was observed in Ukraine before, significantly intensified (Popova 2014). The president not only pressured the Constitutional Court to increase his powers by reversing the 2004 constitutional reforms (Kuzio 2012); he also used his formal and informal control over the judiciary to persecute the political opposition (the widely known case of the prosecution of former prime minister Yulia Tymoshenko was only one among a series of politically motivated criminal charges against former government officials filed by the Yanukovych regime). Having a monopoly control over the informal power levers, Yanukovych used this to dismantle the democratic achievements of the previous period (Kudelia 2012). Among undemocratic trends characterizing his government, the researchers name the weakening of Parliament as an independent legislative body (Kramer et al. 2011), large subordination of law-enforcement agencies to the President (Kudelia 2012, see also Freedom House 2013) and unprecedented politicization of the judiciary (Popova 2014, see also BTI-2014 Ukraine Country Report). Media independence also suffered, and its steep deterioration in 2010–2014 was reflected in incredibly low levels of the country's press freedom indices (Freedom House 2011, 2012, 2013, 2014).

1.2.4. Institutional void, flawed formal rules, and the supremacy of informal institutions

Summing up this brief history of the Ukrainian transformations up to late 2013, we may agree with Kudelia (2012) that the role of informal institutions in the regulation of elite relations within the state and with important non-state groups (e.g., oligarchic clans) never faded away over the last two decades in Ukraine. Besides, no significant progress was achieved in building the fundamental institutions of the state. It is this institutional void that Kudelia believes to be the main reason why the country's post-communist transformation was in fact reduced to what he calls "a vicious cycling between shallow democratization and autocratic reversal" (Kudelia 2012). An integral part of this institutional inadequacy was the persistent weakness of Ukraine's state institutions of horizontal accountability, in particular the judiciary, as well as the substantial subordination of the latter to the executive, together with major state oversight and controlling bodies (D'Anieri 2007; Malygina 2010). To a great extent this was an outcome of purposeful efforts of Ukraine's post-Soviet elites competing for the privilege to monopolize their control over government resources and rent-generating positions, and seeking to weaken the state in order to exploit it (Kudelia 2012).

One more noteworthy outcome of these efforts, as it follows from the study of formal institutions and informal politics in Ukraine by Kerstin Zimmer (2008), was an unclear and contradictory legal framework which made a fertile soil for the prevalence of informal institutions in the regulation of Ukraine's politics and economy. According to Zimmer, legal regulations in Ukraine are often flawed and insufficient to regulate respective behavior, but this does not result from ignorance or transformation frictions. On the contrary, an insufficient legal framework is designed purposely to create uncertainty and to serve as an instrument to exercise control and power. Importantly, Zimmer assumes that formal and informal rules are not neatly separated in Ukraine. Instead, formal rules are intentionally designed in such a way that informal patron-client relations must be used to act successfully and that all actors are rendered potentially vulnerable (Zimmer 2008).

Flawed and entangled legal regulations are thus an indispensable condition for Ukraine's consistent supremacy of informal regulations. As it results from the study by Keith Darden (2002), imperfect laws are a necessary element which enables the inner workings of the Ukrainian state as regulated largely by informal institutions. According to Darden, in Ukraine and many other highly corrupt countries, "the law is not intended to be followed" and "some laws are drafted so as to insure non-compliance" (Darden 2002, 7).

Darden's study illuminates the twisted logic followed frequently by Ukrainian formal institutions and the particular merger of formality and informality characteristic for the Ukrainian institutional landscape. Here, according to Darden, the defects of formal rules are often deliberate, and are designed to use law enforcement mechanisms for punishing violation of informal rules, which *de facto* regulate the relationships between state leaders and key societal groups. Indeed, Darden argues that it is not formal legal institutions that constitute, for example, the contract between decision-making principals and state agents in what he calls a 'corrupt' state. Instead, the "contract" between them is "an *informal* one that is not grounded in the law" (Darden 2002, 8). The essence of this informal contract can be the privilege of deriving informal rents from public office granted by state leaders to subordinate officials in exchange for their compliance and loyalty. Violation of such 'contracts' is sanctioned in Ukraine via the selective use of formal regulations. These regulations, as mentioned before, are intentionally made contradictory, fuzzy, and inconsistent to force people into non-compliance and make virtually everyone a potential law offender (Darden 2001, 2002, 2008). This puts a hook in the mouth of many office holders, entrepreneurs and private individuals: in case they break the informal contracts with decision-making principals, they can be formally sanctioned for breaking the abovementioned defective laws.[25]

Needless to say, a necessary condition for the entire corrupt mechanism to work is weakness and/or the lack of independence

---

25 This does not mean, however, that each violation of an informal contract is necessarily sanctioned through law enforcement bodies. As Helmke and Levitsky (2006) pointedly noted, informal institutions are effectively maintained and enforced via highly visible (if infrequent) episodes of rule-breaking and sanction. According to these researchers, widely observed efforts to punish deviations from informal rules, communicate respective informal rules to relevant actors and discourage others from breaking these rules.

of the judiciary, law enforcement, and public agencies of control and oversight. These state institutions and agencies, instead of being used for their intended purposes, often become an instrument for enforcing informal contracts among the political/economic elites, and, more generally, serve as an important factor of transmission, enforcement and, in effect, reproduction of informal institutions (see Darden 2002; Zimmer 2008; Malygina 2010).

The above brief outline of Ukraine's institutional transformation makes us assume that the media could be just one among many institutions which were (and probably still are) subject to attempts to be appropriated, redefined, or misused by the Ukrainian political/economic elites. This assumption seems all the more plausible since the role of the media in Ukraine's political life was and remains rather significant (see e.g., Dyczok 2006, 2009). This is because along with the weakness of horizontal checks of the executive power (D'Anieri 2007), the country is characterized by at least one relatively effective institution of vertical accountability: namely, elections. Indeed, as international human rights watchdogs as well as political scientists admit, elections in Ukraine are quite competitive and generate genuine uncertainty (see e.g., Freedom House 2002–2013; O'Donnell 1996; Way 2004). No wonder then that the ruling elites make significant attempts to tilt the field of electoral competition in favor of their representatives (Way 2004). This includes the efforts to get control over the media. Ukrainian political/economic elites believe the media to be a powerful instrument of shaping and manipulating public opinion, including that related to elections and candidates (Dyczok 2006). Therefore they invest much effort and resources to control the TV, press, and, recently, also the Internet (see e.g., Åslund 2005; Dyczok 2006, 2009).

The next chapter will carry out a detailed analysis of politics-media relationships in Ukraine in the period under study.

Chapter 2
Media capture in post-communist Ukraine

The previous chapter provided the larger context of this study, and shed light on the internal logic of Ukraine's political process, as well as on general obstacles to democratization shaped (or, in some cases, retained) in Ukraine in the course of state capture by private interests. This chapter goes into greater depth and explores what media-politics relations look like within this particular logic and what the implications of state capture in Ukraine are for the media and their independence.

The central role in the theoretical basis for this chapter is played by the concept of media capture. Media capture, according to Mungiu-Pippidi (2008) is a companion, or complementary phenomenon for state capture. As discussed in the previous chapter, state capture has profoundly marked the situation in Ukraine in the period under study (1994–2013). This chapter helps to answer the following questions: Who are the captors of private media in Ukraine?[26] What impact does media capture have on the content of Ukrainian media? What methods do media captors use to make the media serve their particular interests? What factors may further (or restrain) media capture in Ukraine?

---

26 I focus my attention on private media, because private media enjoy absolutely the highest popularity ratings among Ukrainian audiences (see for ex., Ukrainian TV ratings in 2001–2013 at: http://www.telekritika.ua/page/ratings/?&articles_p=1). Within this group I specifically concentrate on television as the most popular mass medium in Ukraine, especially in discussing the effects and tools of media capture in Ukraine. This is justified by the fact that in the researched period television significantly outstripped the rest of the media as a source of the news in Ukraine. For instance, the survey conducted by the Democratic Initiatives Foundation in May 2013, showed that 90 percent of Ukrainians cited television among their top three sources of political information (www.dif.org.ua/ua/events/hdvhwidhvhdfvjkhj.htm, accessed August 18, 2013).

The second part of the chapter focuses on certain media-related institutions and regulatory frameworks, ones which are supposed to fairly regulate media-politics relationships, but often become obstacles to the democratic performance of Ukraine's media. Thus, here I pay attention, on the one hand, to the design and capacity of these structures—and on the other to how they were used or misused (and sometimes even modified according to their immediate interests) by different Ukrainian governments.

***

The discussion in this chapter elaborates the previous chapter's assumption that because media and politics are too interconnected in Ukraine and other post-Soviet states, explanation of these countries' incomplete media reforms after the fall of the Soviet Union cannot be reduced to the media-centered analysis often proposed in media studies. Indeed, among the concepts typically used to explain "why the media are as they are" in post-communist Europe and Eurasia are media legislation, the media market, state intervention, political culture, and the professionalization of journalism. However, these concepts create an incomplete picture, one that omits important factors influencing the media in countries which are not (fully) democratic (Downing 1996; Curran and Park 2000).

The history of Ukraine's media transformations provides several examples illustrating the limitations of media-centered explanations of media change in post-Soviet countries. One of them is the decline in media freedom following the election of Viktor Yanukovych to the presidency in 2010. This change, registered by international organizations like Reporters Without Borders, Freedom House, and others, cannot be explained by media-related determinants of media freedom such as the condition of the media market, media legislation or a professional journalistic culture, none of which has undergone significant change since 2010. This section helps to explain this matter and other swerves in the trajectory of Ukraine's media change with the help of the conceptual instruments from comparative politics introduced in the previous chapter, as well as the concept of media capture.

Media capture is defined by Mungiu-Pippidi (2012, 40-41) as "a situation in which media have not succeeded in becoming autonomous and manifesting the will of their own, nor able to exercise their main function, notably of informing people. Instead, they have persisted in an intermediate state, with vested interests, not just the government, using them for other purposes." Media capture manifests itself in the form of a concentrated, opaque ownership of media outlets, with important political actors controlling the media (Mungiu-Pippidi 2008). Moreover, its major inherent feature is the prevalence of informal influence on the media, since media capture, in essence, means indirect control of the media through informal techniques (Mungiu-Pippidi 2008; Besley and Prat 2002). As mentioned in the previous chapter, in such countries as Ukraine, where "informal (patrimonial) and formal (bureaucratic) logics of action coexist" (Malygina 2010, 10), informal rules and practices often subvert or undermine new formal regulations introduced after the abandonment of communism, thereby raising barriers to the rule of law and successful democratic reforms in general. This statement especially applies to the relationship between private media groups and politics, one of the areas most affected by the dominance of informal institutions in post-communist countries (Guasti and Dobovsek 2011; Gel'man 2004).

The concept of media capture was initially developed on the basis of evidence from various countries in Latin America, Asia, and Europe (Italy) (Besley and Prat 2005; Prat and Stromberg 2011; Corneo 2006). More recently, scholars have applied it to the analysis of media in the democratic laggards of post-communist Europe, especially Romania (Mungiu-Pippidi 2008; 2012).[27] It seems to be quite relevant for analysis of the state of media freedom in Ukraine.

---

[27] In latest publications, the term of media capture started to be used also to characterise media systems in more successful Central-Eastern European democracies, mostly whith regard to such problems as oligarchization of media ownership (Stetka 2015) or party colonization of the media (Bajomi-Lazar 2015).

Reports by international and Ukrainian media monitoring organizations regularly point to such Ukrainian problems as the opacity of media ownership and its excessive concentration, as well as the unofficial influence of private political and economic interests on media content (MSI-Ukraine 2008, 2009, 2011). Publications on political reforms and regime change in Ukraine describe the Ukrainian political system as oligarchic, with state institutions extensively privatized (or captured) by economic-political elites who use them to support, generate, and maximize profits (Åslund 2005; Puglisi 2003; 2008).

Recent Ukrainian history, with its several changes of institutional design—particularly in 2004, 2010, and 2014 when constitutional amendments reducing the president's formal powers were introduced, then reversed, and finally brought back in—offers a remarkable opportunity to see how such changes can affect the media. Here I focus especially on which opportunities the presidencies of Viktor Yushchenko (2005–2010) and Viktor Yanukovych (2010–2014) gave to different actors to make the media serve their purposes. I expect this comparison to highlight factors that foster or suppress media capture in Ukraine.

Though this chapter examines Ukraine's media and media-politics relationships in the recent past, in the following discussion I often use the present tense to signal that the described state of affairs remained largely unchanged following the period under study (1994–2013) and until the moment when this book went to print in 2016. Nevertheless, I would like to underline that the findings below relate chiefly to the years 1994–2013. Still, where possible I have tried to note what changes (or lack of thereof) took place after Ukraine's Eurorevolution in late 2013–early 2014. For this, I mainly relied on footnotes.

2.1. Media capture in Ukraine: actors, methods, and effects

2.1.1. Who are the captors of private media in Ukraine?

According to Mungiu-Pippidi (2008) and Corneo (2006), actors that can capture media include the government and vested political interests. Media capture is seen as complementary to state capture; vested interests are not interested in the media per se but in the possibility of using them to capture the state. The development of media-politics relationships in post-communist countries can take one of three forms: (1) competitive politics and media pluralism, as in the Central European democracies; (2) oligarchization and media capture, characteristic of semi-democratic and semi-authoritarian regimes; or (3) a return to strict censorship and controlled media, as in outright dictatorships (Mungiu-Pippidi 2008, 91). According to Mungiu-Pippidi, path 2 and path 3 can coexist; for example, private media take path 2 while public ones fall under government control, taking path 3.

How does this theory apply to Ukraine? In the period under study Ukraine had two types of media in terms of ownership: state and municipal media, and private media. Since then, in 2014–2015 Ukraine made substantial progress in the realm of public service broadcasting, which started to be created on the basis of state television and radio broadcasters. Moreover, the way was paved to privatization of the state and municipal print media: in November 2015 the Parliament (passed the corresponding law "On reforming state and communal print mass media"). The process of the print media's privatization will, however, last at least 3 years, and in the meantime some municipal authorities will still enjoy full control over the media they own.

In the researched period Ukrainian state-owned and municipal media approached Mungiu-Pippidi's path 3 of direct control by the relevant authorities. The appointment and dismissal of government media's top managers were a political issue (MSI-Ukraine 2006/2007, 2008, 2011). Because public media relied on state and municipal budgets for their financing, most of them focused on the political interests of the relevant state institutions (MSI-Ukraine 2006/2007, 2010). Municipal media often drew most of their information from officials' and politicians' press conferences and briefings (MSI-Ukraine 2010). During electoral campaigns, the authorities generally used 'their' media as propaganda tools at both the national and the local levels (see e.g., MSI-Ukraine 2008). State and municipal media were generally less popular than private outlets, at least at the national level. For example, in 2011, the then state-owned *UT-1* (which was converted into a public service broadcaster in 2015) was only ninth in the broadcast rankings (GfK Ukraine 2011). Therefore, this study concentrates on the private media sector.

Ukraine's private media display almost all the features attributed by media researchers to captured media (Mungiu-Pippidi 2008, 91): media ownership is highly concentrated; it is nontransparent; and the people who own the media are mostly connected to or directly involved in politics. As the latest studies show (see, for ex., Dovzhenko 2015) this situation underwent no basic changes after the EuroMaidan protests. A feature specific to Ukraine is that private media are, as a rule, owned by industrial-financial magnates, commonly referred to as 'oligarchs,' whose main business interests are outside the media sector—namely, in gas, metal, coal, energy, food processing, and other areas (Dyczok 2006; Dutsyk 2010). As described in Chapter 1, they emerged during the period of *nomenklatura* privatization in the early 1990s, in which the former communist elite transformed its bureaucratic power into financial power, intensifying the collusion between big business and politics (Puglisi 2008; Wolowski 2008). They maintain close political ties (see Table 1), because incomes from their main businesses, opportunities to extend their business empires through privatization of state-owned enterprises, along with the chances to safeguard their property in the conditions of general weakness of the rule of law characteristic to Ukraine depend heavily on political decisions (Melnykovska and Schweickert 2008).

Table 1

Major Media Owners in Ukraine and Their Engagement in Politics (June 30, 2013)

Owner	Major media	Involvement in politics
InterMediaGroup (Serhiy Liovochkin, Dmytro Firtash)	61 percent share of Ukrainian independent TV corporation (*Inter* TV channel) 90 percent share of *Kino*TV (*Enterfilm* TV channel) 90 percent share of *Music*-TV (*Enter music* TV channel), *K1*, *K2*, *Megasport* TV channels 60 percent share of *NTN* TV channel 90 percent share of Ukrainian News Information Agency	Serhiy Liovochkin Feb. 2010–2013: head of presidential administration Dmytro Firtash 2007–2013: financial support for different political parties and politicians
StarLightMedia Group (Viktor Pinchuk)	*ICTV* TV channel *STB* TV channel *Novy* TV channel *Fakty i kommentarii* daily newspaper *Sobytiia i liudi* weekly newspaper Controlling interest in Ekonomika publishing house: daily *Delo*, weekly *Invest gazeta*, and other niche publications Shares in music channels *M1*, *M2* Shares in *Russkoe radio*, *Hit-FM*, *Kiss-FM*	Viktor Pinchuk 2002–2006: member of parliament Before the 2006 parliamentary election, Pinchuk announced that he would never stand for election if Yushchenko guaranteed to protect his property rights. It seems symptomatic that he did not take part in this election. Although Pinchuk has not directly participated in politics since 2006, he maintains close relationships with important political players in Ukraine. For example, top-ranking Ukrainian officials regularly attend summits he organizes in Yalta and Davos. According to *Ukrainska pravda*, Pinchuk financed the Arseniy Yatseniuk Open Ukraine Foundation for two years (Nayem 2009). The newspaper also reported that Vitali Klitschko was cooperating with the Viktor Pinchuk Foundation (Leshchenko 2012). *Ukrainska pravda* also assumed that in the parliamentary elections of 2012 Pinchuk financed several candidates from three political parties: the Party of Regions, Batkivshchyna and Udar (Leshchenko 2012).
Rinat Akhmetov Group (Rinat Akhmetov)	*Ukraina* TV channel *Segodnia* daily newspaper Regional newspaper *Salon Dona i Basa* News website KID (http://zadonbass.org)	Rinat Akhmetov Viktor Yanukovych's main financial supporter during the 2004 presidential elections; a major entrepreneur and influential member of the Party of Regions (Olszanski 2010)

1+1 Media Group (Ihor Kolomoisky)	1+1 TV channel 2+2 TV channel SITI TV channel TET TV channel Kino TV channel		Ihor Kolomoisky Kolomoisky acknowledged that he financed Viktor Yanukovych in the 2004 presidential elections (Nayem and Leshchenko 2008). He also allegedly supported Yulia Tymoshenko (Siumar 2008). He financed the Our Ukraine political party in the 2006–2007 parliamentary elections (Nayem and Leshchenko 2008) and allegedly supported Klitschko's Udar party in the 2012 parliamentary elections (Leshchenko 2012).

Sources: Media ownership—Dutsyk 2010, Leshchenko (December 6, 2006) and later publications in *Ukrainska pravda*; oligarch's involvement in politics—my own research.
Note: Because the list of big media owners in Ukraine is constantly changing for political reasons, this study supplies specific dates for its data on media ownership structure.

In 1994–2013 media ownership was not transparent in Ukraine.[28] Although the Law on Television and Radio Broadcasting obliged the National Television and Radio Broadcasting Council of Ukraine (NTRBC) to provide information about media owners, the council fulfilled its task only in part. The NTRBC Web site provided some information about owners of media outlets, but it provided only the company names: as a rule, foreign enterprises registered in offshore zones (Dutsyk 2010).

Nevertheless, since the mid-2000s media ownership has become somewhat less opaque. Whereas in the 1990s businessmen concealed that they owned (or influenced) media, in the 2000s with increasing frequency they publicly declared their ownership of media assets. In addition, several journalistic investigations and studies by independent researchers disclosed the real owners of popular nationwide media (Leshchenko 2006; Dyczok 2006; Dutsyk 2010). According to these and other sources, in 2013 the major media owners in Ukraine were Viktor Pinchuk, the founder and main owner of one of Ukraine's leading steel industry groups; Rinat Akhmetov, a coal and steel magnate and the country's richest man; Ihor Kolomoisky, the leading partner of a banking and industrial conglomerate engaged in the steel, chemical, and energy industries; Dmytro Firtash, a Ukrainian gas trader who was for years a key figure in the multibillion-dollar Russian natural gas trade to Ukraine; and Serhiy Liovochkin, former senior adviser to Leonid Kuchma and the head of the presidential administration under Viktor Yanukovych (2010–2014). That said, official data confirming this information were not available to the public, making it difficult to document who owns what in the Ukrainian media market.[29]

---

28 At the time of writing, substantial positive changes concerning transparency of media ownership have taken place in Ukraine. On September 3, 2015 the Law on transparency in media ownership was adopted by the parliament of Ukraine and then, on September 10, 2015 it was signed by the president.
29 This state of affairs did not change principally after Ukrainian EuroMaidan in late 2013–early 2014. For example, the opinion poll conducted in 20 May–2 June 2015 by Kyiv International Institute of Sociology (KIIS) showed that only 19 percent of Ukrainians consider that information about who is a real owner of

In the researched period media ownership in Ukraine was characterized by a high degree of concentration. From the mid-1990s Ukraine's media market was ever more dominated by big media companies, ones which in time became large media corporations. Among them are: the InterMediaGroup, whose ownership was kept in the hands of individuals loyal to the state and thus changed regularly; the StarLightMedia Group, owned by former president Kuchma's son-in-law Viktor Pinchuk; the Rinat Akhmetov Group bearing the name of its owner; and the 1+1 Media Group purchased in late 2000s by Ihor Kolomoisky (Dyczok 2014a). (Table 1). According to data from 2011, audience shares of TV channels belonging to these groups were, respectively, 20.47 percent, 25.3 percent, 9.99 percent, and 14.16 percent—that is, 70 percent altogether. InterMediaGroup and StarLightMedia Group received the lion's share of television advertising.[30] For example, in 2009, national television channels pulled in 2.1 million hryvnias (UAH) in advertising revenues, of which InterMediaGroup and Pinchuk's StarLightMedia Group accrued almost 1.6 million UAH—75 percent of the whole (Prodaieva 2010a). Ukrainian tycoons who sought to influence public opinion also dominated the print media (Table 2). Two of the three most widely read Ukrainian dailies, *Segodnia* and *Fakty i kommentarii* belonged to Rinat Akhmetov and Viktor Pinchuk, respectively (Dutsyk 2010). According to the latest publications, this state of affairs has remained basically unchanged also since Ukraine's pro-democratic revolution in 2013–2014 (Dovzhenko 2015).[31]

---

a nationwide TV channel is "fully available" or "rather available." From 58 percent to 84 percent of respondents did not know who are the owners of major Ukrainian TV channels. The only exception was *5 Channel*, belonging to president Petro Poroshenko; as much as 75 percent of the respondents could correctly name its owner.
30 Based on information from GfK Ukraine, June 2011.
31 However, some changes have happened in the newspaper sector, where another leader appeared, namely the free newspaper *Vesti* published by the Multimedia Publishing Group reportedly funded by Yanukovych's associates Kurchenko and Oleksandr Klimenko. There are also assumptions that the Group has ties to Russian funding (MSI-Ukraine 2015, 223).

Table 2
Ownership of Top Four National Dailies (2010)

Newspaper	Owner
Fakty i kommentarii	Viktor Pinchuk
Argumenty i fakty	Boris Lozhkin
Segodnya	Rinat Akhmetov
Komsomolskaya pravda v Ukrainie	Boris Lozhkin, Ihor Kolomoisky

Sources: Konrad-Adenauer-Stiftung (KAS). "Ukrainian Media Landscape-2010", 2011, www.kas.de/ukraine/ukr/publications/23004/, Konrad-Adenauer-Stiftung (KAS), The KAS Democracy Report – 2008: Media and Democracy. Vol. II., www.kas.de/wf/en/33.14855/

The medium that remained and continues to remain relatively free from the grasp of Ukrainian tycoons is the Internet, which the Ukrainian economic-political elite up to 2014 never perceived as a significant means of influencing public opinion. For example, the popular and influential *Ukrainska pravda* news site belongs to its editor-in-chief, Olena Prytula (Obozrevatel 2013). Not surprisingly, the Internet, being freest from political/economic control, serves Ukrainians as a source of independent news. Ukrainian tycoons do own some important online resources, however, mainly the Web sites associated with their broadcast and print media. Serhiy Kurchenko—who in 2013 bought the largest newspaper holding in Ukraine (UMH Group), specializing also in Internet media, from Boris Lozhkin—became an owner of one of the biggest Ukrainian Internet portals *Bigmir.net* and the high-ranking news Web site *Korrespondent.net*.

These big businessmen do not see their media assets primarily as a profitable business. Though opinions vary as to the state of affairs in the late 1990s and throughout the 2000s, in the 2010s the majority of Ukrainian and international experts claimed that television channels, including top-ranking ones, were not sustainable businesses (EED 2015:41). Maksym Lazebnyk, head of the Ukrainian Advertising Coalition, insisted in 2011 that "there are no profitable TV channels in Ukraine today, big or small" (Grytsenko 2011). In 2012 Boris Lozhkin, then big media owner himself, also stated that television was unprofitable for Ukrainian tycoons (Mediananny 2012). He explained this by the following assumption:

> "[they] do not regard television as a business. They consider it a kind of supplement to their other businesses, one that provides, in their view, certain solutions for their main businesses." (Ibid.)

What calls no doubts, media assets serve their owners as a means of accumulating political influence, something they can convert into opportunities to develop or support their main businesses (Dutsyk 2010; Matuszak 2012). Hence we can assume that private media in Ukraine belong to Mungiu-Pippidi's category of media captured by vested interests closely intertwined with politics.

The state also influences the content of private media in Ukraine. The state had a particularly significant impact on media under Kuchma, when the administration censored media with the use of *temnyky* (Dyczok 2006).[32] It dropped—but did not disappear—after the success of the Orange Revolution, when Yushchenko's Secretariat used different methods to discipline disobedient media, including sanctions issued by the National Broadcasting Council (Ligachova 2006). During the Yanukovych presidency, *de facto* censorship has returned: despite the absence of *temnyky,* the homogeneity of news on central TV channels caused media and human right watchdogs to believe that Ukrainian media were again orchestrated from above (Ivanov et al. 2011). We can assume, therefore, that the state is another captor of private media in Ukraine.[33]

In Ukraine, admittedly, like in many other post-Soviet countries, the state is not a single actor or an actor with certain broadly consistent core interests and positions. It is rather an aggregate of competing economic, political, and bureaucratic interests (Wolowski 2008; Fisun 2012). Because the main motive for political

---

32 The term refers to unofficial instructions issued by the Kuchma administration to the main media outlets 'recommending' what events to cover and how.
33 The state of media independence in Ukraine noticeably improved after the fall of president Viktor Yanukovych's government in February 2014, as evidenced by the reports the reports of Freedom House and International Research and Exchange Board (Freedom House 2015, MSI-Ukraine 2015). In particular, political pressure on state-owned outlets decreased, as did the level of government hostility and legal pressure faced by journalists.

participation is access to state resources and opportunities for rent seeking, different political actors and groups compete with one another to capture state institutions (Wolowski 2008; Fisun 2012). As outlined in Chapter 1, especially attractive in this sense is control over (or closeness to) the executive branch, which controls such precious resources as control over large sectors of the economy, patronage (control of government jobs), and control of regional governments (D'Anieri 2007). It also has at its disposal the powerful (albeit chiefly informal) mechanisms of media control, including influence on media regulatory and monitoring organs, control of law and administrative enforcement, and considerable influence on the judiciary (D'Anieri 2007; Way 2004). Thus, in speaking about the state as a media captor in Ukraine in this chapter, I have in mind, first and foremost, the executive branch.

As elaborated in Chapter 1, the Ukrainian executive branch has undergone several important formal changes in the time span analyzed in this book (1994–2013); these changes affected both the political situation in the country and press freedom. The first one was the result of the decided upon during the 2004 Orange Revolution amendments to the 1996 constitution. These amendments shifted significant powers from the president to the prime minister (and the parliament). This development redistributed not only formal but also informal power within the executive branch (Hale 2011), creating two pyramids of power (instead of one, headed by the president, characteristic of Kuchma's time in office), competing with each other to control the state. President Yushchenko's time in office also brought a noticeable improvement of media freedom and the interruption of centralized control of the media by the presidential administration. The *temnyky* policy stopped, and violence against journalists became rarer. Political interference with the media did not stop altogether, however, and the media in Ukraine remained 'partly free' in Freedom House's classification. Greater media independence was also not accompanied by lower corruption and better governance (Freedom House 2006, 2007, 2009). This state of affairs reflected the persistence of capture of state institutions by private interests (Hale 2011; Malygina 2010).

The next significant change in formal executive arrangements took place after Viktor Yanukovych won the presidential election in 2010. Soon after taking office, Yanukovych revived the powerful Kuchma-style presidency by revoking the 2004 constitutional amendments and returning Ukraine to a hyper-centralized constitutional model that strongly empowers the president (Kudelia 2013). Under Yanukovych, media independence has considerably eroded, a development attributed by some commentators to excessive interference in news coverage by oligarchic media moguls, now more afraid of conflict with the ruling class than under Yushchenko (Kudelia 2011). Direct and indirect government control of the media also grew.[34]

Media ownership, or at least control over the content of the most powerful private media, is a desirable resource in Ukraine—and one that is contested from time to time. Every Ukrainian president from Kuchma to Yanukovych has tried to make effective use of the media by favoring his allies' companies or appointing new owners to existing firms.[35] Under Kuchma, the main media outlets in Ukraine—above all, the national television stations—became the property of people from the president's immediate entourage: for example, his son-in-law, Viktor Pinchuk, or Ihor Pluzhnikov, an ally

---

34 The most recent constitutional amendments related to power distribution between the president and the cabinet in Ukraine are not considered in this study because they happened later than the period under study in this book. In early 2014, a few days after overthrow of Viktor Yanukovych's presidential powers, the Constitutional reform of 2004 was resumed. The role of the president was weakened similarly as after the Orange Revolution, and the parliament's prerogatives strengthened significantly. This increased the political weight of oligarchs who since the 1990s had been influencing the key political parties. The dismantling of the power vertikal built by Yanukovych positively impacted the state of media freedom and pluralism in Ukraine (see: Freedom House 2015, MSI-Ukraine 2015). At the same time, Ukrainian media monitoring organizations point out that the practice of instrumental use of media by their owners continues (Dovzhenko 2015).

35 I do not consider the presidency of Leonid Kravchuk here because big media empires emerged in Ukraine not until under Leonid Kuchma (see Dyczok 2006).

of the pro-presidential Social-Democratic Party of Ukraine (United) led by the head of Kuchma's presidential administration Viktor Medvedchuk (Dyczok 2006; Kuzio 2009). In Yushchenko's case, such attempts resulted in a change of ownership at the two largest television channels—*Inter* and *1+1* (Dutsyk 2010; Nayem and Leshchenko 2008; Siumar and Taran 2005). Under Yanukovych, the leader in TV ratings *Inter* again underwent a change in ownership (Dzerkalo Tyzhnia 2013). Besides, the president's older son Oleksandr reportedly joined the circle of big media owners (Neef 2012). Also the person from Oleksandr Yanukovych's surrounding, a young businessman Serhiy Kurchenko who had never been interested in media business before, unexpectedly became a new Ukrainian media mogul in 2013. Yanukovych also took significant steps to ensure that his political group would control broadcasting after the switchover to digital television. In 2011, the National Broadcasting Council selected one company as Ukraine's nationwide provider for digital multiplexes: a previously unknown company, Zeonbud, whose owners were hidden in offshore zones (Rachkevych 2011). Speculation was running high in Ukraine that people close to president Viktor Yanukovych and his allies were behind the company (Shcherbyna 2012). Whether or not this was true, the situation in which a single provider has the monopoly on digital television gives Ukrainian authorities the exclusive opportunity to control television in the future.[36]

Does this mean that only two actors—the groups of vested interests who own the media and the state—define media content in Ukraine? Not entirely, as can be seen from media performance in the period of relative freedom from political pressure after the Orange Revolution. Since then, Ukrainian media content has become saturated with hidden political (less often, economic) advertising,

---

36 Following the EuroMaidan, Zeonbud remained a monopolist of digital format TV programs distribution.
Ukraine's State Antimonopoly Committee confirmed this in its Decision on December 23, 2014, in which Zeonbud was declared a monopoly (http://medialaw.org.ua/en/news/zeonbud-is-recognized-to-be-a-monopolist/).

known as *dzhynsa* (see e.g., Belyakov 2009; Ligachova 2008b). Ukrainian media experts have estimated that before elections prepaid political materials account for up to 80 percent of all media content (Poludenko and Semenchenko 2008). According to Ligachova, the spread of *dzhynsa* is troubling because the media do not bring audiences essential news, but instead promote the interests of those who can pay for hidden advertising. In Ukraine, these people predominantly represent the political and economic elite. Big media owners and their associates, therefore, make up the first group of media captors—namely, vested interests closely connected with politics.

2.1.2. How does media capture affect Ukrainian media content?

Captured media fail to perform their main function: providing society with information. Instead, they serve the interests of their captors—governments or vested interests networked with politics (Mungiu-Pippidi 2008). They manipulate information on behalf of their masters, who can use them as an information weapon against political opponents. They also trade in influence. For example, in Romania private media may offer favorable treatment of the government in exchange for state advertising (Ghinea and Avădani 2011).

In nationwide media the impact of the interests of the first kind of media captors (owners) on media content is not always obvious. The oligarchs who own influential media may offer the support of their news outlets to other political players, notably those in power, in exchange for political decisions favorable to their businesses. On other occasions, the owners' impact on what their media print or air becomes visible. For example, Ukrainian oligarchs often use their media to promote themselves and their close allies. Viktor Pinchuk regularly advertises the activity of his foundation, including its philanthropic programs and political projects such as the World Economic Forum meetings in Davos. In 2011, Pinchuk used his media to whitewash his father-in-law, Leonid Kuchma, against whom criminal proceedings had been instituted in March 2011 for abuse of power and office that led to the death of the journalist Georgi Gongadze. In May 2011, two television channels belonging to Pinchuk transmitted a twenty-six-minute fragment from the film *Battle for Ukraine*, which Pinchuk had allegedly commissioned from Andrei Konchalovsky, a popular Russian filmmaker living abroad. The film depicted the murder of Gongadze as the result of a skillful intrigue against Kuchma financed mainly by the United States (*Ogonek* 2011). Kuchma's defense attorneys asked investigators to attach the film as evidence in the case (*Ogonek* 2011).

Owners also make use of private media for their own ends by organizing information campaigns in support of their business interests. One example of such a campaign was the 'war' that the *Inter* TV channel conducted against Prime Minister Yulia Tymoshenko in 2009. In January 2009, Tymoshenko signed an agreement with Russia that removed the private company RosUkrEnergo from the Russian-Ukrainian gas trade (Englund 2010). The co-owner of RosUkrEnergo, Dmytro Firtash, was at the time supposedly also a shareholder of *Inter*. The channel's newscasts sharply criticized the gas contract signed by Tymoshenko and accused her government of stealing gas from RosUkrEnergo. Firtash, who earlier had avoided the cameras, several times appeared personally on *Inter* TV programs and accused the government of mismanagement and messing things up.[37]

As for the impact on media content of the other 'captor,' the state, it may manifest itself in an imbalance between the amount of attention devoted by media to the authorities and the opposition,

---

37 After the EuroMaidan revolution Ukrainian oligarchs continued to use their media for political ends. A common practice in post-Maidan Ukraine is that of oligarchic media wars. The oligarchic media, primarily nationwide TV channels, became a battlefield between the oligarchs in their fight for political influence and resources (Dovzhenko 2015). One important reason for the oligarchs to instrumentalize their media for political purposes since the rise of the new pro-European government in 2014 was also the desire to stop the government in its attempts to lessen their impact on Ukraine's economy and/or challenge the monopoly position some of them had in various industries (Ligachova 2014).

and the way in which each of them is presented and evaluated. According to the AUP, which monitors the national televised news in quantitative terms, Yanukovych and his allies dominated the news since he won the presidential election in 2010 until the late 2013.[38] In particular, the share of airtime granted in news programs to members of the ruling coalition in December 2010 was 70 percent, whereas only 26 percent of the coverage went to the opposition (AUP 2011). In the first half of 2011, this disproportion increased: media coverage of the Party of Regions and its allies ranged between 76 percent and 84 percent of total news coverage, whereas the opposition received between 14 percent and 16 percent.

Telekrytyka, a watchdog analyzing the qualitative aspect of informational television programs, documents such indicators of government influence as coverups of the misdeeds of those in power, biased and/or one-sided news coverage that favors the ruling party and the government, unbalanced viewpoints, and manipulation of public opinion.[39] According to Telekrytyka, in 2010–2013, Ukrainian television channels often ignored facts inconvenient to the government—especially antigovernment protests, reduced living standards, violations of freedom of speech, and the property of high officials (such as the president's vast luxury estate at Mezhyhiria).

During Yushchenko's presidency, Ukrainian media watchdogs also detected symptoms of state influence on the media, which Natalia Ligachova (2006), who is in charge of Telekrytyka's Web site and magazine,[40] called 'mild control.' In particular, the AUP (Mar. 2006) noted how the president and his party, Our Ukraine, dominated most popular nationwide television channels

---

38 The Academy of Ukrainian Press monitors television news together with the Institute of Sociology of the Ukrainian Academy of Sciences.
39 For examples, see www.ua/mediacontinent/monitoring/telenovini. In October 2015 Telekrytyka abandoned the website http://www.telekritika.ua. Starting in January 2016, it now publishes its monitorings at http://detector.media Telekrytyka abandoned the website telekritika.ua, which since then belongs exclusively to 1+1 media Group.
40 *Telekrytyka* print magazine was published in 2004–2010.

before the 2006 parliamentary election. Telekrytyka documented that several of the most popular television channels similarly manipulated public opinion to favor the president in covering issues important to him and his entourage, such as the scandal surrounding RosUkrEnergo and the shooting of Prosecutor Kuzovkin in 2006, in which the president's son Andrii allegedly took part (Telekrytyka 2006; Ligachova 2006). An important indicator of private broadcasters' lack of autonomy from the authorities was the journalists' failure to undertake well-founded investigations of government corruption, mismanagement, and abuse of office (Ligachova 2006).[41]

Even so, Yushchenko's general approach to influencing private media differed from his successor's. Above all, the media did not concentrate their attention on one political camp, as they had under Kuchma's presidency, but were divided among several political forces. This division became particularly evident in 2006, when the constitutional amendments of 2004 restricting the president's powers came into force and the president became one of several competing power centers. In the same year, the Anti-Crisis Coalition led by the Party of Regions was formed after the parliamentary election; and Viktor Yanukovych, Yushchenko's main rival in the 2004 presidential elections, became prime minister. After these events, news broadcasts more or less evenly divided their airtime and attention between Yushchenko's Our Ukraine and Yanukovych's Party of Regions (AUP Oct. 2006, May 2007). In qualitative terms, different channels gave preference to different high officials. The division of media attention among different power centers continued after Yulia Tymoshenko succeeded Yanukovych as prime minister in 2007 and the "War of Prime Minister Yanukovych

---

41 Ligachova differentiates between serious journalistic investigations aimed at holding public officials accountable and petty attacks more aimed at helping media owners soften up the authorities in their negotiations with big businesses.

Against President Yushchenko" gave way to the "War of Prime Minister Tymoshenko Against President Yushchenko."[42]

A second feature that characterized media content under Yushchenko was the instability that many media outlets—especially the most popular channels, *Inter* and *1+1*—displayed in their attachment to this or that political actor. For example, *Inter* shifted from supporting the president to backing his rivals many times, which some media experts attributed to bargaining associated with its owners' primary economic interests—in particular, the security status of RosUkrEnergo.[43]

Natalya Ligachova (2007a) has explained the unsteady support that most private nationwide television channels offered to individual parties or politicians in the late 2000s by noting that the political field and its alignment with economic interests were not stable under Yushchenko, and the division into 'orange' and 'white-blue' elite groups increasingly blurred. According to this argument, such fuzziness and instability gave rise to the possibility that any two forces might align within the economic and political elite, including media magnates. Therefore, it did not make sense for owners who sought to use their media to further their interests to adhere to one politician or party; instead, they chose temporary information campaigns in favor of politicians and/or office holders based on expediency.

This situation with the Ukrainian media during Yushchenko's presidency exemplifies Duncan McCargo's concept of *partisan polyvalence*, developed to characterize political links with the media in Southeast Asia. By partisan polyvalence, McCargo (2012) has in mind the behavior of media outlets that do not remain loyal to particular political actors over the long term, but shift their loyalties depending on economic support as well as general power shifts within

---

42   On shifts of media support in 2005–2007, see Katasonova 2007. On the political sympathies expressed on popular television channels during the 2010 presidential campaign, see Telekrytyka 2010.
43   Private communication from Otar Dovzhenko, a Ukrainian media expert (Skype, September 8, 2012).

a clientelistic system. This type of relationship between media and politics helps newspapers ensure their own survival and access to key political figures in political environments where the state is weak and divided against itself and rival power groups use the media in their political struggle.

2.1.3. What methods do media captors use?

According to the theory of media capture, the instruments used by the captors for subverting the media to their particularistic interests predominantly fall in the realm of *informal practices* (Mungiu-Pippidi 2008, 93). Mungiu-Pippidi claims that post-communist governments do not have diverse opportunities to control the media with the help of formal regulations, which are strongly influenced by international actors. This thesis resembles Andrei Richter's view of post-Soviet countries: that the legal frameworks for journalism guaranteeing freedom of mass information have proven their long-term viability in these countries; although their democratic media laws mostly "incorporate not realities but aspirations" (Price 2000, cited in Richter 2008, 308), the fundamental change of media legislation in an undemocratic direction has not taken place in the region (Richter 2008). This statement holds true for the condition of media law in Ukraine in the period under study,[44] as Ukrainian media legislation is considered rather liberal and in terms of legal guarantees may be considered the second most developed country of the former Soviet Union, including the Baltic states (Richter 2008).

What instruments of media capture does the state use? Studies mention such techniques as granting benefits to media companies in exchange for favorable treatment (Mungiu-Pippidi 2008;

---

44 A notable exclusion is the short period during the EuroMaidan Protests when the Ukrainian parliament adopted the set of laws which substantially limited the freedoms of speech, press, and association. The bill was passed in Ukrainian parliament (Verkhovna Rada) on 16 January 2014. On 17 January, Viktor Yanukovych signed the bill into law despite an outcry from Western governments and international organizations. The laws were cancelled by the parliament on January 28, 2014.

Karklins 2002).⁴⁵ The benefits include state subsidies, bailouts from debt, preferential distribution of state advertising, and tax-breaks for media owners. In Ukraine, where the major media owners are business people who draw most of their profits from other industries, the government offers similar benefits for media loyalty (excluding state advertising), but tailors them to the owners' main businesses: metals, gas, banking, and so on.⁴⁶ Thus Ukrainian oligarchs who own media outlets exchange information support for the government for privileges given to their key businesses (Mediasapiens 2012). According to Ukrainian media experts, the government achieves control over private media primarily via informal agreements of this type.⁴⁷

Ukrainian oligarchs may have additional reasons to use their media for maintaining good relations with the government. The state has several tools, such as selective use of financial or administrative sanctions, that could adversely affect their key businesses. Therefore the oligarchs often choose to be loyal to the government in exchange for protection of their businesses from administrative pressure. Moreover, because of corruption, many Ukrainian businesses were founded or purchased (or received licenses) in violation of the law, which gives the government an opportunity to blackmail big business people with the threat of lawsuits.⁴⁸

To put it differently, the means used by the state to influence oligarchs are well known 'carrots' and 'sticks.' 'Carrots' include granting media owners access to state resources, or giving them an opportunity to extract rents. 'Sticks' is, first, depriving them of this opportunity, and, second, harassing their main businesses (energy, oil, food, transport) with the help of inspecting organs (such as tax inspection), law enforcement, or the judiciary. The same sticks, especially selective enforcement of formal laws as well as selective

---

45   Methods used to control state-owned media are outside the scope of this study.
46   On sources of rents for Ukrainian oligarchs, see Melnykovska and Schweickert (2008).
47   Private communication from Otar Dovzhenko (Skype, September 8, 2012).
48   Darden (2001) describes this tool, employing the concept of 'blackmail state.'

inspections for compliance with tax, employment, and other regulations, are also implemented for influencing media. Importantly, in case of the media, the state has an additional instrument of compulsion, namely media regulating bodies, in particular a license regulating organ (the National Television and Radio Broadcasting Council). The main type of carrots generated by the latter is that of broadcasting licenses. Sticks include license withdrawal (or threats to withdraw) as well as other penalties issued by media regulating bodies (in more details these instruments of state interference with media freedom will be discussed in Section 2 of this chapter).

It is worth noting that the use of law-enforcement and regulatory and inspection agencies for disciplining disobedient media, along with other abovementioned informal methods of political control over the press, have become a recurring practice for the Ukrainian authorities during the years of Ukrainian independence. These methods became an important element of state-media relationships during the presidency of Leonid Kuchma, and later were reproduced both under a more democratic Yushchenko, and under an evidently authoritarian Yanukovych. This continuity might indicate that the abovementioned practices were in some sense institutionalized in the regulation of relationships between the state and the media, or became, if not usual, then at least possible ways for the politics dealing with the media. This couldn't but impact the relationships between the media and the authorities in Ukraine, which in the case of the media most obviously reveals itself in the form of self-censorship in the coverage of political events.

Because the state has in its disposal significant instruments for influencing both oligarchic businesses and the private media belonging to oligarchs themselves, Ukraine's big media owners often cooperate with the state in preventing the media from holding the authorities accountable. This phenomenon usually results in what Richter (2008) called "in-house censorship"—obstruction of the publication or transmission of journalistic output that the powers that be will not like. Editors in chief and top managers, who are well paid for loyalty to their bosses, usually play the key role in bringing media content into line with the authorities' demands (Ligachova 2007a; Dovzhenko 2011a).

In addition to in-house censorship, media owners and top managers also take more radical steps to constrain politically undesirable journalistic output. They fire independent-minded journalists and editors or even close rebellious media outlets (MSI-Ukraine 2011; 2012). Due to fear of reprisals, Ukrainian journalists commonly resort to self-censorship, since in a fluctuating and insecure labor market with a weak professional organization, they are highly vulnerable employees.

According to free speech advocates in Ukraine, media owners' efforts to curb critical coverage of the authorities by their media intensified after Viktor Yanukovych became president in 2010. As early as the spring of 2010, journalists of several Ukrainian mainstream media were announcing that their reports had been censored by managing editors. Media monitoring organizations also expressed concern about the increase of inter-organizational pressures on journalists. In response to these trends, the most active Ukrainian journalists and media representatives launched a "Stop Censorship" movement in May 2010, which has remained an important advocate of press freedom in Ukraine ever since.

International observers have attributed the intensification of owners' control over the media in 2010–2013 and the greater subordination of the largest Ukrainian media holdings to the government to the consolidation of power under Yanukovych (Freedom House 2011). Since the 2010 reversal of the 2004 constitutional reform restricting presidential power and other measures aimed at consolidating authority in the hands of the president and his allies, the then leaders of Ukraine did have much more power to issue both positive and negative sanctions against Ukrainian oligarchs, including media owners. This shift expanded both the level and the scope of state capture as the restoration of the 1996 constitution gave Yanukovych and his surrounding a more centralized and extensive power to influence rules and the conduct of different state institutions such as the legislature, courts, or bureaucracy.

The consolidation of power in Ukraine in presidential hands in 2010–2013 may also explain the state's more extensive use of two additional methods of media control: sanctions from supervisory agencies (especially the National Television and Radio Broadcasting Council), and the misuse (or selective use) of the judiciary and law-enforcement agencies. From the beginning of his presidency, Yanukovych tried to extend his control of the national broadcasting regulator. In June 2010, Ukraine's parliament, already controlled by the pro-presidential Party of Regions, added four new members to the National Television and Radio Broadcasting Council.[49] All candidates put forward by the opposition and relevant non-governmental organizations were rejected. The new National TV and Radio Broadcasting Council, consisting chiefly of persons loyal to the president, helped him significantly lessen the reach of the opposition's *TVi* and *5 channel* and prepared the ground for the exclusive access to viewers of regime-friendly broadcasters after the digital switchover planned for 2015.[50]

As for the judiciary, Yanukovych made significant inroads on its independence at the very beginning of his presidency in 2010. The Law of Ukraine on the Judiciary and the Status of Judges adopted by the Ukrainian parliament in 2010 increased presidential power over courts of general jurisdiction, reduced the power of the Supreme Court, and opened the door to politicization of the selection process for judges (Futey 2011). The Ukrainian lawmaker Hryhoriy Omelchenko noted the then tendency in Ukraine to collapse the judiciary into the executive branch and to remove the judicial power (Futey 2011). Ukrainian and international think tanks and hu-

---

49   After its 2010 victory, the Party of Regions formed a new parliamentary majority, extending the pro-government coalition with the support of dozens of deputies from opposition factions. The party managed this by combining a controversial interpretation of the Constitution (one endorsed by the Constitutional Court) with pressure on and/or cooptation of opposition deputies, who joined the coalition without changing their faction (Olszanski 2010).
50   This switchover never took place as planned. In the time of writing this book in 2015 Ukraine still has yet to complete the switch to digital TV.

man rights organizations also noted the decline of judicial independence in Ukraine during president Yanukovych's time in office (BTI 2012; Freedom House 2011, 2012).

The independent media in Ukraine had fully experienced the effects of this trend. Courts and prosecutor's offices played an important role in stripping the oppositional *TVi* and *5 channel* of frequencies in 2010 and in the intimidation of the online newspaper *Livyi bereh* and the *TVi* channel before parliamentary elections in 2012 (Julliard and Vidal 2010; Kievukraine 2012). Instead of protecting media freedom, the judicial system and law-enforcement agencies had increasingly become means of harassing independent media. According to Victoria Siumar, the then executive director of the Institute of Mass Information, what distinguished the assaults on media and journalists after Yanukovych became president in 2010 was that journalists' rights were often violated by the very agents tasked with defending them: the police, officials, and the Department of Civic Protection (EU-Ukraine 2012).

Various publications have underlined the importance of judicial independence for press freedom (Keith 2002; Guseva et al. 2008). An environment without an independent judicial system may deprive journalists of protection from powerful office holders seeking to silence critical media. Subordinate courts and judges can be used to prevent media from holding those in power accountable. Studies on state capture demonstrate that incumbents appropriating state institutions often constrain judicial independence as a means of raising their immunity from prosecution while extracting private benefits from the state and of restricting political competition (Grzymala-Busse 2008).

Completing our list of methods used by media captors requires us to address the widespread phenomena of bribery: more precisely, illegal payment for hidden advertising. Since president's Kuchma centralized control of the media ended in 2005, illegal payments, colloquially used in Ukraine *dzhynsa*, have become a central means of media instrumentalization (Belyakov 2009). Since then, Ukrainian media content has become saturated with hidden political (less often, economic) advertising (see e.g., Belyakov 2009; Ligachova 2008). Being most tangible in pre-electoral times, *dzhynsa* was widespread also in-between elections when it could reach up to 40 percent in local TV-newscasts (see for ex., Sokolenko 2013). Nor was hidden advertising in Ukraine limited to sporadic orders for a propaganda article or video. Entire news packages and programs were sold on Ukrainian television (Tsetsura and Grynko 2009). Telekrytyka reported that even before the 2006 parliamentary elections television channels offered candidates a package of services that included positive coverage, regular appearances on the air, the blockage of critical materials launched by the candidate's rivals, and even minimal attention to other candidates (Dovzhenko 2008).[51]

Both types of media captors discussed in this book—vested political interests and the state—used bribery to make the media serve their interests in the researched period (1994–2013). Ukrainian media experts claim that not only politicians, but also civil servants and public institutions purchased propaganda materials from the media (Telekrytyka 2012). The National Bank of Ukraine regularly ordered *dzhynsa* from various news outlets in 2012 and 2013.[52] Ukrainian presidents allegedly resorted to *dzhynsa* as well. For example, in August 2012, the editor of the popular regional newspaper *Express* declared that he had received an offer of several million Ukrainian hryvnias in exchange for regular positive coverage of president Yanukovych's activities for the period leading up to the presidential elections scheduled for 2015 (Vybory.mediasapiens 2012).[53]

---

[51] Concealed advertising never disappeared from Ukrainian media also after Ukraine's Maidan revolution in late 2013–early 2014. As the monitorings by Ukrainian media supporting organizations demonstrate, only before the early presidential election in May 2014 was the content of Ukrainian media mostly free from ordered materials. However, already during electoral campaign for the early parliamentary election in October 2014 Ukrainian TV and newspapers were again overloaded with *dzhynsa* (see, for ex., Ieremenko 2014).
[52] Private communication from Otar Dovzhenko (Skype, September 8, 2012).
[53] These elections were not held because the date was moved to 25 May 2014 after the EuroMaidan protests.

The nongovernmental organizations monitoring media content in Ukraine reported that the amount of concealed advertising in Ukrainian media never changed between Viktor Yushchenko's and Viktor Yanukovych's presidencies.[54] Whereas under the more liberal rule of Viktor Yushchenko the flood of *dzhynsa* in the media mainly resulted from bribery, Ukrainian media experts suggested that in 2010–2013 force could also be used to persuade the media to disseminate concealed advertising promoting the authorities (Dovzhenko 2010a). The numerous reports from Ukrainian media watchdogs about bribery attempts associated with the Yanukovych regime that became public since 2010, however, indicated that graft continued to be common in media-political relationships in Ukraine under Yanukovych's rule, similar to the post-Orange period.

2.2. Disabling environment: media regulators and media law

2.2.1. Regulatory and monitoring bodies

Let's now have a closer look at formal institutions regulating the media, their design and capacity, as well as the way these institutions were (mis)used in Ukraine during the period under study. One type of institution in the realm of media-politics relationships, which are significant from the point of view of control over media by the elites, is that of media regulating and monitoring bodies. As the studies of media transformations in former communist countries in CEE and FSU indicate, these institutions are often used for curbing media freedom (Dragomir 2003). Marius Dragomir, in his study of media reforms in post-communist Europe, shows that post-communist governments employ two main strategies to exert influence upon media via institutions: they either adapt existing broadcasting councils whose real task is to regulate the activities of TV and radio in the name of the public good, or they establish new monitoring institutions similar to the censorship committees of the communist era.

---

54 For media monitoring results that measure, among other things, levels of concealed advertising, see www.telekritika.ua/media-continent/monitoring/.

Ukraine's primary media regulating authority in the domain of television and radio broadcasting is the National Television and Radio Broadcasting Council (NTRBC). It was created in 1994 as a public regulatory body, with a remit to supervise broadcasters and grant licenses. Though the Council is supposed to be an independent body, throughout the two decades since 1994 it was often criticized for serving the political interests of the government of the day. One of the factors which may explain this is the composition of the regulator as defined by the Ukraine's legislation. Namely, the procedure of appointment of the NTRBC members, as stipulated by the Ukrainian Constitution, presupposes that one-half of the members is appointed personally by the president, and the other by the Verkhovna Rada (the Parliament of Ukraine). According to the analysis of the Law of Ukraine regulating the activity of the Broadcasting Council, carried out in 2007 by Eve Salomon and Karol Jakubowicz for the Media Division of the Council of Europe at the request of the Ukrainian authorities, this process of appointments of the NTRBC members inevitably leads to appointments being made on the basis of political affiliations, with the members of the National Council taking decisions on political grounds (Salomon and Jakubowicz 2007). One more defect of the procedure under which four members of the media regulator are appointed by the president and another four by the Parliament, as pointed out by Taras Shevchenko (2004), the director of the Kyiv-based Media Law Institute, is that it gives the president an advantage over the parliament in forming the media regulator. This is because if the parliament appointed at least one person loyal to the president, then the latter would master the majority of votes.

Indeed, for most time of its existence, the NTRBC was controlled by the incumbent presidents and their administrations. As for the members of the Broadcasting Council appointed by the parliament, very often they were the protégées of big oligarchic groups interested in having their 'representatives' in the media regulating body in order to safeguard and advance their media businesses.

The two-decade history of the Council shows that it is controlled by the Ukrainian media captors not only by means of appointing loyal people as Council members. The media regulator can be subjected also to other, more informal, pressures. For example, during the time president Viktor Yanukovych was in office, NTRBC members were reportedly the subject of informal pressure by the Secret Service of Ukraine (SBU), which was headed in 2010–2012 by Valerii Khoroshkovskyi, then owner of the InterMediaGroup (Dovzhenko 2010b). A bright illustration of this pressure was the case of disputing the allocation of terrestrial broadcast frequencies by the NTRBC which happened in the early days of Yanukovych's presidency. Then the channels from InterMediaGroup (then loyal to Yanukovych) challenged the frequencies which were allocated to the Yanukovych-unfriendly *TVi* and *5 channel* just before the end of president Yushchenko mandate, specifically on 27 January 2009. Soon after Yanukovych succeeded, Inter Media's channels started to question the decision of the NTRBC regarding the frequencies' allocation. Different methods were used to make the NTRBC cancel this decision. One of these methods was harassment of the NTRBC members. In the middle of the arguments around the frequencies' allocation the SBU demanded that the Council provided personal files of some NTRBC members as well as the documents on the tender for the broadcasting licenses. It is probably in result of this pressure that soon after one of the Council's members, Tetiana Mokridi, resigned from her post (Dovzhenko 2010b). The rest agreed to 'cooperate' with the new authorities and finally voted for disowning the 27 January allocation (Julliard and Vidal 2010).

From its early days, the NTRBC was accused of manipulating the procedures for awarding and canceling TV and radio licenses to further the political and economic interests of the ruling political groups. This was claimed, for example, in thirty lawsuits filed by journalists in 2002.[55] In the years of Yanukovych's presidency, the NTRBC repeatedly proved to be an instrument of political control

---

55 For details, see www.pressreference.com/Sw-Ur/Ukraine.html, accessed September 20, 2015.

over broadcasting. Besides playing, as mentioned above, one of the key roles in withdrawing the frequencies earlier allocated to oppositional *TVi* and *5 channel*, it also refused to award a license for satellite broadcasting to TV channel Info-24, founded by managers and journalists of *TVi*. The Council also took a series of decisions which would ensure the then power holders and their allies an unquestioned dominance in Ukrainian broadcasting after the digital switchover planned for 2015 in case the EuroMaidan revolution never occurred (Kramer et al. 2012).

The other problem with the National Television and Radio Broadcasting Council is that the licensing regulations are unclear, ambiguous, or in some cases even conflicting. In 2008 the Ukrainian experts participating in the Media Sustainability Index panel even called legal provisions for licensing broadcasters "one of the most shadowy of state regulations" (MSI-Ukraine 2008, 193). This creates the conditions under which it is relatively easy for the regulator to selectively enforce formal rules. Not surprisingly, both Ukrainian and international media watchdogs often criticize NTRBC for awarding and renewing licenses to companies that violate licensing agreements, as well as for granting and cancelling licenses for political reasons (see e.g., MSI-Ukraine 2002, 2008, 2010). Moreover, the licensing of broadcast media is a very nontransparent and shadowy process (Ivanov 2005). Since the regulations concerning licensing of broadcasters are unclear and ambiguous, it is hard to know what conditions must be met in order to get a license and exactly what actions are in violation of the licensing requirements.

This leads to a situation where practically every broadcasting company bends the regulations to some degree. Consequently, the regulatory power of the NTRBC is a convenient tool for the punishment of dissenting broadcasters. As *Telekrytyka* magazine characterized the state of affairs, "as far as every channel is violating the law or its license to a certain extent, the NTRBC may be a universal tool of influence on television businesses like the tax administration or fire inspectors," government agencies traditionally used to harass businesses (MSI-Ukraine 2009, 199).

As already mentioned, some post-communist states also influence the media through new monitoring entities created officially for some respectable purpose, such as the protection of state secrets, but in fact fulfilling the functions of censorship bodies (Dragomir 2003). The recent history of post-communist countries yields several examples of such institutions: the Inspection Agency of State Secrets in Uzbekistan, which reviews and approves the publication of news stories; the Turkmen State Committee for the Protection of State Secrets, which *de facto* screens critical and opposition views in the media; the State Inspectorate to Protect the Freedom of the Press and Mass Information at the Russian Ministry of Press and Mass Information, which functions as a censorship body (Dragomir 2003, 9–10; de Smaele and Vartanova 2007, 344). In Ukraine, this tendency was exemplified by an infamous institution named the National Expert Commission for the Protection of Public Morality (NEC).

The NEC was created by the Cabinet of Ministers of Ukraine in November 2004 shortly before Yushchenko was elected president. Its declared aim was "to ensure the realization of state policies in the sphere of the protection of public morality" (Law of Ukraine on the Protection of Public Morality 2004). The design of this institution made it completely dependent on the government. The Cabinet of Ministers appointed the head of the NEC[56] and approved the composition of its membership. The duties of the NEC included supervision of adherence to the Law on the Protection of Public Morality, monitoring of TV, radio, video, and other information products with regard to their compliance with the regulations on protection of

---

56 This practice was illegal and resulted from a contradiction in the text of the Law on the Protection of Public Morality. Article 18 of the law stated that the membership of the NEC must be approved by the Cabinet of Ministers upon a submission by the head of the NEC, but that the head of the NEC is to be elected by the members of the NEC.

public morality, and prevention of the distribution of materials containing scenes of violence and pornography (Law of Ukraine on the Protection of Public Morality 2004).

The Law on the Protection of Public Morality on which the functioning of the Commission was based, contained a number of vague clauses concerning freedom of expression and information distribution.[57] Some of them run counter to Article 10 of the European Convention on Human Rights.[58] According to Professor Dirk Voorhoof of Ghent University, who carried out an expert analysis of the law for the Council of Europe in 2004, this legislation was unclear and ambiguous and had a very wide purview of application. Consequently, the NEC had the potential to become a true weapon against independent media.

The NEC was initially conceived as an expert agency whose main function was to analyze media products based on morality guidelines. However, after being a 'sleeping' structure in the first years of the Orange government, it unexpectedly became an influential media-controlling body by 2008. For example, it effectively prohibited further airing of *The Simpsons* by issuing a verdict that the cartoon series might provoke juvenile delinquency. Based on its evaluation, the National Television and Radio Broadcasting Council warned TV channels not to air *The Simpsons* under penalty of a fine or even license withdrawal. NEC complaints similarly led to the cancellation of several comedy programs and serials, including a Russian adaptation of the American sitcom *Married ... with Children*. It also prohibited the screening of Sacha Baron Cohen's film *Bruno* and seized copies of the Ukrainian novel *The Woman of His Dreams* by the winner of the Shevchenko Prize, Oles' Ulianenko.

During the presidency of Viktor Yanukovych there was an attempt to use the National Expert Commission for the Protection of

---

57 See the conclusions of the round table "Mass Media and Protection of Public Morality: European Standards in Public Morality and Child Protection" (unian.ua 2010).
58 Ibid.

Public Morality as an instrument for constraining freedom of the Internet in Ukraine. In 2011 the Verkhovna Rada adopted in the first reading the draft Law № 7132 on Amendments to the Law on the Protection of Public Morality which *de facto* introduced censorship of the Internet. The amendments, among other matters, would oblige providers without even a court order to block content which the National Commission for the Protection of Public Morality deemed harmful to public morality. The bill sparked a wave of protests from Ukrainian and international media- and human rights organizations. Statements of concern were issued by Ukrainian Helsinki Human Rights Union, the Ukrainian journalistic movement "Stop Censorship!," International Federation of Journalists, Reporters Without Borders and many other organizations. The draft law was criticized for providing overly vague definitions of offensive media content, as well as for giving extraordinary powers to the NEC. If the amendments had been adopted, the Commission would have been allowed to issue orders to block websites and access to content within 24 hours without a court order or any provisions for website owners/content authors to appeal. The scandalous bill was withdrawn by the Verkhovna Rada on 21 June 2012.

Ukrainian cultural and media activists initiated numerous campaigns in favor of elimination of the National Commission. However, the Commission was preserved by successive Ukrainian governments for more than a decade. It was liquidated not until after the fall of the Yanukovych regime and the election of a new, more democratic Parliament in 2014.[59]

2.2.2. Media-related laws

Throughout the years of Ukraine's independence its legislation framework for freedom of the media has been regularly assessed by media scholars and international media monitors as one of the

---

[59] Ukrainian parliament voted for the bill liquidating the Commission on January 10, 2015.

most liberal in the post-Soviet area. For example, in 2007, the Moscow Media Law and Policy Institute published the comparison of legal frameworks for media in the countries of the former Soviet Union, including the Baltic states, where Ukrainian media legislation was recognized the second most developed from the standpoint of legal guarantees of mass media freedom (Richter 2007). However, the implementation of this legislation has proved more problematic (see, for ex., Richter 2002; Freedom House 2013b).

First of all, media laws were often misused in post-communist Ukraine, and this practice has not disappeared to this day. A handbook example here is a defamation law which was recurrently used by Ukraine's public office holders, politicians, and big businessmen against media freedom. For example, in 1999, during president Kuchma's time in office, more than 2250 lawsuits on defamation were filed against various media in Ukraine. The total amount of money sought as compensation in these defamation cases was more than 90 billion hryvnia (US$ 16.82 billion), which represented nearly twice the amount the national government planned to earn in 2000 (Associated Press 2000 as quoted by Richter 2002). Lawsuits on defamation were extensively used by Ukraine's elites to punish independent media also after the Orange Revolution and under Viktor Yanukovych's presidency. Editorial staff often lost such defamation cases not least because of the lack of judicial independence and corruption in courts (see e.g., MSI-Ukraine 2008, 2010, 2013).

One more problem is quality of media-related statutes. The Ukraine's office holders often employ legal drawbacks and loopholes to impede media independence and democratic performance. For example, under the presidency of Viktor Yushchenko NTRBC often used the language quota regulations to punish disloyal broadcasters. These regulations limited the amount of broadcasting in languages other than Ukrainian, but they were inconsistent. For example, Article 10 of the Law on TV and Radio Broadcasting (as amended in 2006) treated the Ukrainian quota differently in two separate paragraphs. Whereas Paragraph 3 required that every non-

Ukrainian film or program be dubbed in Ukrainian, Paragraph 4 established a 75 percent quota on Ukrainian-language programming for national broadcasters, which meant that it was acceptable that some non-Ukrainian programs (as much as 25 percent of total broadcasting time) were not dubbed (Law of Ukraine on Television and Radio Broadcasting 2006). The inconsistency of these regulations gave the NTRBC an opportunity to enforce the law selectively.

The next problem with media regulating laws in Ukraine is that they are frequently changed. This causes additional problems for media organizations and makes them vulnerable to state pressure. According to the Konrad Adenauer Stiftung Democracy Report for 2008, Ukraine's media law was modified and supplemented as many as ten times during the preceding five years (KAS 2008). In 2008, for example, the NTRBC introduced new provisions on production and language quotas in broadcasting (National Television and Radio Broadcasting Council 2008). These raised the quota of Ukrainian-language broadcasting from 75 percent to 80 percent. Editorial offices were troubled, because it was difficult to follow the new requirements on startup: broadcasters calculated that to meet the new NTRBC demands, they had to spend an additional $200 million to translate foreign-language programs (mostly Russian) into Ukrainian (Fokus 2008).

However, the language quota change in license provisions and the subsequent NTRBC monitoring of national TV channels did not mean that every channel with a broadcast schedule that did not satisfy the 80 percent Ukrainian language rule was deprived of its license. Channels *1+1*, *NTN*, *Ukraine*, and *Novy*, according to the NTRBC monitoring, did not fulfill the Ukrainian-language requirements, but they were not punished at all. The sanctions (or, to be more precise, a warning on sanctions) were received only by the *Inter* channel, which was not loyal to then-president Viktor Yushchenko. As the president had *de facto* control of the NTRBC up to mid-2009, he was able to use amendments to discipline broadcasters.

A separate issue is that of the regular attempts of Ukrainian law-makers to change media legislation for the worse, that is, to introduce legal restrictions on press freedom. For example, in 2012 the Ukrainian parliament approved in the first reading a bill criminalizing libel (nota bene, over the previous decade libel had been a civil-law issue in Ukraine). The bill was introduced by the MP from the pro-presidential Party of Regions Vitalii Zhuravskii, who in 2010–2012 served as the staff advisor to president Yanukovych. It was only due to the storm of criticism among media and media-support organizations in Ukraine and abroad that the bill was in the end not adopted.

Amending and making laws relating to media independence happen to be a highly politicized and problematic process in Ukraine. Although Ukrainian media law is generally positively evaluated when compared to corresponding legislation in other post-Soviet states, this does not mean that it is flawless. More than that, international human rights and media development organizations many times have pointed to numerous deficiencies in Ukraine's legislation framework for media freedom, in particular the lack of regulations concerning public service broadcasting, access to public information or media ownership transparency. However, the developments around these bills has demonstrated that Ukrainian elites were extremely reluctant to adopt these laws, since the latter could threaten the mode of media-politics relationships which shaped in Ukraine in the first years of transformation and whose essence was media capture by private interests.

One of the brightest examples is the long history of adoption of the law on public service broadcasting in Ukraine. The first attempt to adopt it was made in 1997. That was when the bill on the system of public broadcasting in Ukraine was passed in the Parliament, but then-president Leonid Kuchma vetoed it. Viktor Yushchenko, who won the election in 2005, placed the creation of Ukrainian public broadcaster among his most often repeated election promises. However, when in November 2005 the bill on public broadcasting was voted on in the Parliament, there were members of the president's Our Ukraine party who never supported the bill with their votes. Besides, Yushchenko himself openly declared that he was not a fan of the idea to liquidate state broadcasting on which basis the public broadcasting had to be created. Up to the end of his presidency he remained an advocate of the idea to preserve the state TV in parallel to the creation of public broadcasting in Ukraine (Dovzhenko and Derkach 2011).

Nor was the law on Public Broadcasting enacted in 2010–2013, when Ukraine's president was Viktor Yanukovych. The bill was passed in the Parliament in the first reading in July 2013, but it never proceeded to the second reading till the end of Yanukovych's presidency in February 2014. Importantly, the bill was criticized by the Office of the OSCE Representative on Freedom of the media for some significant flaws built in its content. As the Representative on Freedom of the Media, Dunja Mijatović noted, the bill never excluded a dangerous possibility of parallel existence of the public and the state broadcaster (Tyzhden 2013). Finally, after about two decades of unsuccessful attempts, the law was adopted only after the overthrow of president Yanukovych and the rise of the new pro-European government in early 2014. It came into force in May 2014.

The greatest problem with legal frameworks for media in Ukraine is that, under conditions of a corrupt and politically-dependent judiciary, the regulations aimed at protecting media independence are often abused. Courts and law enforcement agencies, in their turn, are often reluctant to protect media and journalists from attacks. Media and journalists have little chance to defend their rights in courts. The situation with crimes against journalists was most dramatic in Ukraine under the authoritarian rule of president Kuchma, when journalists disappeared and even died under suspicious circumstances (the best known case is surely Georgi Gongadze's murder, which happened in 2000). However, after the Orange Revolution and under Yanukovych's rule, harassment and intimidation were still not rare, and these crimes were not properly investigated (see e.g., Julliard and Vidal 2010). The most striking example was the lack of progress in the investigation of the Gongadze murder, but there was also a number of instances where the perpetrators of other crimes against journalists were not convicted or sent to prison. According to Viktor Danylov, the director of the OGO Publishing House, "Crimes against journalists gain broad resonance in the media, but actually there are no completed investigations and prosecution of the guilty" (MSI-Ukraine 2008, 194). The impunity of those who assault journalists has led to a state of permanent tension and fear among media professionals, making them resort to self-censorship.

Ukraine's state of affairs—namely, its lack of proper protection of media independence despite rather progressive laws on the books—seems to support Katrin Voltmer's thesis about the limitations of the widespread opinion that "the less the state regulates media, the better." When commenting on media development in emerging democracies, Voltmer points out that the role of the state *vis-à-vis* the media is not necessarily antagonistic and lack of state regulation does not necessarily mean more freedom for the media (Voltmer 2008, 37–38). On the contrary (as it also results from the foregoing analysis) a state unable or unwilling to pass and, what is extremely important, enforce laws providing freedom to the mass media may be detrimental for the development of media autonomy and freedom.

This thesis is quite consistent with the findings about the role of formal *vs* informal institutions in Ukrainian politics presented in Chapter 1. Ukraine's comparatively liberal media laws often *de facto* do not govern media-politics relations, and are regularly abused and misused. This is because the agencies responsible for enforcement of formal laws are far from independent from the private interests that capture the state in Ukraine. Interactions between media and politics are commonly regulated by informal agreements and rules instead. State captors seek to use formal institutions for enforcement of the informal agreements between them and the media (or media owners). In effect, formal institutions (in this case, media laws) are selectively used to punish the media and journalists disloyal to the authorities. This also concerns the cases when media-protecting laws are violated, and their violators are not prosecuted and enjoy impunity. Such cases serve to discourage journalists from fairly performing their professional duties and encourage them instead to follow 'unwritten rules' of politically-dependent journalism as well as informal media-politics agreements.

Chapter 3
The media market and ownership, and economic dimension of media capture in Ukraine

The capture of private Ukrainian media by oligarchs dependent on political favor and the overflow of paid-for materials in news coverage would be much less possible if Ukrainian media were a profitable business. Indeed, in the new European democracies where media are rated by international organizations as 'free,' advertising budgets and the purchasing capacity of media consumers are significantly higher than in Ukraine. This chapter presents the main features of the Ukrainian media market and media ownership in comparison with the situation in other post-communist countries; it also analyzes certain specific barriers which prevent private Ukrainian media from becoming financially viable and politically independent. Moreover, it aims at clarifying what 'media market' means in the circumstances of Ukraine's deformed market economy typified by close intertwinement between business and political elites.

3.1. The Ukrainian media market

3.1.1. Size and wealth

With a population of about 42 million, Ukraine could have a large, dynamic media market. According to ZenithOptimedia, Ukrainian television has the second-largest (after Russia) audience in the region: 18.6 million viewers (Onufrienko and Mironova 2008). Before the global economic crisis began in the fall of 2008, Ukraine had the fastest-growing advertising market in Europe, one expanding at an average of 30 percent per year and becoming more and more attractive for investors, both domestic and foreign (Kalinina 2009).

However, compared to other European countries, the Ukrainian media market is largely underdeveloped. The country's weak economy does not produce enough market resources to ensure the development of a private, advertisement-financed media sector. The advertising budget in Ukraine is low in comparison with the ad budgets of countries with populations of comparable size. For example, in 2008 the total TV advertising budget in Ukraine amounted to about $500 million, which was half the size of the total advertising budget in neighboring Poland, and forty times smaller than in Germany (Kalinina 2009). Per capita advertising spending in Ukraine is among the lowest in the region—$19.50 in 2012, whereas in Poland, the Czech Republic, and Hungary it was $62.90, $145.00, and $84.10, respectively (Austin et al. 2012).

Since Ukraine is a TV-viewing nation, the largest share of advertising money (more than 45 percent) goes to broadcast media.[60] Newspapers, meanwhile, comprise only around 7 percent of the advertising market, which is very small compared to the more common 30–40 percent in neighboring countries. Indeed, the 7-percent level cannot ensure the newspapers' financial independence.[61] This is one of the reasons for the underdeveloped print media market in Ukraine, where newspaper circulation (74 readers per 1,000 inhabitants) is comparatively low among the post-communist countries.[62] As for the TV advertising market, only nationwide channels have a good chance of attracting scarce advertising money, since the ad-

---

60 The shares of TV advertising revenues in the total advertising market are calculated on the basis of data provided by the All-Ukrainian Advertising Coalition quoted in MSI-Ukraine (2010).
61 The share of newspaper advertising revenues in the total advertising market is calculated on the basis of data provided by the All-Ukrainian Advertising Coalition quoted in MSI-Ukraine (2010). The data on advertising revenue shares in the media sector in Central and East European countries come from Peruško and Popović (2008, 172).
62 Compare, for example, to newspaper circulation in Hungary (194 per 1,000 people) or the Czech Republic (89 per 1,000). See www.pressreference.com, accessed September 20, 2015.

vertising budget is very unevenly divided between national and regional TV channels. For example, in 2010 the advertising budget of national TV channels totaled $342 million, whereas regional stations received only $14.7 million in advertising money (MSI-Ukraine 2011, 214).

Advertising income is difficult to obtain because the advertising 'pie' has to be divided among too many players. The Ukrainian media market is overcrowded, with more than twice as many non-satellite national television channels as neighboring Poland (Onufrienko and Mironova 2008).[63] As a result, commercial TV channels in Ukraine wage a fierce battle for ad revenue, often by resorting to the commercialization and tabloidization of their content.

3.1.2. Dependence on political advertising

The lack of a developed advertising market and the low average income of the Ukrainian population make it difficult for print media to reap profits from sales. In consequence, Ukrainian media are dependent on political advertising. Since 2000, Ukraine has held national elections almost every two years, and political advertising (both direct and indirect) has become one of the leading sources of advertising money. For example, during the 2010 presidential election campaign the share of political advertising during the final five months of the year (August–December 2009) accounted for as much as 23.5 percent of all television advertising income in 2009.[64] Bearing in mind that this figure is based on data for direct political ads—and thus does not take into account the hidden advertising

---

63 These numbers predate the digital switchover in Poland in 2010.
64 According to the monitoring of political advertising in the 2010 presidential elections conducted by the public organization Telekrytyka, Ukrainian TV channels were paid a total of 470 million hryvnias for political advertising in August–December 2009 (Zakusylo 2010). The total TV advertising market in Ukraine in 2009 was 1940 million hryvnias (Vakaliuk and Lazebnik 2009).

widely used by presidential contenders—one may assume that political advertising accounts for an even larger share of total TV ad revenue. This is an important difference between Ukraine and other post-communist countries. For instance, spending on political ads in Poland during its parliamentary and presidential elections in 2005 accounted for only about 15 percent of the total TV advertising market.[65] In mature democracies, the share of political advertising in media ad revenues is even lower. In the United States, the share of TV political advertising in total television ad revenues oscillates between 2.6 percent and 7.6 percent.[66] In European democracies like France, the United Kingdom, and Sweden, paid political advertising is banned or heavily restricted (Johnson 2009).

3.1.3. Unfinished privatization

Two significant factors that hindered fair market competition in the Ukrainian media market in the period under study were unfinished privatization and the continued existence of state-owned and municipal media outlets. At the moment of writing this book Ukraine had only started to create its public broadcasting (which became a real prospect only after the Maidan revolution and the overthrow of Viktor Yanukovych in 2014), and to privatize hundreds of state-owned and municipal print media which had continued to exist in

---

[65] According to the Polish marketing and sales monthly *Brief*, no. 1 (2006, 16), a total of 37 million złoty was spent on political TV spots during the six-month parliamentary and presidential election campaigns in Poland. The country's total TV advertising market in 2005 was 2.47 billion złoty (Starlink Media House 2006).

[66] These data for 2003–8 concern local television stations in the United States, which historically get around 60 percent of political ad dollars (Pew Research Center Project for Excellence in Journalism 2009).

Ukraine in the post-communist period.[67] [68] So, it would be right to state that for more than 20 years of transformation the country's media were essentially divided into two sectors: private and state-owned (including municipal and communal media). Ukrainian national and local governments have been in no hurry to privatize the remaining state-owned outlets because they frequently used them for self-promotion and in power struggles.

The unfinished privatization of the media has inhibited media democratization across post-communist Europe. The states where the media partly remained for a long time (or even still continue to remain) in the hands of national or local authorities—Albania, Macedonia, Croatia, Bosnia and Herzegovina, Moldova, Armenia, Belarus, Russia, and the Central Asian states—are all states with low scores in the international press freedom rankings (see e.g., Freedom House 2006–2014).

When Viktor Yushchenko became president in 2005 after the Orange Revolution, he declared that the privatization of state and municipal media was one of his major goals. However, no significant action ensued from these promising words. In 2006—fifteen years after the start of the post-communist transformation—as many as half of all newspapers and magazines in Ukraine still belonged to the state (Dyczok 2006). The state also owned thirty-five television and radio outlets, including the nationwide *UT-1* television channel and three radio channels (MSI-Ukraine 2005). Apart from this, there were nearly 815 municipal television and radio companies controlled by local governments (KAS 2008). In addition, there were still more than 100 state-owned newspapers, as well as more

---

67 On April 7 president Petro Poroshenko signed the Law on Amending Certain Laws of Ukraine related to Public Television and Radio Broadcasting of Ukraine, which in fact cleared the way for the launch of public service broadcasting in Ukraine.
68 Municipal media are not treated separately because in Ukraine they are very close to the state-owned media in the sense of their dependence on government entities. For example, under Ukrainian law, municipal media can only be set up by local governments subordinated to the central government. The finances of municipal media in Ukraine are heavily dependent on local budgets.

than 800 municipal newspapers, awaiting privatization; together they constituted almost 22 percent of all Ukrainian periodicals (KAS 2011).[69]

The municipal media were used in the interests of local authorities. One of the most well-known cases is that of the ex-mayor of Kyiv, Leonid Chernovetskyi, who, for practical purposes, had transformed the capital city's media into his personal public relations firm (Telekrytyka 2008). During the pre-term municipal electoral campaign in 2008, Kyiv print and TV outlets heaped lavish praise on Chernovetskyi, while smearing his rivals' reputations (Bulavka and Shevchenko 2008). Similar practices were widespread across the county.

Although state- and municipally-owned media were generally less popular than privately-owned outlets, at least at the national level,[70] many retained a considerable audience share in distant or poorly populated areas where they were the only media available. Three state-owned nationwide radio channels have managed to keep a relatively large part of their listeners because of their exclusive access to a system of wire radio broadcasting traditionally popular in Ukraine (especially in rural areas) from Soviet times (Kulyk 2010, 198). The same was true for municipal newspapers, which often were the only papers in some rural areas.

State-owned and municipal media, posed unfair competition against privately owned print media, at least on the local and regional markets (see MSI-Ukraine 2006–2007, 2008). Unburdened by the need to earn money for their survival, they offered much lower rates to advertisers and lower prices for readers and subscrib-

---

69 Since the fall of Yanukovych's government in 2014 this situation began to change. As mentioned in the previous chapter, in the TV and radio sector, state broadcasters began to be transformed into a public broadcaster. As for the state and municipal print media, on November 24, 2015 the Ukrainian parliament adopted the Law on Reforming State and Communal Print Mass Media, paving the way to their privatization.
70 See previous chapter.

ers, indirectly undermining the financial sustainability of their privately owned rivals. Moreover, at the regional level state and municipal media waged unfair competition on the labor market because the salaries they offered journalists and, more important, their pensions were calculated according to the public-servant scale. Thus jobs at state-owned media—especially local print media—were more lucrative than those offered by private media (MSI-Ukraine 2004, 2005, 2006–2007).[71]

3.1.4. Foreign investments

The state is not a good media manager. Ukrainian state and municipal newspapers, which were preserved by the authorities for more than two decades, relied primarily on government support and had no concept of how to run media as a business (see e.g., MSI-Ukraine 2008, 198; MSI-Ukraine 2009, 207). The same was true for state and municipal radio and TV, which in addition lacked new equipment and technologies. The example of other post-communist countries that have managed to create a developed media market shows that substantial investments are needed to turn old-style publications into outlets capable of winning audiences and competing in a free market. The Czech Republic, Hungary, Poland, and the Baltic states solved their funding problems by relying on foreign investments. For example, the Polish *Rzeczpospolita*, an official government daily up to 1989, became a high-quality, high-circulation newspaper after the French firm Socpresse bought 49 percent of its shares and poured $4.5 million into its renewal (Klimkiewicz 2004).

In addition to bankrolling the modernization of outdated communist-era media or launching new outlets to help diversify the market, Western businesses also bring industry expertise, professional management, education, and training. Students of media and de-

---

[71] There are several exceptions to this rule, but they mainly concern popular television presenters and entertainers who get unusually high fees from private TV channels.

mocracy often criticize Western media corporations in Central-Eastern Europe for putting profit ahead of quality,[72] but they acknowledge that foreign owners have extensively contributed to the development of independent, pluralist media in the region.

For example, Miklós Sükösd, of the Media Diversity Institute (London), believes that foreign ownership effectively ensured that the government would not interfere with Hungary's print media, which were privatized by German and Austrian investors (Sükösd 2000, 152). Marius Dragomir, senior manager and publications editor for the Open Society Program on Independent Journalism, claims that without Western players in the media markets of Eastern and Central Europe to keep the debate about media freedom alive and ease the legal environment concerning the media, the situation would have been much more problematic (Dragomir 2003, 40).

Western investments in media have been much lower in Ukraine than in Poland, Hungary, or the Baltic states. The rare exceptions include glossy magazines and the Internet, the only type of media in Ukraine where foreign capital is extensively represented. In many Central-European countries (Poland, Czech Republic, Hungary, Slovakia), Western media companies invest in daily and weekly newspapers, sectors that are unattractive in Ukraine because of their low profitability. The only popular nationwide news outlet that ever belonged to a Western investor was *Korrespondent* magazine, whose former primary owner, Jed Sunden, is a US citizen, but in April 2011 he sold his media holding, KP media, which included *Korrespondent*, to the Ukrainian big media owners, Boris Lozhkin and Petro Poroshenko, who in turn sold the magazine to an alleged crony of then-president Viktor Yanukovych, Serhiy Kurchenko, in 2013 (Finance.ua 2011; Kononczuk 2013).[73]

---

72 See, for example, Wyka (2009, 136), Dragomir (2003, 35–40), Sükösd (2000, 151–52).

73 Until 2009, Jed Sunden also owned the quality English-language newspaper *Kyiv Post*, one of the first truly independent newspapers in Ukraine. In July 2009, he sold the paper to Mohammad Zahoor, a United Kingdom citizen and an owner of the ISTIL Group. In 2008, because of the economic crisis, Sunden

During the years of Ukrainian independence foreign capital has sometimes entered the Ukrainian TV market as well, but it was Russians, not Westerners, who managed to stay there for a longer period.[74] In general, however, Ukrainian television was and continues to be dominated by Ukrainian businessmen.

To be precise, Western companies did make substantial investments in Ukrainian TV in the late 1990s and early 2000s, but they gradually began to leave the market, selling their shares to Ukrainian entrepreneurs. For example, the US company Story First Communications was one of the co-founders of *ICTV* (International Commercial Television), a national TV channel, but in 2000 it sold the channel to the Ukrainian tycoon Viktor Pinchuk, the son-in-law of then-president Leonid Kuchma. Similarly, the US company Central European Media Enterprises (CME), which in 1996 cofounded *1+1*, one of the most popular Ukrainian TV channels, and became its 100-percent owner in 2008, sold the channel in early 2010 to the Ukrainian oligarch Ihor Kolomoisky.

Western investors stay away from the Ukrainian media market because of the lack of stable, transparent business regulation, the widespread corruption, and the uneasy relationships between the media and politicians. For example, the above-mentioned Jed

---

also closed two news outlets he had only recently founded: the metro daily *15 Minutes* and the weekly news magazine *Novynar*.

74 For example, 29 percent of the shares of *Inter* TV channel, one of the long-time leaders of the Ukrainian broadcast ratings, were held by the Russian state company Russian Channel One, from the time the channel was founded in 1996 till early 2015. Then the channel's main shareholders, the Ukrainians Dmytro Firtash and Serhiy Liovochkin purchased the Channel One's 29 percent stake for $100 million, as *Inter* reported in the Securities and Stock Market Commission's information disclosure system on February 4, 2015. The transaction was carried out two weeks after the new bill (which prohibited Russian investors from owning equity capital in Ukrainian TV channels) was registered in Ukrainian parliament.
The example of *Inter* does not mean however that Russian-owned media in Ukraine were not squeezzed out of the market by Ukrainian business close to politics, as in the case with Western-owned media. For example, in 2003 Viktor Pinchuk successfully bought *Novy Kanal* from the Russian "Alfa-group." The next year he also bought *STB* channel from its founder, the Russian oil company Lukoil (Telekrytyka 2010).

Sunden, the former co-owner of the KP media holding and founder of the leading English-language weekly *Kyiv Post*, was detained at Boryspil Airport in early 2000 and declared *persona non grata*. He was allowed to enter Ukraine only after diplomatic intervention from Washington (Kyiv Post 2005).

An additional barrier to foreign investors, especially in television, is that the main players in the broadcasting sector are not primarily driven by market logic. This distorts market competition. As mentioned before, the owners of Ukrainian TV channels are entrepreneurs, but media outlets are not an important source of capital for them. They see TV as a medium in which they can accumulate political influence and 'convert' it into opportunities to develop or support their main businesses. They invest generously in their media holdings and fight for the high ratings that determine how much influence a channel has, but obtaining an (immediate) profit is not necessarily what motivates them. For example, in 2010 Telekrytyka estimated that Rinat Akmetov's *Ukraina* TV channel, which the oligarch transformed from a local into a nationwide channel in 2003 and which underwent an expensive reorganization following 2005, had never turned a profit (Prodaieva 2010b).

The inhospitable business climate created by the politically-motivated behavior of media owners is not a unique Ukrainian problem, as it can also be found in other countries with the symptoms of media capture. The experience of foreign media owners in such countries as Bulgaria, Romania, and Serbia shows that foreign investors in their media industries have very similar problems with those who have tried to invest in Ukrainian media. For example, the CEO of the WAZ Media Group Bodo Hombach, when explaining the Group's pullout from Romania and Serbia in 2010, claimed that "the close intertwining of oligarchs and political power" was "poisoning the market" in these countries, leading to the diminishing of free market competition in the media sector of southern Europe.[75] As Hombach complained, "oligarchs in the Balkans are buying ever

---

75 The Bodo Hombach's newspaper interview, as quoted by Stetka (2012).

more often newspapers and magazines in order to exert political influence, not in order to win money." A very similar picture can be observed in Ukraine, where oligarchs do not hesitate to pay overpriced sums for broadcasting licenses, to invest in disproportionately expensive equipment to overrun their competitors,[76] or to take other steps that seem illogical from the point of view of normal market behavior. This is because political goals take precedence over profits.

3.1.5. The Russian factor

Besides the abovementioned internal obstacles to the development of Ukrainian media market—such as the weak media market, unfinished privatization, and the deficit of foreign investments—there also exists a significant external one. Namely, Ukrainian media face tough competition from the Russian media market. Throughout the years of Ukrainian independence this has significantly restricted the development of Ukraine's media market. Indeed, the impact of the Russian media market was partly reduced only recently, when—after Russia's annexation of Crimea in 2014 and the start of fighting with Russia-backed separatists in the Donetsk region—Ukraine suspended several of the most propagandistic Russian broadcasts on its territory. Also prohibited was television broadcasting of many Russian movies and television serials, especially those that glorify Russia's armed forces or law-enforcement agencies.

In 1995–2013, however, there were very few (if any) barriers for Russian media in Ukraine. The Russian newspapers *Komsomolskaya pravda*, *Izvestia*, and *Argumenty i fakty* were very popular (Kuzio 2009); *Argumenty i fakty* was the second most widely-circulated newspaper in the country (see Table 2). Russian TV channels were also popular. They were available in Ukraine via cable and satellite, and in some areas via terrestrial television (in US usage,

---

76 For example, Ukrainian business oligarch and media baron Rinat Akhmetov invited for the design and equipment of his TV Centre for Information and Programs in 2011 international companies and specialists which took part in building TV studios for FOX, CBS, and RTL (myNews-in.net 2011).

broadcast television). This was especially true for the eastern territories of Ukraine bordering with Russia and populated mostly by Russian-speaking inhabitants, as well as the south of Ukraine, also populated by Russian-speakers. In the Crimea, more than half the population got its news from Russian TV channels, which were the more trusted media in the region when compared with Ukrainian and Crimean media (National Security and Defense Magazine 2009).

Products of the Russian media industry made their way to Ukrainian audiences not only via Russian TV channels. Ukrainian TV schedules were heavily padded with Russian serials, reality shows, and gala concerts. Russian soap operas and comedy shows were constantly among the most popular programs in Ukraine's TV ratings.[77] In comparison with the somewhat parochial domestic media product, the Russian TV industry offered programs of higher quality and variety. Ukrainian TV channels willingly purchased Russian programs and serials because the latter ensured them high viewership. This created unfavourable conditions for the development of the Ukraine's own production.

After Russia occupied Crimea in 2014 and started to support pro-Russian separatists in Donetsk and Luhansk, the attitude of Ukrainians to Russia has become more negative, something reflected in the steep decline of trust toward Russian TV channels.[78] However, private Ukrainian TV channels did not reduce the share of Russian TV serials and films in their schedules until June 4, 2015 when the law establishing a barrier for some types of Russian TV

---

77 Weekly Ukrainian TV ratings in 2004–2013 are available at http://www.telekritika.ua/page/ratings/?&articles.
78 According to data from Kyiv International Institute of Sociology, the share of Ukrainians having a positive attitude to Russia decreased from 85 percent in February 2013 to 36.5 percent in December 2014 (KIIS 2015). As far as the trust of Russian media is concerned, it also dropped dramatically. For example, whereas in October 2009 only 17.2 percent of Ukrainians never trusted to Russian media completely (Razumkov 2013), in October 2014 this amount grew to 48.5 percent (KIIS 2014).

content in Ukrainian TV came into force.[79][80] According to research conducted by the civic group Vidsich in September 2014, the average share of Russian content on top-10 Ukrainian TV channels amounted then to more than 40 percent (compare to 41 percent of Ukrainian content); on Akhmetov's *Ukraina* it reached 87 percent, and on Firtash/Liovochkin's *Inter*—67 percent (texty.org.ua 2014).

The presence of a stronger media market in the neighborhood that intrudes on a country's information space is typical of several other post-communist countries. It can be found in the Balkan region, where the media of Macedonia, Montenegro, and Bosnia-Herzegovina face strong competition from Serbian and, sometimes, Croatian newspapers, TV, and radio. It is also experienced in some former Soviet countries (Moldova, Belarus, Latvia, Lithuania, Estonia), which experience the intrusion of Russian media into their markets. In all these cases, the neighboring media entering the country's market are supported by a larger audience and a correspondingly larger advertising market, and thus compete with national producers under non-equal conditions.

What is special in this respect about Ukraine (as well as some other non-Baltic former Soviet republics, such as Belarus or Moldova) in comparison with other countries is the extraordinarily large scale of the neighbor's presence in its media market. For example, whereas in Lithuania in 2007 the share of Russian programs, TV series, movies, and talk shows in the broadcasting time of major TV networks ranged from 1 percent to 31 percent,[81] in Ukraine it was much higher. According to the data from the State Committee of Television and Radio Broadcasting of Ukraine quoted by Radio

---

79 The statute of Ukraine On Amendments to Certain Statutes of Ukraine to Protect Information Television and Radio Sphere of Ukraine, N 159–VIII, 5 February 2015. Published in *Holos Ukrainy* (Голос України) official daily on 4 April 2015, № 61.
80 An interesting discussion about the abundance of Russian soap operas on Ukrainian TV and its economic aspect was published in 2014 by Forbes Ukraine (available at: http://www.telekritika.ua/daidzhest/2014-05-13/93567).
81 The results of the Lithuanian Media Content Survey conducted by Nerijus Maliukevicius (Institute of International Relations and Political Science, University of Vilnius) in 2005–7, as quoted in Maliukevicius (2007).

Free Europe in 2009, up to 80 percent of the broadcast time of Ukrainian radio and TV channels was filled with non-Ukrainian product (Kaspruk 2009). The lion's share was Russian product. Even more dramatic was the picture of the book market in Ukraine. According to market research commissioned by the Renaissance Foundation in 2007, as well as assessments by experts from the Ukrainian Publishers and Booksellers Association, about 85 percent of the books sold in Ukraine were produced in Russia (Khaminich and Pylypenko 2009).

3.2. The dark side of media privatization and commercialization in Ukraine

3.2.1. Oligarchic media ownership

What distinguishes the Ukrainian market from the media markets in many other countries of post-communist Europe and Eurasia is the structure of its media ownership. As illuminated in Chapter 2, the most popular Ukrainian media are concentrated in the hands of a specific type of owners, namely industrial and financial magnates with good political connections, often called 'oligarchs.' Their main interests are outside the media sector; they seek to control media to influence politics and protect their businesses, given Ukraine's weak state, unreliable institutions, and lack of the rule of law. Political influence also may lead to commercial privileges and advantages as state property continues to be privatized.

This type of media ownership is in no way specific to Ukraine or the post-Soviet region. Media owners referred to as 'oligarchs' in Ukraine or Russia are known in media and communication studies as "media/industrialist moguls," (Tunstall and Palmer 1991), "tycoons" (Mazzoleni 1991) or "industrialists" (Hallin and Mancini 2004; Hallin and Papathanassopoulos 2002).[82] A specific feature of these media owners is that they "are primarily captains in some

---

82 A recent overview of the studies of the types of big media owners in the Western world was made in Stetka (2012).

other [than media] industrial field, but in addition own and operate major media interests" (Tunstall and Palmer 1991, 105–6). Media/industrialist moguls are distinguished from big media owners well known in the history of European media as 'media barons,' for whom media are the main business and the main sphere of investments. Different from the latter, they invest in the media not (so much) in search for profits, but for the sake of wielding influence in the political world. The owners of the first type are described in European media studies mostly based on the examples from Greece and Italy, which are known for their obstacles to media freedom and pluralism compared to other Western democracies (Tunstall and Palmer 1991; Hallin and Mancini 2004; Hallin and Papathanassopoulos 2002). According to Peter Humphreys, they "were to be found most thickly on the ground in countries where established media interests were weaker and where they were therefore presented with a relatively open field" (Humphreys 1995, 209). The effect of media ownership by media/industrialist moguls on democratic functions of the media is generally accessed as negative. When exploring this, Daniel Hallin and Paolo Mancini use the term 'instrumentalization.' They point out that instrumentalization, or instrumental use of media by outside actors—economic actors seeking political influence, parties, or politicians is one of the main characteristic features of media-politics relationships in such countries as Italy or Greece (Hallin and Mancini 2004). Papathanassopoulos, when describing the Greek media system, where industrialists dominate media ownership, points out that the media are used there as "a vehicles for negotiating with and pressuring the government of the day, rather than representing the public discourse of society" (Papathanassopoulos 1999, 401).

In post-communist Central-Eastern Europe this particular type of media ownership is common in the countries with weak media markets (Macedonia, Albania, Bulgaria, Romania) (see country reports in Hrvatin and Petković 2004). The same countries are characterized by notably lower indices of press freedom as compared with CEE democratic frontrunners like Poland or Estonia. After the

2008 economic crisis hit the media and advertising markets in the CEE region, a growing number of such owners also started to appear in advanced new democracies, where—since the privatization of the early 1990s—private media were mostly in the hands of national and foreign companies for which media was the main business (Stetka 2012). In 2008–2011 several big international media players withdrew from CEE media markets, often selling their media stakes to local big businessmen with other-than-media background. The cases of the entry of domestic players of this kind into the media markets of successful new European democracies are a cause of concern among analysts (see e.g., Stetka 2012, 2015).

In post-Soviet media studies the phenomenon of instrumental use of the media by private interests is well documented in the study of news-making in Russia in the 1990s by Olessya Koltsova from the National University Higher School of Economics. She introduced the terms 'internal' and 'external' media ownership to differentiate between the two types of owners which appeared in Russia after privatization of the media in the early 1990s. According to Koltsova, internal media owners confine their activities to media organizations and are guided mainly by their interest in earning a profit from their media business. External owners, in contrast, are "interested first of all in their political capital or in the development of other kinds of business for which they need the advertising propaganda resource of the mass media" (Koltsova 2006, 75).

The external ownership of media outlets constrains the independence and pluralism of the media because of the political and economic interests of their owners. Koltsova notes that internal media owners, whose primary aim is profit maximization, predominantly control the financial aspects of their media business and never interfere in the area of content. This is not the case for external owners, for whom the media is a tool with which to realize their political and economic goals. They can overlook some financial mismanagement, but steadfastly exercise control over content (Koltsova 2006).

As indicated in Chapter 1, in Ukraine, 'fat cats' began to seize portions of the media market in the mid-1990s. This trend intensified after 1998, when the global financial crisis significantly weakened private media companies. Their establishment was possible after the adoption of laws in 1990–1991 abolishing the Communist Party's monopoly on the media and allowing private ownership of media organizations. If before 1998 many broadcasting companies functioned as conventional, middle-sized business structures and were relatively free and independent, the crisis—combined with growing political pressure by the Kuchma administration—forced them to sell their shares to politically and economically powerful oligarchic clans. Within a year or two, the main nationwide Ukrainian TV channels (*Inter, ICTV, Novy, STB*) fell under the control of industrial magnates and financial-political groups, most of whom were members of the entourage of president Kuchma. [83] Oligarchs bought media outlets not necessarily as financial investments. Instead, they did so as a means of accumulating political capital and enhancing their personal prestige. Oleksandr Bohutskyi, general director of *ICTV*, noted that in the 1990s owning a TV channel or at least a radio station was a status symbol for Ukrainian businessmen (Onufrienko and Mironova 2008).

Ironically enough, although private ownership is considered an important condition for the independence of the media,[84] the process of media appropriation by large financial-industrial groups in Ukraine was accompanied by a reduction of their autonomy and freedom. Indeed, the period when oligarchic clans gained ownership or control in the media sector, coincided with the second term of president Kuchma (1999–2004), which was characterized by a

---

83 An important exception is that of the *1+1* channel, which until 2007 was co-owned by its co-founders, Oleksandr Rodnianski, a Kyiv-born film maker, businessman Borys Fuksman, and the American company Central European Media Enterprises Ltd. This does not however exclude the fact that the channel was one of the main pro-Kuchma media resources during parliamentary elections-2002 and presidential elections-2004 (Ligachova 2007c, see also Dovzhenko 2011a).
84 See, for example, Keane (1991, 1–51).

constant reduction of media independence (Freedom House 1999–2004). The Orange Revolution, even despite the significant progress in media independence it engendered, nonetheless did not allow Ukraine to move from 'partly free' to 'free' media. Indeed, the temporary improvements were soon replaced by the quick regress of press freedom under Viktor Yanukovych. This trajectory of media development, fairly well corresponding to Mungiu-Pippidi's 2-nd path of media evolution in post-communist countries (under which the media, even after a promising beginning, end up captured) also supports the thesis by Katrin Voltmer about the ambiguous outcomes of media privatization in emerging democracies. As Voltmer puts it:

> The outcomes of privatization of the media depend to a large degree on the market structure in which they operate. If the purchasing power of the wider public is weak, then the advertising market will also be underdeveloped, thus forcing the media to seek funding from alternative sources. Usually this is the state, political parties of political entrepreneurs who still expect support for their own interests in response. (Voltmer 2008)

3.2.2. Concentration of media ownership and its nature in Ukraine

The problem with media ownership in Ukraine is not only that it is dominated by oligarchs, but also that it is concentrated. As Table 1 demonstrates, the major owners on the Ukrainian media market own media 'empires' that encompass TV and radio, newspapers, news websites, and other kinds of outlets. As of 2013, Rinat Akhmetov owned the high-ranking national TV channel *Ukraina*, the national daily *Segodnya*, the Internet portal Segodnya, a printing house in Vyshgorod, the regional TV channel *Donbas*, and a number of local media outlets in the Donetsk region. Viktor Pinchuk was the owner of four national TV channels—*ICTV, STB, Novy*, and the *M1* music channel—the largest-circulation daily *Fakty i kommentarii*, shares in the popular radio stations *Russkoe radio*, *Hit-FM*, *Kiss-FM*, and other media. Ihor Kolomoisky owned the national *1+1*, *TET*, and *Kino TV* channels, several newspapers and magazines, was a co-owner of the UNIAN news agency, as well as the media holding Glavred, which included several Internet sites and news outlets.

Karol Jakubowicz described the appropriation of the media market by a handful of oligarchic groups in some countries of post-communist Europe and Eurasia as a 're-monopolization.' In his view, the abolition of state media monopolies (de-monopolization), media differentiation, democratization, and the professionalization of journalists constitute the minimum of what would ensure qualitative change in post-communist European and Eurasian media as compared to the situation under communist rule (Jakubowicz 1995). In some countries, such as Poland, the Czech Republic, Slovenia, and Estonia, the process of de-monopolization was relatively successful and resulted in the creation of a developed media market with diverse, privately-owned outlets independent both financially and generally (Jakubowicz 2007). In many of the former Soviet republics, the media were in fact 're-monopolized' by media groups headed by oligarchs closely associated with (or part of) the political elite.

Media concentration is not exclusive to Ukraine among the countries of post-communist Europe and Eurasia. Levels comparable to that of Ukraine can be found in Hungary, Poland, Lithuania, and Estonia (Peruško and Popović 2008). What differentiates these countries from Ukraine, however, is that their dominant media owners are most often foreign companies (Downey 2012). Unlike Ukrainian owners, for whom media assets are a means to influence politics, these foreign firms are independent from politics and have no interest in utilizing their media for political purposes.

When commenting on the differences in media concentration between the democratic front-runners in Central-Eastern Europe and the laggards like the Balkan states (excluding Slovenia) or former Soviet republics, Jakubowicz assumed that in the latter group media concentrations were mostly politically-driven. According to him, this is different in the first group of countries, since media concentration there was promoted solely by market mechanisms (Jakubowicz 2005). The evidence provided by the studies of Ukrainian media appears to support Jakubowicz's assumption, at least in the part concerning the group of democratic laggards. As Dutsyk (2010) points out, indeed not only business interests, but, notably, also political matters were the most important moving forces for this process in Ukraine. Rather similar developments were observed in Russia, where the process of media concentration was, according to Ivan Zassoursky, highly politicized (Zassoursky 2000).

The media market in Ukraine is subject to anti-trust legislation, but in practice media monopolies are not regulated. The government's anti-trust agency is unable to effectively combat the monopolization of the media market (MSI-Ukraine 2009, 206). As noted above, Ukrainian media moguls conceal their ownership of the media with the help of offshore entities and figureheads. As a result, the process of media concentration does not come up against any significant government barriers. This also indirectly supports the thesis that the concentration of media ownership in Ukraine is the outcome of political, not only market forces.[85]

An important aspect of media concentration in Ukraine, as in the rest of the world, is editorial concentration, or concentration of media content production. This takes place, for example, when media content for several news outlets belonging to a single owner is produced in one place. According to Zrinjka Peruško and Helena Popović from Zagreb University, this mode of editorial concentration significantly endangers the diversity and pluralism of media content, as only one viewpoint is presented in different media (Peruško and Popović 2008). Ukrainian tycoons do practice editorial concentration, and its consequences are negatively assessed by the independently-minded journalists and media monitoring organizations.

In particular, significant organizational changes enhancing editorial concentration were accomplished in 2007–2009 in such

---

85 In September 2015 some hope appeared that the state of affairs regarding this issue will improve, i.e., when the Law on Transparency in Media Ownership was adopted in Ukraine.

large Ukrainian media groups as InterMediaGroup, the owner of several TV channels (including the highly popular *Inter*), and Ihor Kolomoisky Group. Reorganization at *Inter* started with the liquidation in 2007 of the unit which produced the news for the channel. Simultaneously within the InterMediaGroup was created the separate production studio National Information Systems (NIS), producing the news for all the channels of the Group, including *Inter*. The official explanation for this reorganization was optimization of news production within the group and the fight for higher TV ratings (Telekrytyka 2007). Ukrainian media watchdogs, however, criticized this move by InterMediaGroup, claiming that it created conditions for centralized control over the news by the Group's owners and top managers. Otar Dovzhenko in his commentary for Telekrytyka pointed out that organizational changes like this in big Ukrainian media companies were chiefly a way of creating fully dependent and guided-from-above units of news production (Dovzhenko 2010a). From the moment it was created, NIS had a complicated bureaucratic structure, and, according to some journalists, the news stories created by the production studio's employees were to be checked and accepted not only by news editors, but also by top managers. An investigation carried out in 2012 by the then-respected Ukrainian weekly *Korrespondent*[86] found out that in the news programs by *Inter* "even an innocent video about cats and dogs could not be aired without approval of the top managers" (Korrespondent 2012).

---

86 *Korrespondent* was founded in 2002 by the American Jed Sunden, and from the very start it was a quality medium. In 2012 it was sold to Boris Lozhkin and Petro Poroshenko who promised not to interfere into the journal's editorial policy. Indeed, the journal's critical approach to the coverage of political events and their commentary underwent no basic changes in 2012–2013 when they were the owners. In 2013, however, Lozhkin and Poroshenko had to sell the outlet to Serhiy Kurchenko from the inner circle of president Yanukovych. After this, the most prominent journalists of *Korrespondent*, led by its editor from 2003 Vitaly Sych, left the journal's editorial office. After that, the journal became the mouthpiece of the Yanukovych's regime.

3.2.3. Implications of oligarchic media ownership

The structure of Ukraine's media ownership, with major media concentrated in the hands of media owners having good political connections and interested in the media as a tool of realizing their political/economic goals, has some important implications for the development of the country's media market. First, the market 'overpopulation' (an effect of setting up or maintaining media businesses based on political rather than market goals) reduces chances to run a sustainable media business in Ukraine. This is because Ukraine's already low advertising budget has to be distributed among too many market players. For example, in Odesa, the city in southern Ukraine, there are as many as twenty-seven private local television channels (Kabachii 2015). This is a disproportionately large number for a city with a population of around one million inhabitants. The excessive number of market players then further weakens the market and makes media dependent on big business and politics.

Second, because the market is dominated by several large media corporations, market entry is no easy task for newcomers, which is especially true for the broadcasting sector.[87] This problem is aggravated by the fact that the licensing process in Ukraine is heavily politicized (see the previous chapter). The practice of Ukrainian presidents in 1995–2013 of redistributing media ownership in favor of their supporters, described in the previous chapter, well illustrates this problem. In a 2011 IREX panel discussion Kostiantyn Kvurt, board chair of Internews-Ukraine, commented on the issue of barriers for market entry in Ukrainian broadcasting as follows:

---

[87] Though the spread of new technologies recently opened wide prospects for online TV and radio in Ukraine, the problem remains for more traditional broadcasting—terrestrial, cable or satellite. Notably, it is traditional television which, as mentioned before in this book, serves the main source of the news for the lion's share of the Ukrainian audience.

> it is nearly impossible to enter the television market without proper political partners. Politics and business interests drive the process, and the accelerating concentration of capital and resources in the hands of a few business groups does not bode well for newcomers. (MSI-Ukraine 2011)

As for the implications of oligarchic media ownership for media independence and pluralism, in the case of Ukraine several issues are worth mentioning in addition to the matter of the instrumentalization of Ukrainian media by private interests, which was extensively presented in the previous chapter. First, the experience of Ukraine's media transformations in the post-communist period demonstrates that the structure of media ownership under which the most popular media are concentrated in the hands of a few financial-industrial magnates dependent on political favor carries the risk of establishing centralized control over the media. The rapid deterioration in press freedom under president Viktor Yanukovych after the preceding five years of relatively free and pluralistic media, described in the previous chapter, suggests that having the media concentrated in the hands of a few oligarchs considerably helped the Yanukovych team to curb the relative independence of the media.

Russia experienced a similar reverse development in the early 2000s that established centralized state control over the most significant media, further suggesting that oligarchic media ownership may facilitate the process of reversing the democratization of the media in post-communist countries. In the 1990s, Russia owed the relative pluralism and independence of its media to their ownership by several oligarchs whose interests did not always coincide with the interests of the Kremlin and who used their media outlets to criticize the government and further their economic and political goals. In the early years of his presidency, Vladimir Putin methodically attacked the media empires owned by his critics and redistributed their holdings among state-controlled businesses or oligarchs loyal to the Kremlin (Becker 2004). For example, Gazprom, the state-controlled gas monopoly, acquired the popular nationwide NTV channel owned by Vladimir Gusinsky, whereas *ORT*, the TV channel with the widest reception area in Russia, passed from Kremlin critic Boris Berezovsky to Kremlin-connected Roman Abramovich (Dunn 2009). These high-profile cases cowed other independent media, which began to self-censor content and avoid challenging the regime, practices now widespread among journalists in Russia. Today's Russian media are obedient servants of the regime, manipulating public opinion in the interests of the Kremlin.

Another issue regards the implications of oligarchic media ownership for media pluralism. In studies of the transformations of the media and political systems in former Soviet countries one may find the thesis about the positive impact of this type of ownership on the plurality of perspectives in post-Soviet media. In particularly, Ellen Mickiewicz, when commenting on the commercial television concentration in the hands of powerful oligarchs in pre-Putin Russia, points out that the oligarchic media displayed a greater degree of independence than did the sector of state broadcasting (Mickiewicz 2000, 99–105). According to Mickiewicz, the then relative autonomy of Russia's commercial TV stations rested on the power and influence of Russian oligarchs who owned them, and if media resources were not concentrated in the hands of a few highly influential owners, private broadcasters might not have had enough capacity to "compete with, and challenge governmentally managed news" (Ibid., 120). In 2000, when Mickiewicz's study was published, the author could not know yet how easy this relative pluralism of oligarchic media could be transformed into uniform news coverage orchestrated from the president's administration, though she noted that there existed a risk of curtailing this pluralism in case of "collusion of media 'oligarchs' or between them and the government" (Ibid., 105). The media developments under Putin's presidency have produced extensive evidence for the latter.

However fair the above argument about the (relative) pluralism which can be ensured by oligarchic media is, one should be aware that this pluralism is rather constrained. To put it differently, this pluralism is limited to the political/economic interests of the biggest oligarchic groups. In Ukraine the media owned by oligarchs serve at best as a mouthpiece for big business and political groups; not incidentally, Ukraine's media expert Natalia Ligachova uses the term 'oligarchic pluralism' about them (Ligachova 2015). Ligachova points out that this restricted pluralism deprives Ukrainian citizens of a chance to receive complete, verified, and comprehensive information on current events from the TV, which is, as mentioned before, the main source of news for the lion's share of Ukrainians. Commenting on the oligarchic media, which has changed little, according to her, after the revolutionary events in 2013–2014, Ligachova points out that they narrow the field of information to the matters related to the private interests of the oligarchs. At the same time they under-report, miss, or distort the stories and information society needs:

> *Inter* and *Ukraina* will tell us what villains Kolomoisky and Yatseniuk are, *1+1*—what monsters Firtash, Liovochkin, Pinchuk, Kuchma are. But in [Ukrainian] TV-space there is still lack of equally powerful resources which could help audiences gain a proper perspective on what's going on [in the country]. (Ligachova 2015)

3.2.4. Market-driven tabloidization or 'political yellowing'?

When comparing media systems in more and less reformed countries of former Soviet bloc, scholars of post-communist media often assume that their development in the post-communist period is determined by divergent kinds of factors. In particular, it is supposed that the main agent which shapes media systems in less reformed countries like Ukraine or Bulgaria is politics (Jakubowicz 2001, 2005). By contrast, in such democratic frontrunners as Poland and Estonia, it is basically the market which determines their media transformations (Jakubowicz 2001; Dyczok 2009). The media market, according to scholars of CEE media, has not only evidently positive, but also negative consequences for media freedom in more advanced new European democracies. They include, in particular, the concentration of media ownership which may endanger the pluralism of opinions in public discourse as well as excessive commercialization and tabloidization of media content.

As far as the thesis about the primary role of politics in the transformation of the media in less reformed countries (like Ukraine) is concerned, it is hardly contentious. At the same time, I believe that the impact of the market on media change in these countries should not be underestimated. As we could see above, in Ukraine the privatization of the media in 1990s enabled people to obtain access to relatively diverse information and opinion about current events. On the other hand, similar to the media in the rest of the world, the commercial media in Ukraine also became subject to such global trends as the concentration of media ownership (which we addressed earlier in this chapter) and the tabloidization of the media.[88] Importantly, media tabloidization in Ukraine, like the concentration of media ownership, has its own character.

The tendency toward the commercialization and tabloidization of media content, which was observed in Ukraine after the rise of private media in the early 1990s, and manifested itself predominantly in filling the airwaves with foreign films and series, became the subject of particular concern on the part of Ukrainian media critics after the Orange Revolution. The media experts were unhappy about the noticeable changes in news programs, namely their excessive concentration on crime, accidents, and catastrophes (Ligachova 2008b, 2007b; Dovzhenko 2006; Dankova 2008). Simultaneously, political and economic news started to receive less attention than before, with a noticeable tendency to their over-dramatization (often at the expense of fairness and accuracy of reporting), and 'showization' (Ligachova 2008b, 2007b; Dovzhenko 2006; Dankova 2008). Moreover, the media critics were concerned over how the share of entertainment programs was growing, whereas information-analytical, educational, and cultural programs were disappearing from private TV channels. In the last years of Yushchenko's incumbency the amount of political talk-shows also shrank, which only started to appear on Ukrainian TV after the Orange Revolution and were popular among audiences (see e.g., Dovzhenko 2009b).

---

88 For an analysis of Ukraine's media market in the perspective of global trends see: Dyczok 2014b.

These negative tendencies persisted also after Yanukovych succeeded Yushchenko as president in early 2010. Immediately after Yanukovych came to power, the owners of several TV channels decided to get rid of political talk-shows and other political programs they aired. For example, Akhmetov's TV channel *Ukraina* ceased airing the talk-show by popular TV host Savik Shuster, whereas Poroshenko's *5 Channel* suspended the political talk show "Ya tak dumayu" (I think so) with Anna Bezulyk.[89] Additionally, the duration of newscasts dropped, and news reports themselves became ever more depoliticized. For example, the share of home news in news programs of major nationwide TV channels lessened from 38 percent in October 2005 to 16 percent in June 2012 (AUP Oct. 2005; June 2012). At the same time, the major TV channels focused on the development of their own entertainment production. Already by late 2010, each of them had in its weekly schedule up to ten different talent, reality, culinary and other non-political shows (Dovzhenko 2011b).

Commercialization and tabloidization of media content in Ukraine, as in the rest of the world, is connected with market competition and the desire of media organizations to attract the widest possible audience. In particular, intense tabloidization in Ukrainian TV after the Orange Revolution can be explained by the fact that though the majority of big nationwide TV channels became privatized during Leonid Kuchma's presidency, they had little chance to start functioning as business projects during Kuchma's time in the office, because they were essentially instruments of state propaganda orchestrated by the president's administration. Only after the success of the Orange Revolution, when centralized control over the media (including as state-owned and private outlets) significantly decreased, did media owners get an opportunity to treat their media outlets as businesses (Ligachova 2007b; Dovzhenko 2008). No surprise, therefore, that it was at this moment when private TV

---

89 Characteristically, soon after Shuster's program disappeared from *Ukraina*, the host started a new talk-show, this time at the state owned *UT-1*.

channels started an intense fight for ratings, simultaneously seeking ways to attract the widest possible audiences (Ligachova 2007b).

That being said, it cannot be denied that many decisions of the top-managers regarding the choice and content of the programs broadcast on Ukrainian TV channels since 2005, and especially after 2010, have not been consistent with market logics (though the managers themselves often tried to explain these decisions by economic reasons above all). For example, the refusal to run political talk-shows traditionally popular among Ukrainian TV-audiences in the end of Yushchenko's presidency and under the rule of Yanukovych can hardly be explained by the market demands. A telling example is Savik Shuster's show: when in 2010 it was cancelled by *Ukraina*, the program had consistently high ratings (Dovzhenko 2011c).

Similarly, it would be difficult to explain in terms of commercial matters (only) the abrupt depoliticization of newscasts at almost all major Ukrainian TV channels after the victory of Yanukovych in the presidential elections of 2010, and substitution of hard news with criminal chronicles and other soft news. Here the most realistic explanation seems to be that of Natalia Ligachova, who stated that this depoliticization was primarily the result of the authorities' (informal) political pressure on the media, which made media owners and top-managers reluctant to provide accurate, fair, and complete coverage of current affairs, especially concerning politics. According to Ligachova, only because it became too risky for broadcasters to catch the attention of viewers by the news per se, that is, information necessary to understand what actually was going on in the country, did TV channels try to hold them by means of such catchy issues as crime and other 'yellow' stories (Ligachova 2012). This version seems especially plausible in view of the fact that Ukrainians did seek political news in the media in the period discussed. In particular, according to the results of the opinion poll by the Gorshenin Institute in October 2010, as much as 72 percent of

Ukrainians were interested in political news and information programs, and only 14.3 percent did not have such an interest (Gorshenin Institute 2010).

The problem of the tabloidization and expansion of the lowest-common-denominator content in commercial media is well known in the developed democracies, as well. These countries have already elaborated certain instruments which moderate the effects of excessive rampant commercialization of the private media and profit maximization to the detriment of public-interest content. These instruments include limits on media concentration, a tradition of public service broadcasting, as well as regulatory agencies answering to a pluralistic political system and engaged in the protection of the public interest instead of serving the short-term political/economic interests of ruling elites. Different from these countries, in Ukraine these instruments are very weak, if at all existent. In the period analyzed in this book Ukraine had no public broadcasting, the regulations limiting media concentration were insufficient and poorly enforced, and effective regulatory agencies were also lacking. The National Broadcasting Council, which was expected, according to its formal tasks, to promote socially responsible broadcasting, failed to tame the reckless commercialization of content at Ukrainian TV and to prevent them from getting rid of analytical, cultural, and educational programs in their TV schedules.

What is more, the Council often directly contributed to extreme commercialization and tabloidization of broadcasting. For example, in 2009 it allowed the owners of *1+1* channel to substantially change its program strategy and thus *de facto* approved the channel's switching from an information-analytical profile to what Angelika Wyka (2009) calls 'dumbing down,' or 'super-commercialization/tabloidization' (Wyka 2009). Specifically, in the process of renewing of the channel's license, the Broadcasting Council allowed *1+1* to introduce basic changes into the program strategy, based on which the license was issued. This allowed the channel to halve the share of information-analytical programs, to remove from the schedule cultural programs, and to get rid of the obligation to cover the activity of the Parliament (which was written in the previous version of the program strategy) (Telekrytyka 2009). Moreover, to 12-hour daily increased the share of airtime devoted to airing of 'foreign audiovisual products.' By the latter the channel's top-managers in essence understood cheap Russian and American series. Significantly, the channel was not a low-popular or niche broadcaster, but one of the leaders in the TV-ratings and one of the three Ukrainian channels with the biggest reach (more than 90 percent of the territory of Ukraine). Therefore the Council's decision had consequences for a significant share of the country's TV audience.

The decision was sharply criticized by Ukraine's media monitoring organizations. The media watchdog Telekrytyka accused the regulator of letting a nationwide TV channel be turned into a "box with cheap films and soap operas" (Dovzhenko 2009a). Media experts stressed that this case was not the only example when the country's main broadcasting regulator appeared to be unwilling or unable to protect the Ukrainian public from rampant commercialization and tabloidization of the media. For example, in 2008 Telekrytyka analyzed the licenses of major Ukrainian TV channels and came to the conclusion that the channels usually granted noticeably less airtime to information-analytical, publicist, scientific, and educational programs than was presupposed by their license requirements, and the NTRBC regularly turned a blind eye to these violations (Ligachova 2008b). The Telekrytyka experts also concluded that when confronted with the desire of media owners to fill air time with cheap entertainment at the expense of socially important quality content, the Broadcasting Council took rather the side of the media owners, not that of the public. The reason, according to Telekrytyka, was that the NTRBC *de facto* served the interests of the Ukrainian government, interested primarily in the political loyalty of commercial broadcasters. This loyalty was 'exchanged,' with media owners being given a free hand in maximizing their audiences by means of broadcasting a lower common-denominator content (Ligachova 2008b).

Tabloidization of the media, which is not only market- but also politically-driven, is characteristic not only for Ukraine. For example, Russian researchers point out that for media owners in Russia, switching to entertaining formats was one of just a few ways to preserve their media outlets under Putin's centralized control over the media. Ilya Kiriya and Elena Degtereva (2010) described this particular type of tabloidization, characterized by departure from political topics and switching instead to an entertainment content, as follows:

> Commercial way of financing (by income and advertising) on the one hand, and serious limitations of socio-political and informational broadcasting on the other hand, were the reasons for predomination of entertaining formats on Russian TV. [...] Neutral entertainment programs are both profitable and politically safe for the broadcasting media, especially for commercial TV channels. (Kiriya and Degtereva 2010, 44)

In a very similar way, in Ukraine the tabloidization of the media in the years of the country's independence, especially in 2010–2013, was conditioned not only by market demands, but just as much by the political considerations of media owners.

Conclusion: New obstacles to media reform in post-communist Ukraine

The three months of the EuroMaidan protests in Ukraine in 2013–2014 made evident certain key characteristics of the Ukrainian state formed over the country's more than two-decades of post-communist transformations. These characteristics became imprinted into the structure of the state's core political and economic institutions. What Ukrainians and the international community could therefore witness during those dramatic events included: the shortage of institutional check on the executive, who felt free to take arbitrary and even anti-constitutional decisions regarding public gatherings and rallies; inadequate law enforcement, which used excessive force against the protesters but was unable to catch the perpetrators of kidnappings, torture, and brutal beatings of protesters; and politicized courts issuing unjust verdicts against activists on orders from above.

These and similar deficiencies and distortions to a great extent spawned the EuroMaidan revolution in late 2013–early 2014.[90] Together with Putin's subsequent incursion into Crimea and the armed clashes in Donbass, it constituted a critical juncture which opened a new window of opportunity for Ukraine to redesign its basic institutions and finalize the much-needed democratic reforms (Kudelia 2014). However, realization of the reforms, including those in the media realm, requires a clear understanding of the problems to be solved. Importantly, these problems are significantly different from those which Ukraine and other post-communist countries faced directly after the collapse of the Soviet bloc in 1989–1991. This book attempts to contribute to understanding some of these new problems, particularly those which prevent the media in

---

90 According to the study of Olga Onuch, the main demands which brought Ukrainians to the Maidan in November 2013–February 2014 were "not just EU accession, but safeguards for basic rights and an end to systemic elite corruption" (Onuch 2014, 51).

Ukraine from becoming more pluralistic, independent, and responsive to the interests of the society.

This study has showed that the choice to depart from the transition paradigm within which the analysis of media change in post-communist Eurasia is usually carried out may be useful for understanding the essence and character of this change. The concepts of *state capture* and *informal institutions* applied in comparative politics for the study of the societies in the 'gray zone' between authoritarianism and democracy, as well as the concept of *media capture* recently introduced in post-communist media studies for the same purpose, help comprehend the specific constellation of politics, economics, and the media that formed in Ukraine during the more than two decades of its transformation since independence in 1991. They also contribute to the analysis of new and hybrid patterns of the media-politics relationships which proliferate in Ukraine and generally throughout the post-Soviet area, but are difficult to grasp by means of traditional approaches in post-communist media studies, as long as the latter see these patterns only as deviations from the democratic norm and not as manifestations of a norm of its own, one worthy of separate explanatory models and categories.

As the studies into Ukraine's transformations cited in this book highlight, for the greater part of the transformational period Ukrainian society existed in the conditions of a captured state where the key state institutions were 'privatized' by self-interested political/economic elites who in fact were the main drivers of institutional change in the country. The outcomes of this change included: (1) weak and insufficiently independent agencies of horizontal accountability, especially the judiciary and various supervisory state agencies; and (2) fuzzy and defective legislation, especially in the realms principally important for distribution of power and resources (such as the laws regulating elections, party financing, and the media). Both of these phenomena were significant barriers for advancing democratic consolidation in Ukraine because they created a fertile soil for the persisting prevalence of informal institutions (such as rent-seeking, selective use of law, and the exchange of government privileges for political loyalty) in the regulation of Ukraine's politics and economy, as well as the media. They contributed to the maintenance of a neo-patrimonial state, under which lax regulations allowed the informal extraction of state resources by the state's captors (that is, higher echelons of the bureaucracy and ruling oligarchic clans) and their poorly restricted control over politics, the economy, and the media. These agents received considerable profits from partial economic and political reforms, therefore they deliberately affected the shaping of institutions in such a way so as to hamper completion of these reforms.

One additional barrier to the progress of the reform process which arose in Ukraine since its independence in 1991, was that of the deformed market where the country's key economic sectors were monopolized by oligarchic clans and competition was significantly constrained by their interests. This was a market where a leading position was achieved not due to purchasing power in an open market, but due to corruption and access to resources owing to political influence.

Both of these institutional deficiencies, marked by weak institutions and foggy rules, along with the market's deformations, also hampered the reform of the media. On the one hand, media organizations became a victim of selective enforcement of formal rules as well as ubiquitous regulation of media-politics relationships by non-transparent, informal rules and agreements serving media captors and, on the other hand, the highly concentrated and distorted market.

Recent publications and analyses from academic scholars and international organizations (Freedom House, the International Monetary Fund, and others) show that though several important improvements have been introduced in Ukraine's legislation, governance, and economy since the country's revolutionary events in 2013–2014, much of the above regarding the barriers to democratic reforms is still relevant at the moment this book goes to print in 2016. This especially concerns the deficit of judiciary independence, lack of basic change in electoral law and regulations concerning political parties, as well as the remaining significant impact of the oligarchs on the economy and economic freedom.

Beyond the abovementioned general obstacles to media democratization, during the years of Ukraine's transformation there also appeared certain media-specific barriers to media reform. As demonstrated in this study, these barriers were formed by the joint influence of politics, on the one hand, and the market on the other. Moreover, it must be noted that these barriers remained largely intact at the time of writing this book.

The first two barriers are related to the structure of media ownership that formed in Ukraine following 1991. Starting from the late 1990s in Ukraine an oligarchic media ownership took form, with the major nationwide media divided between a handful of media groups owned by powerful Ukrainian oligarchs, or well-connected big businessmen. The first obstacle to the development of media reform in Ukraine created by this circumstance is the **dominance of politicized ownership** in the media market. As described in this book, for Ukrainian oligarchs the media are neither their main business, nor the source of significant revenues: rather, they are a means for influencing politics and promoting their own political/economic interests. That such a big part of the media is in the hands of businessmen from outside the media industry is a result of not only political considerations: it is also caused by the poor condition of Ukrainian media market. Its low advertising budget gives little opportunity to run a sustainable media business. In turn, the dominance of politicized ownership in the media significantly contributes to maintenance of this state of affairs. Since media enterprises are set up or maintained because of political, not market reasons, the market is overpopulated. This further impairs both profitability and the autonomy of the media. In this way the dominance of politicized media ownership impedes the rise of economically (and hence, also politically) independent media.

The dominance of politicized media ownership in the Ukrainian media market is detrimental to the ability of the media to exercise its democratic services, especially information and watchdog functions. Because the main Ukrainian media owners obtain most of their income from other than media industries, their profits and the security of their business empires in the context of a politicized judiciary and weak rule of law largely depend on political decisions. Because the state has the means to adversely impact both the key businesses and the media of big business people, Ukrainian media owners would rather cooperate with the state than challenge it. As a result, media owners and top managers try to restrict media criticism of top officials through in-house censorship, the replacement of journalists and/or editors with each new political constellation, and even the elimination of television programs or press outlets not deemed sufficiently loyal to the authorities.

Since Ukrainian politics is rather unstable, however, owners may also use their private media in the political struggle—especially in moments of political crisis when the state is divided against itself and rival power groups compete with one another for political and financial resources. In these situations, media owners may back one political group or another. However, major nationwide television channels in particular often exhibit partisan polyvalence: a shift of loyalties depending on economic support as well as general power shifts within the political establishment.

This intra-elite struggle in which oligarchic media play an important role enable, on the one hand, the relative pluralism of Ukraine's mainstream media (a no-go subject for one TV channel or newspaper may be a scoop for another). On the other hand, this is a very limited pluralism, restricted to the interests of oligarchic clans fighting for the capture of the state and its resources. What it is lacking is genuine and consistent representation of the interests of broader Ukrainian society in the media. The role imposed on society by the oligarchic media is reduced to that of spectators rather than participants of political life.

The second barrier to media reform in Ukraine that relates to the structure of media ownership is **ownership concentration**. Concentration of media ownership is a global trend, however in Ukrainian conditions it has a unique character. Namely, concentration here (as in some other post-Soviet countries, in particular in Russia) is conditioned not only by economic, but also by political causes. Concentration of big media assets in the hands of powerful Ukrainian oligarchs offers a way for them to accumulate significant political influence. This can also be profitable for a corrupt state: when the media market is divided between a few owners dependent on politics, it is easier to get their compliance to serve a ruling political group than would be the case if media owners were more numerous and more independent.

How detrimental such politically-induced media concentration is for free speech is especially obvious in the moments when the state is strong enough to force conformity on media owners. The past decade of media history in Russia and the curbing of media freedom in Yanukovych's Ukraine, as described in this book, give convincing proof that this kind of media ownership enhances the risk of introducing centralized control over the media. One more disadvantage it carries within itself is the threat to pluralism: as mentioned above, the concentration of media ownership in the hands of politicized media owners essentially narrows the spectrum of interests represented in public debate. Last but not the least, the concentration of media ownership in the hands of owners with other-than-media interests hinders fair market competition and creates unfavorable conditions for the producers of genuinely independent news outlets.

A further barrier to media freedom that emerged in Ukraine since independence in 1991, one conditioned by both political and market factors, has been that of **media commercialization**. This became especially pronounced in 2007–2009, when major Ukrainian media owners, driven by a desire to broaden their audience, carried out basic reorganizations of their media companies. From this time on the decisions over programming and the quality of news in major nationwide media started to heavily depend on audience measurements. This worsened such tendencies as trivialization and personification of political news, as well as tabloidization and depoliticization of TV programs.

The problem is that, similar to media concentration, the processes of depoliticization and tabloidization of media content in Ukraine were not only market-, but also politically-driven. For example, the idea to reduce the time of TV newscasts to avoid problems with the authorities was first employed in 2003 during Leonid Kuchma's Presidency. Oleksander Tkachenko, then chief editor of the *Novy* TV channel, shortened his news programs so significantly that they often had no space for the topics recommended in Kuchma's *temnyky*.[91] The abrupt depoliticization of news programs after president Viktor Yushchenko was succeeded in 2010 by Viktor Yanukovych, described in Chapter 3, is another example which supports the assumption that the above processes might have hidden political motives in Ukraine. In this regard Ukrainian media experts even coined the term 'political yellowing' (Dovzhenko 2012). Natalia Ligachova called the tabloidization in Ukraine a "mode of censorship", under which "natural criticism of the media was substituted by their tabloidization" (Ligachova 2008b).

Concentration of media ownership and the tabloidization of the media are global phenomena, but differently than in Ukraine, in developed democracies they are not amplified by other than market considerations. Besides, in contrast to advanced democracies, the effects of market logic on the media in Ukraine are not moderated by media-protecting state policies. The instruments that limit the harmful effects of media concentration and commercialization in the West (such as the institute of public service broadcasting or formal limits on media concentration) were never developed (or enforced) during the nearly quarter-century of Ukraine's independence. They became the subject of concern for policy makers only after Ukraine's Eurorevolution in late 2013–early 2014.

---

91 Private communication from Otar Dovzhenko (Skype, September 8, 2012).

One more set of obstacles to press freedom formed by the conjunction of political and economic factors in Ukraine lies in the realm of **institutionalized rules and practices (both formal and informal)** that regulate both the relationships between media owners and editorial offices, as well as between media organizations on the one hand and the state and political actors on the other. We may observe here the rise of new forms, ones different from those of the communist-period and ones which shaped, to a greater or lesser extent, the performance of Ukrainian media in the period under study. One example of these new forms is an informal practice of hidden advertising (colloquially called *dzhynsa*) described in this book. The rise of *dzhynsa* was conditioned by politics (that is, the belief of politicians that publicity may ensure them electoral success) and also by the market—namely, the shortage of advertising money. According to the assessments of media-supporting NGOs, *dzhynsa* brings media considerable money, at levels which are sometimes bigger than those of regular advertising revenues (Dovzhenko 2010a; Yerevan Press Club 2011). What is troubling about *dzhynsa* is that it has become if not a normal, then at least a common way of making political news. Correspondingly, it often sets the templates for relationships between journalists and politicians involved in communicating political issues to the public. For example, in 2007–2013 Ukrainian politicians (both pro-governmental and oppositional) often complained that they had little chance to appear in the news unless they bribed media. Similarly, media monitoring organizations frequently raised the alarm that, especially during electoral campaigns, even newsworthy events involving candidates were covered for money. This indicates that the informal practice of concealed advertising has become a functioning pathology that structures the relationships between media and politics. The reports of the Ukrainian monitors having appeared at the time of writing this book prove that *dzhynsa* remains a significant problem for Ukrainian media after 2013 as well (Mnich 2014; Mediasapiens 2015b).

However significant the above barriers to completing media reform in Ukraine are, the changes that have taken place in Ukraine since the Euromaidan show that success is still possible. Although analysis of these changes lies beyond the scope of this book, even bare acquaintance with them allows us to see that significant progress has been achieved. In less than two years Ukraine has managed to pass laws so vitally important for media independence as the law on public broadcasting, on the transparency of media ownership, and the privatization of state and municipal printed media. At the same time, the struggle around these changes, as well as the problems with their implementation, shows how significant is the resistance to them on the part of groups uninterested in the reforms.

The adoption of the Law of Ukraine on Public Television and Radio Broadcasting, which had been unsuccessfully debated in the Ukrainian Parliament for almost two decades, was a real breakthrough in Ukraine's media democratization. For it gave Ukrainians a chance to create an alternative to the heavily commercialized and interests-led oligarchic media. The law was passed in May 2014, and in April 2015 the Parliament adopted the amendments which introduced a procedure for reorganizing state-owned broadcasters into public ones. The latter cleared the way for the creation of the public broadcaster in practice. At the moment of completing this book, the Ukrainian PSB is still in the making: on January 6, 2016 the second phase of reform of the formerly state television began, on the basis of which the public broadcaster is being created. The management of public television expresses concern over the impediments to reform raised by several state institutions. For example, the sum allocated in the 2016 state budget for funding the public broadcaster is significantly less than what was presupposed by the Law.

Another important improvement in Ukraine's media legislation was adoption of the law guaranteeing transparency of media ownership in September 2015. The work on the bill was a good example of cooperation between MPs, media-monitoring NGOs, and media experts. However, according to the latter, the final version of the law was not flawless. For example, Ihor Rozkladai, a lawyer from the Media Law Institute who was a member of the working group drafting the bill, pointed out that when the bill was considered in the second reading the Parliament managed to build into it certain loopholes that made it less effective than it could have been.[92] Fortunately, bigger risks were avoided. For example, the majority of MPs rejected an amendment which would have allowed offshore companies to set up TV stations. Experts from the Telekrytyka media watchdog, who presented their analysis of the law in a separate report (Zakusylo et al. 2015), pointed to certain obstacles in implementing the law. One of them is that the country's media regulator, the National Television and Radio Broadcasting Council, does not have enough human and financial resources to check multiple documents on the structure of media ownership submitted by media organizations.

Besides these and other developments in the regulatory environment for Ukrainian media, some positive changes also occurred in the Ukrainian media landscape. A number of new independent media projects, many of them web-based (and therefore relatively cheap), have been launched and successfully developed in post-Maidan Ukraine, both on the national and regional levels. They were created outside of the old system of corruption and therefore provide an alternative to the oligarch-driven media—if not for the whole of Ukrainian society, then at least for its creative minority. The study of these changes will no doubt contribute to our understanding of the prospects for media democratization in Ukraine and other countries with protracted or delayed media reform.

---

92 Private communication from Ihor Rozkladai (Skype, October 30, 2015).

Bibliography

Åslund, Anders. 2015. *Ukraine: What Went Wrong and How to Fix It.* Washington, DC: Peterson Institute for International Economics.

Åslund, Anders. 2014. "Ukraine's Enemy Within." *The Wall Street Journal*, October 1. Accessed October 3, 2014. http://www.wsj.com/articles/ukraines-old-internal-enemy-1412191062.

Åslund, Anders. 2005. "Comparative Oligarchy: Russia, Ukraine, and the United States." *CASE Network Studies and Analyses*, no. 296. Accessed December 21, 2015. http://papers.ssrn.com/sol3/papers.cfm?abstract_id=1441910.

Åslund, Anders, Peter Boone, and Simon Johnson. 2001. "Escaping the Under-Reform Trap." *IMF Staff Papers*, 48:88–108.

AUP (Academy of Ukrainian Press). 2011. "Monitorynh politychnykh novyn: osnovni rezul'taty, Hruden' 2010–Cherven' 2011." (Monitoring of Political News: Main Results, December 2010–June 2011) Accessed August 14, 2013. www.mediaosvita.com.ua/sites/mediaosvita.com.ua/files/andriyche/dec-feb-apr-june.pdf.

AUP (Academy of Ukrainian Press). October 2005; March 2006; October 2006; May 2007; June 2012. "Monitorynh politychnykh novyn: osnovni rezul'taty." (Monitoring of Political News: Main Results) Accessed August 14, 2013. www.aup.com.ua/?cat=monitoring and subcat=newst and menu=newst.

Austin, Anne, Jonathan Barnard, Eleonora Galli, and Nicola Hutcheon. 2012. *Adversiting Expenditure Forecasts, June 2012*. London: ZenithOptimedia.

Bajomi-Lazar, Peter. 2015. "Political Actors and the Colonisation of the Media." In *Media and Politics in New Democracies: Europe in a Comparative Perspective*, edited by Jan Zielonka, 73–84. Oxford: Oxford University Press.

Becker, Jonathan. 2014. "Russia and the New Authoritarians." *Demokratizatsiya* 22(2):191–206.

Becker, Jonathan. 2004. "Lessons from Russia: A Neo-Authoritarian Media System." *European Journal of Communication*, 19(2):139–163.

Belyakov, Alexander. 2009. "Censorship by Money' on Freedom of Speech in Ukraine." *Critique*, 37(4):601–617.

Bennich-Björkman, Li. 2009. "The Communist Past: Party Formation and Elites in the Baltic States." *Baltic Worlds* 2(3–4):29–36.

Berglund, Sten, and Joakim Ekman. 2013. "The Diversity of Political Regimes." In *Handbook of Political Change in Eastern Europe*, edited by Sten Berglund, Joakim Ekman, Kevin Deegan-Krause, and Terje Knutsen, 1–13. Cheltenham: Edward Elgar Publishing.

Besley, Timothy, and Andrea Prat. 2002. "Handcuffs for the Grabbing Hand? Media Capture and Government Accountability." *LSE STICERD Research Paper no. PEPP07.* Accessed August 14, 2013. http://papers.ssrn.com/sol3/papers.cfm?abstract_id=298049.

Beumers, Birgit, Stephen Hutchings, and Natalia Rulyova, eds. 2009. *The Post-Soviet Russian Media. Conflicting Signals.* New York: Routledge.

Böröcz, József. 2000. "Informality Rules." *East European Politics and Societies,* 14(2):348–80.

Bratton, Michael. 2011. "Neo-Patrimonialism." In *International Encyclopedia of Political Science Vol. 1,* edited by Badie Bertrand, Dirk Berg-Schlosser, and Leonardo Morlino, 1679–1681. Thousand Oaks: SAGE Publications, Inc.

Bratton, Michael, and Nicholas van de Walle. 1994. "Neopatrimonial Regimes and Political Transitions in Africa." *World Politics,* 46 (4):453–489.

BTI (Bertelsmann Stiftung's Transformation Index). 2014. "BTI 2014-Ukraine Country Report." Gütersloh: Bertelsmann Stiftung. Accessed September 3, 2015. https://www.bti-project.org/fileadmin/files/BTI/Downloads/Reports/2014/pdf/BTI_2014_Ukraine.pdf.

BTI (Bertelsmann Stiftung's Transformation Index). 2012. "BTI 2012-Ukraine Country Report." Gütersloh: Bertelsmann Stiftung. Accessed August 14, 2013. www.bti-project.de/fileadmin/Inhalte/reports/2012/pdf/BTI%202012%20Ukraine.pdf.

Bulavka, Yevhen, and Yuri Shevchenko. 2008. "Rol media u kyivskykh vyborakh: 'Nichoho ne bachu. Nichoho be chuju. Nichoho nikomu ne skazhu'" (The Role of Media in Kyiv Elections: "I Hear Nothing; I See Nothing; I Say Nothing"), *Telekrytyka,* May 30, 2008. Accessed September 21, 2011. www.telekritika.ua/media-suspilstvo/expert/2008-05-30/38709/.

Capello, Maja, ed. 2015. *Regulation of Online Content in the Russian Federation.* IRIS extra, Strasbourg: European Audiovisual Observatory.

Carothers, Thomas. 2002. "The End of the Transition Paradigm." *Journal of Democracy* 13(1):5–21.

Collins, Kathleen. 2006. *Clan Politics and Regime Transition in Central Asia.* New York: Cambridge University Press.

Coman, Ioana, and Peter Gross. "Uncommonly Common or Truly Exceptional? An Alternative to the Political System-Based Explanation of the Romanian Mass Media." *The International Journal of Press/Politics* 17(4):457–479.

Corneo, Giacomo. 2006. "Media Capture in a Democracy: The Role of Wealth Concentration." *Journal of Public Economics* 90(1):37–58.

Curran, James, and Myung-Jin Park, eds. 2000a. *De-Westernizing Media Studies.* London: Routledge.

Curran, James, and Myung-Jin Park. 2000b. "Introduction." In *De-Westernizing Media Studies,* edited by James Curran and Myung-Jin Park, 2–15. London: Routledge.

D'Anieri, Paul. 2007. *Understanding Ukrainian Politics: Power, Politics and Institutional Design.* Armonk, New York: M.E. Sharpe.

Dankova, Natalia. 2008. "TSN na-vi-shcho?" (TSN, Why?) *Telekrytyka*, November 6, 2008. Accessed August 16, 2016. http://www.telekritika.ua/telekanaly/2008-11-06/41783.

Darden, Keith A. 2008. "The Integrity of Corrupt States: Graft as an Informal State Institution." *Politics & Society*, 36(1):35–60.

Darden, Keith. 2002. "Graft and Governance: Corruption as an Informal Mechanism of State Control." *Leitner Program Working Papers*, 2. Accessed August 25, 2014. http://www.yale.net/leitner/resources/docs/2002-02.pdf.

Darden, Keith A. 2001. "Blackmail as a Tool of State Domination: Ukraine under Kuchma." *East European Constitutional Review* 10:67–71.

de Smaele, Hedwig. 2012. "Russian Media and Democracy." In *Media Transformations in the Post-Communist World: Eastern Europe's Tortured Path to Change*, edited by Peter Gross and Karol Jakubowicz, 133–148. Lanham: Lexington Books.

de Smaele, Hedwig. 2007. "Mass Media and the Information Climate in Russia." *Europe-Asia Studies*, 59(8):1299–1313.

de Smaele, Hedwig. 2005. "Is There a Life after Death for Four Theories of the Press?" Paper presented at the First European Communication Conference, Amsterdam, November 25–26.

de Smaele, Hedwig. 1999. "The Applicability of Western Media Models on the Russian Media System." *European Journal of Communication*, 14(2):173–189.

de Smaele, Hedwig, and Elena Vartanova. 2007. "Russia." In *Western Broadcast Models: Structure, Conduct & Performance*, edited by Leen d'Haenens and Frieda Saeys, 341–359. Berlin: Mouton de Gruyter.

Diamond, Larry. 2002. "Thinking about Hybrid Regimes." *Journal of Democracy* 13 (April):21–35.

Dobek-Ostrowska, Bogusława, and Michał Głowacki, eds. 2015. *Democracy and Media in Central and Eastern Europe 25 Years On.* Frankfurt am Main: Peter Lang.

Dobek-Ostrowska, Bogusława, and Michał Głowacki, eds. 2011. *Making Democracy in 20 Years: Media and Politics in Central and Eastern Europe.* Wrocław: University of Wrocław Press.

Dobek-Ostrowska, Bogusława, and Michał Głowacki, eds. 2008a. *Comparing Media Systems in Central Europe: Between Commercialization and Politicization.* Wrocław: University of Wrocław Press.

Dobek-Ostrowska, Bogusława, and Michał Głowacki. 2008b. "Introduction." In *Comparing Media Systems in Central Europe: Between Commercialization and Politicization,* edited by Bogusława Dobek-Ostrowska and Michał Głowacki, 9–24. Wrocław: University of Wrocław Press.

Dobek-Ostrowska, Bogusława, Michał Głowacki, Karol Jakubowicz, and Miklós Sükösd, eds. 2010. *Comparative Media Systems: European and Global Perspectives*. Budapest: CEU Press.

Dovzhenko, Otar. 2015. "Media Serfdom in Ukraine." *openDemocracy*. Accessed August 16, 2016. https://www.opendemocracy.net/od-russia/otar-dovzhenko/media-in-ukraine-set-free-to-be-slaves.

Dovzhenko, Otar. 2012. "Zhovta gariachka." (Yellow Fever) *Mediasapiens*. Accessed August 16, 2016. http://osvita.mediasapiens.ua/ethics/standards/zhovta_garyachka/.

Dovzhenko, Otar. 2011a. "À La Guerre Comme à La Guerre." *Telekrytyka*, January 11. Accessed August 14, 2013. www.telekritika.ua/spec_tk/ukrainski_zmi/20 11-01-11/59041.

Dovzhenko, Otar. 2011b. "Shcho zanadto, to zanadto." (What's Too Much Is Too Much) *Telekrytyka*, February 12. Accessed August 16, 2016. http://www.telekr itika.ua/otar_col/2011-02-12/60112.

Dovzhenko, Otar. 2011c. "Gostri zapytannia, tupi vidpovidi." (Sharp Questions, Stupid Answers) *Telekrytyka*, March 7. Accessed December 28, 2015. http://www.telekritika.ua/telekontinuum/2011-03-07/60865.

Dovzhenko Otar. 2010a. "Vid dzynsy do politychnoho dyktatu." (From *Dzhynsa* to Political Dictate) *Mediasapiens*, November 29, 2011. Accessed August 14, 2013. http://osvita.mediasapiens.ua/material/vid-dzhinsi-dopolitichnogo-diktatu.

Dovzhenko, Otar. 2010b. "Sluzhba bezpeky korporatyvnykh interesiv." (The Service of Security of Corporate Interests) *Glavcom*, April 13, Accessed August 16, 2016. http://glavcom.ua/articles/518.html.

Dovzhenko, Otar. 2009a. "Jakshcho ne mozhna, ale duzhe hochetsia." (If You Can Not, but Really Want) *Telekrytyka*, November 12. Accessed August 14, 2013. http://www.telekritika.ua/otar_col/2009-11-12/49206.

Dovzhenko, Otar. 2009b. "NeVchasno. Pidsumky." (Malapropos: Summing Up) *Telekrytyka*, January 1. Accessed August 16, 2016. http://www.telekritika.ua/telebachennya/2009-01-01/42977.

Dovzhenko, Otar. 2008. "Ukrainskiie media segodnia: iz garema v bordel'." (Ukrainian Media Today: From Harem to Brothel) *Dzerkalo Tyzhnia*, May 23. Accessed August 14, 2013. http://gazeta.zn.ua/POLITICS/ukrainskie_media_ segodnya__iz_garema_v_bordel.html.

Dovzhenko, Otar. 2006. "Krov na pershii shpalti." (Blood on the First Page) *Telekrytyka*, September 6. Accessed August 16, 2016. http://www.telekrit ika.ua/monitoring-archive/2006-09-06/7466.

Dovzhenko, Otar, and Andrii Derkach. 2011. "Hromadska mriia." (Public Dream) *Telekrytyka*, January 19. Accessed August 16, 2016. http://www.telekritika.ua/ukrainski_zmi/2011-01-19/59316.

Downey, John. 2012. "Transnational Capital, Media Differentiation, and Institutional Isomorphism in Central and Eastern European Media Systems." In *Central and Eastern European Media in Comparative Perspective: Politics, Economy and Culture*, edited by John Downey and Sabina Mihelj, 63–88. Burlington: Ashgate.

Downey, John, and Sabina Mihelj, eds. 2012. *Central and Eastern European Media in Comparative Perspective: Politics, Economy and Culture*. Burlington: Ashgate.

Downing, John. 1996. *Internationalising Media Theory: Transition, Power, Culture. Reflections of Media in Russia, Poland and Hungary 1980–1995*. London: Sage.

Dragomir, Marius. 2003. *Fighting Legacy: Media Reform in Post-Communist Europe*. Washington, DC: Atlantic Council of the United States.

Dunn, John. 2009. "Where Did It All Go Wrong? Russian Television in the Putin Era." In *The Post-Soviet Russian Media: Conflicting Signals*, edited by Birgit Beumers, Stephen Hutchings, and Natalia Rulyova, 42–55. New York: Routledge.

Dutsyk, Diana. 2010. "Media Ownership Structure in Ukraine: Political Aspects." In *Public Service Broadcasting: A German–Ukrainian Exchange of Opinions. Results of the Conference on October 20, 2010 in Cologne, Germany*, edited by Olexii Khabyuk and Manfred Kops, 29–40. Accessed August 14, 2013. http://rundfunkoek.uni-koeln.de/institut/tagungen/2010-Cologne/Dutsyk_e.pdf.

Dyczok, Marta. 2015. "Threats to Free Speech in Ukraine: The Bigger Picture." In *Ukraine Twenty Years after Independence*, edited by Giovanna Brogi, Marta Dyczok Oxana Pachlovska, and Giovanna Siedina, 141–155. Rome: Aracne.

Dyczok, Marta. 2014a. "Mass Media Framing, Representations and Impact on Public Opinion." In *Ukraine's Euromaidan: Analyses of a Civil Revolution*, edited by David R. Marples and Frederick V. Mills, 77–94. Stuttgart: ibidem Press.

Dyczok, Marta, 2014b. "Ukraine's Media in the Context of Global Cultural Convergence." *Demokratizatsiya*, 22(2) (Spring):231–254.

Dyczok, Marta. 2009. "Do the Media Matter? Focus on Ukraine." In *Media, Democracy and Freedom: The Post-Communist Experience*, edited by Marta Dyczok and Oxana Gaman-Golutvina, 17–42. Frankfurt: Peter Lang.

Dyczok, Marta. 2006. "Was Kuchma's Censorship Effective? Mass Media in Ukraine Before 2004." *Europe-Asia Studies* 58(2):215–238.

Dyczok, Marta, and Oxana Gaman-Golutvina, eds. 2009. *Media, Democracy and Freedom: The Post-Communist Experience*. Frankfurt: Peter Lang.

Dzerkalo, Tyzhnia. 2013. "Khoroshkovskyi prodal Firtashu *Inter* za 2.5 milliona dollarov" (Khoroshkovskyi Sold *Inter* to Firtash for 2.5 mln Dollars) *Dzerkalo Tyzhnia*, February 1. Accessed August 16, 2016. http://zn.ua/ECONOMICS/horoshkovskiy-prodal-firtashu-inter.html.

EBRD. 2000. *Transition Report*. London: EBRD.

The Economist. 2014. "Planet Plutocrat." *The Economist*, March 15. Accessed September 6, 2014. http://www.economist.com/news/international/21599041-countries-where-politically-connected-businessmen-are-most-likely-prosper-planet.

EED (European Endowment for Democracy). 2015. *Bringing Plurality and Balance to the Russian Language Media Space*. Brussels: European Endowment for Democracy.

Ekiert, Grzegorz. 2012. "Eastern Europe's Postcommunist Transformations." *World Politics Review*, March 20.

Englund, Will. 2010. "Gas Deal Disputed in Ukraine." *Washington Post*, December 11. Accessed June 21, 2012. www.washingtonpost.com/wp-dyn/content/article/201 0/12/10/AR2010121007029.html

EU-Ukraine. 2012. "Viktoriya Siumar: Freedom of Speech in Ukraine 2010–2012: The Main Trends." *EU-Ukraine*, May 15. Accessed May 19, 2013. www.eu-ukraine.o rg/2012/05/viktoriya-siumar-freedom-ofspeech-in-ukraine-2010-2012-the-main-trends.

Finance.ua. 2011. "Poroshenko kupyv zhurnal 'Korrespondent.'" (Poroshenko Has Bought *Korrespondent* Magazine) April 13. Accessed September 21, 2011. http://news.finance.ua/ua/~/1/0/all/2011/04/13/234902/.

Fisun, Oleksandr. 2012. "Rethinking Post-Soviet Politics from a Neopatrimonial Perspective." *Demokratizatsiya*, 20(2):87–96.

Fisun, Aleksandr. 2011. "Ukraiinskaia neopatrimonialnaia demokratiia: formiro-vaniie, specifika i tendencii razvitiia." (Ukrainian Neopatrimonial Democracy: Formation, Specific Character and Tendencies of Development) *OIKUMENA*, 8:119–127.

Fisun, Aleksandr. 2007. "Postsovetskie neopatrimonial'nye rezhimy: genezis, osobennosti, tipologiya." (Post-Soviet Neopatrimonial Regimes: Genesis, Development, Typology) *Otechestvennye Zapiski* 6:8–28.

Fokus. 2008. "Iz ukrainskogo mediaprostranstva postepenno vytestiayetsia russkii yazyk." (Russian Language Is Being Steadily Forced Out of Ukrainian Media Space) *Fokus*, May 6. Accessed September 21, 2011. http://focus.ua/society/ 19287/.

Freedom House. 2015. "Freedom of the Press-2015." Accessed August 16, 2016. https://freedomhouse.org/report/freedom-press/2015/ukraine.

Freedom House. 2014. "Freedom of the Press-2014." Accessed August 16, 2016. https://freedomhouse.org/report/freedom-press/2014/ukraine.

Freedom House. 2013a. "Freedom of the Press-2013." Accessed August 16, 2016. https://freedomhouse.org/report/freedom-press/2013/ukraine.

Freedom House. 2013b. "One Step Forward, One Step Back: An Assessment of Freedom of Expression in Ukraine during its OSCE Chairmanship." *Freedom House*, December 2013. Accessed August 16, 2016. https://freedomhouse.org/sites/de fault/files/FREEDOM%20HOUSE%20One%20Step%20Forward%2C%20One

%20Step%20Back%20-%20Assessment%20of%20FOE%20in%20Ukraine%20ENG_0.pdf.

Freedom House. 2012. "Freedom of the Press-2012." Accessed August 16, 2016. https://freedomhouse.org/report/freedom-press/2012/ukraine.

Freedom House. 2011. "Freedom of the Press-2011." Accessed August 16, 2016. https://freedomhouse.org/report/freedom-press/2011/ukraine.

Freedom House. 2010. "Freedom of the Press-2010." Accessed August 16, 2016. https://freedomhouse.org/report/freedom-press/2010/ukraine.

Freedom House. 2009. "Freedom of the Press-2009." Accessed August 16, 2016. https://freedomhouse.org/report/freedom-press/2009/ukraine.

Freedom House. 2008. "Freedom of the Press-2008." Accessed August 16, 2016. https://freedomhouse.org/report/freedom-press/2008/ukraine.

Freedom House. 2007. "Freedom of the Press-2007." Accessed August 16, 2016. https://freedomhouse.org/report/freedom-press/2007/ukraine.

Freedom House. 2006. "Freedom of the Press-2006." Accessed August 16, 2016. https://freedomhouse.org/report/freedom-press/2006/ukraine.

Freedom House. 2005. "Freedom of the Press-2005." Accessed August 16, 2016. https://freedomhouse.org/report/freedom-press/2005/ukraine.

Fritz, Verena. 2007. *State-building: A Comparative Study of Ukraine, Lithuania, Belarus, and Russia.* Budapest: Central European University Press.

Futey, Bohdan. 2011. "The Suppression of an Independent Judiciary in Ukraine." *Kyiv Post*, December 27. Accessed August 14, 2013. www.kyivpost.com/opinion/op-ed/the-suppression-of-an-independent-judiciary-in-ukr-119708.html.

Gallina, Nicole, and Nicolas Hayoz. 2011. "Beyond Democracy: The Relevance of Informal Power in Eastern Europe." In *1989 in Central and Eastern Europe: Implications and Meanings Twenty Years Later*, edited by Nicolas Hayoz and Leszek Jesień. Bern: Peter Lang.

Ganev, Venelin. 2007. *Preying on the State: The Transformation of Bulgaria after 1989.* Ithaca: Cornell University Press.

Gel'man, Vladimir. 2012. "Subversive Institutions, Informal Governance, and Contemporary Russian Politics." *Communist and Post-Communist Studies* 45 (3): 295–303.

Gel'man, Vladimir. 2004. "The Unrule of Law in the Making: The Politics of Informal Institution-Building in Russia." *Europe-Asia Studies* 56(7):1021–1040.

Gel'man, Vladimir. 2003. "Post-Soviet Transitions and Democratization: Towards Theory Building." *Democratization* 10(2):87–104.

GfK Ukraine. 2011. TV Data. Accessed August 14, 2013. http://www.gfk.ua/imperia/md/content/gfkukraine/tvdata/11_12_tv_channels.pdf.

Ghinea, Cristian, and Ioana Avădani. 2011. "Does Media Policy Promote Media Freedom and Independence? The Case of Romania." In *European Media*

Policies Revisited: Valuing and Reclaiming Free and Independent Media in Contemporary Democratic Systems. MEDIADEM.

Gorshenin Institute. 2010. "Doveriie k SMI v Ukraine." (Trust to Mass Media in Ukraine) http://institute.gorshenin.ua/researches/28_doverie_k_smi_v_ukraine.html.

Gross, Peter. 2008. "Dances with Wolves: A Meditation on the Media and Political System in the European Union's Romania." In *Finding the Right Place on the Map: Central and Eastern European Media Change in a Global Perspective*, edited by Karol Jakubowicz and Miklós Sükösd, 125–143. Bristol, UK, and Chicago, IL: Intellect Ltd.

Gross, Peter. 2002. *Entangled Evolutions: Media and Democratization in Eastern Europe*. Baltimore: Johns Hopkins University Press.

Gross, Peter, and Karol Jakubowicz, eds. 2012a. *Media Transformations in the Post-communist World: Eastern Europe's Tortured Path to Change*. Lanham: Lexington.

Gross, Peter, and Karol Jakubowicz. 2012b. "The Slings and Arrows of Outrageous Fortune: When, How and for What Purpose Is Media Transition and Transformation Undertaken (and Completed) in Central and Eastern Europe?" In *Media Transformations in the Post-Communist World: Eastern Europe's Tortured Path to Change*, edited by Peter Gross and Karol Jakubowicz, 1–14. Lanham: Lexington.

Grytsenko, Oksana. 2011. "TV Channels Good for PR, Not for Profits." *Kyiv Post*, September 12. Accessed August 14, 2013. www.kyivpost.com/content/business/tv-channels-good-for-pr-not-for-profits-112666.html.

Grzymala-Busse, Anna. 2010. "The Best Laid Plans: The Impact of Informal Rules on Formal Institutions in Transitional Regimes." *Studies in Comparative International Development* 45(3):311–33.

Grzymala-Busse, Anna. 2008. "Beyond Clientelism: Incumbent State Capture and State Formation." *Comparative Political Studies* 41:638–73.

Grzymala-Busse, Anna, and Pauline Jones Luong. 2002. "Reconceptualizing the State: Lessons from Post-Communism." *Politics & Society*, 30(4):529–554.

Guasti, Petra, and Bojan Dobovšek. 2011. "Informal Institutions and EU Accession: Corruption and Clientelism in Central and Eastern Europe." Paper presented at ECPR General Conference in Reykjavik, August 2011.

Guseva, Marina, Mounira Nakaa, Anne Sophie Novel, Kirsi Pekkala, Bachir Souberou, and Sami Stouli. 2008. "Press Freedom and Development: An Analysis of Correlations between Freedom of the Press and the Different Dimensions of Development, Poverty, Governance and Peace," UNESCO. Accessed December 27, 2015. http://unesdoc.unesco.org/images/0016/001618/161825e.pdf.

Hale, Henry. 2011. "Formal Constitutions in Informal Politics: Institutions and Democratization in Post-Soviet Eurasia." *World Politics* 63(4):581–617.

Hale, Henry. 2010. "Eurasian Polities as Hybrid Regimes: The Case of Putin's Russia." *Journal of Eurasian Studies* 1:33–41.

Hale, Henry. 2009. *Why Ukraine Produced Post-Soviet Eurasia's Only Democratic Breakthrough as of 2009. Countering Democratic Regression in a Newly Divided Europe and Eurasia*. Retrieved March 16, 2012. http://www.sais-jhu.edu/academics/regionalstudies/europe/conferences/countering-regression/pdf/Hale_Ukraine_101309.pdf.

Hale, Henry. 2006. "Democracy or Autocracy on the March? The Colored Revolutions as Normal Dynamics of Patronal Presidentialism." In *Communist and Post-Communist Studies*, 39(3), 305–329.

Hallin, Daniel C., and Paolo Mancini, eds. 2012a. *Comparing Media Systems Beyond the Western World*. Cambridge: Cambridge University Press.

Hallin, Daniel C., and Paolo Mancini. 2012b. "Comparing Media Systems Between Eastern and Western Europe." In *Media Transformations in the Post-communist World: Eastern Europe's Tortured Path to Change*, edited by Peter Gross and Karol Jakubowicz, 15–32. Lanham: Lexington.

Hallin, Daniel C., and Paolo Mancini. 2004. *Comparing Media Systems: Three Models of Media and Politics*. Cambridge: Cambridge University Press.

Hallin, Daniel C., and Stylianos Papathanassopoulos. 2002. "Political Clientelism and the Media: Southern Europe and Latin America in Comparative Perspective." *Media Culture & Society* 24(2):175–95.

Havrylyshyn, Oleh. 2015. "A Quarter Century of Economic Reforms in Ukraine: Too Late, Too Slow, Too Little." *mBank – CASE Seminar Proceedings* No. 135. Accessed May 14, 2016. http://www.case-research.eu/sites/default/files/publications/mbank-case_135_final_0.pdf.

Hellman, Joel. 1998. "Winners Take All: The Politics of Partial Reform in Postcommunist Nations." *World Politics* 50:203–234.

Hellman, Joel, and Daniel Kaufmann. 2001. "Confronting the Challenge of State Capture in Transition Economies." *Finance and Development* 38(3):31–35.

Helmke, Gretchen, and Steven Levitsky. 2006. *Informal Institutions and Democracy: Lessons from Latin America*. Baltimore: Johns Hopkins University Press.

Helmke, Gretchen, and Steven Levitsky. 2004. "Informal Institutions and Comparative Politics: A Research Agenda." *Perspectives on Politics* 2(4):725–740.

Holmes, Leslie. 2006. *Rotten States? Corruption, Post-communism, and Neoliberalism*. Durham: Duke University Press.

Hrvatin, Sandra, and Brankica Petković, eds. 2004. *Media Ownership and Its Impact on Media Independence and Pluralism*. Ljubljana: SEENMP and Peace Institute.

Humphreys, Peter J. 1995. *Mass Media and Media Policy in Western Europe*. Manchester: Manchester University Press.

Hyden, Goran. 2002. "Why Africa Finds It So Hard to Develop? Reflections on Political Representation and Accountability." Paper presented at the conference Cultural and Political Foundations of Socio-Economic Development in Africa and Asia, Monte Verità, Switzerland, October 6–11.

Ieremenko, Svitlana. 2014. "Regional'ni media dzhynsuiut 'po-novomu.'" (Regional Media are Practicing *Dzhynsa* in a "New Way") *Mediasapiens*, November 13. Accessed August 16, 2016. http://osvita.mediasapiens.ua/monitoring/regional _newspapers/regionalni_media_dzhinsuyut_ponovomu/.

Inglehart, Ronald. 2000. "Culture and Democracy." In *Culture Matters: How Values Shape Human Progress,* edited by Lawrence E. Harrison and Samuel P. Huntington, 80–97. New York: Basic Books.

Ivanov, Valerii. 2005. "A Short Overview of the Situation in Ukraine's Media Field." www.aup.com.ua/upload/1134038407Astrid.pdfwww.aup.com.ua/upload/113 4038407Astrid.pdf.

Ivanov, Valerii, Viktoria Siumar, and Natalia Kostenko. 2011. "Kurs na sterylnist'." (Course Toward Sterility) *Dzerkalo Tyzhnia*, October 8. Accessed August 14, 2013. http://dt.ua/POLITICS/kurs_na_sterilnist-89245.html.

Jakubowicz, Karol. 2012. "Post-Communist Political Systems and Media Freedom and Independence." In *Central and Eastern European Media in Comparative Perspective: Politics, Economy and Culture,* edited by John Downey and Sabina Mihelj, 15–39. Burlington: Ashgate.

Jakubowicz, Karol. 2011. "Democracy at 20? Many (Un) Happy Returns." In *Making Democracy in 20 Years: Media and Politics in Central and Eastern Europe,* edited by Bogusława Dobek-Ostrowska and Michał Głowacki, 15–41. Wrocław: University of Wrocław Press.

Jakubowicz, Karol. 2008. "Finding the Right Place on the Map: Prospects for Public Service Broadcasting in Post-Communist Countries." In *Finding the Right Place on the Map: Central and Eastern European Media Change in a Global Perspective,* edited by Karol Jakubowicz and Miklós Sükösd, 101–124. Bristol, UK, and Chicago, IL: Intellect Ltd.

Jakubowicz, Karol. 2007. *Rude Awakening: Social and Media Change in Central and Eastern Europe.* New York: Hampton Press.

Jakubowicz, Karol. 2005. "Post-Communist Media Development in Perspective." *Internat. Politikanalyse*, Abt. Internat. Dialog. Berlin: Friedrich-Ebert-Stiftung.

Jakubowicz, Karol. 2001. "Rude Awakening—Social and Media Change in Central and Eastern Europe." *Javnost–The Public*, 8(4):59–80.

Jakubowicz, Karol. 1995. "Lovebirds? The Media, the State and Politics in Central and Eastern Europe." *Javnost–The Public*, 2(1):75–93.

Jakubowicz, Karol, and Miklós Sükösd, eds. 2008. *Finding the Right Place on the Map: Central and Eastern European Media Change in a Global Perspective.* Bristol, UK, and Chicago, IL: Intellect Ltd.

Johnson, Dennis W. 2009. *Routledge Handbook of Political Management.* New York: Routledge.

Julliard, Jean-François, and Elsa Vidal. 2010. *Press Freedom in Ukraine: Temptation to Control.* Paris: Reporters Without Borders. Accessed August 14, 2015. https://www.reporter-ohne-grenzen.de/fileadmin/rte/docs/2010/100901_Engl_Ukraine-Bericht.pdf.

Kabachii, Roman. 2015. "Odeski ZMI niby riznomanitni, prote neridko praciuiut za radianskymy lekalamy I zastosovuiut chornyi PR." (Media in Odesa Seem to be Diverse but They Often Practice Soviet Time Journalism and Use Black PR) *texty.org*, December 12. Accessed August 16, 2016. http://texty.org.ua/pg/article/textynewseditor/read/63710/Odeski_ZMI_niby_riznomanitni_prote_neridko_pracujut.

Kalinina, Svetlana. 2009. "Business Sense with Svetlana Kalinina." *Kyiv Post*, August 21. Accessed September 21, 2011. www.cetv-net.com/en/press-center/media/94.shtml.

Karklins, Rasma. 2005. *The System Made Me Do It: Corruption in Post-Communist Societies.* Armonk, New York, and London: M. E. Sharpe, Inc.

Karklins, Rasma. 2002. "Typology of Post-Communist Corruption." *Problems of Post Communism* 49(4):22–32.

KAS (Konrad-Adenauer-Stiftung). 2011. "Ukrainian Media Landscape—2010." Accessed September 21, 2015. www.kas.de/ukraine/ukr/publications/23004/.

KAS (Konrad-Adenauer-Stiftung). 2008. "The KAS Democracy Report – 2008: Media and Democracy. Vol. II." Accessed September 20, 2015. www.kas.de/wf/en/33.14855/.

Kaspruk, Viktor. 2009. "Chy mozhlyva realna derusyfikaciia Ukranny?" (Is Real De-Russification of Ukraine Possible?) *Radio Svoboda*, August 24. Accessed September 18, 2015. www.radiosvoboda.org/content/article/1806505.html?page=1 andx=1#relatedInfoContainer/.

Katasonova, Dusia. 2007. "Sponsory telenovostei." (TV News Sponsors) *Telekrytyka*, September 21. Accessed August 14, 2013. http://www.telekritika.ua/kurilka-tk/2007-09-21/33997.

Keane, John. 1991. *The Media and Democracy.* Cambridge: Polity Press.

Keith, Linda. 2002. "Judicial Independence and Human Rights Protection Around the World." *Judicature* 85(4):195–200.

Khabyuk, Olexii. 2009. "Public Service Broadcasting in Ukraine: To Be or Not to Be?" In *Comparative Media Systems: European and Global Perspectives*, edited by Bogusława Dobek-Ostrowska, Michał Głowacki, Karol Jakubowicz, and Miklós Sükösd, 115–126. Budapest: CEU Press.

Khaminich, Svitlana, and Ganna Pylypenko. 2009. "Knyzhkovyi rynok Ukranny v umovakh ekonomichnon kryzy: stan i mozhlyvosti rozvytku." (Ukrainian Books Market Under the Conditions of Economic Crisis: State and Opportunities for Development) *Ekonomichnyi prostir*, 26:79–87.

Kievukraine. 2012. "100 Journalists Picket Prosecutor General." *Kiev Ukraine news blog,* July 21. Accessed August 14, 2013. http://news.kievukraine.info/2012/07/100-journalists-picket-prosecutor.html.

KIIS (The Kiev International Institute of Sociology). 2015. "How Do the Attitude of Ukrainians to Russia and Russians to Ukraine Has Changed." Accessed August 16, 2016. http://www.kiis.com.ua/?lang=eng&cat=reports&id=502&page=3.

KIIS (The Kiev International Institute of Sociology). 2014. "The Media and Trust to Ukrainian and Russian Media." Accessed August 16, 2016. http://kiis.com.ua/?lang=eng&cat=reports&id=425&page=1.

King, Charles M. 2001. "Potemkin Democracy." *National Interest* 64 (Summer):93–104.

Kiriya, Ilya, and Elena Degtereva. 2010. "Russian TV Market: Between State Supervision, Commercial Logic and Simulacrum of Public Service." *Central European Journal of Communication,* 1(3):37–51.

Klimkiewicz, Beata. 2004. "Poland." In *Media Ownership and its Impact on Media Independence and Pluralism,* edited by Sandra Hrvatin and Brankica Petkovič, 363–402. Ljubljana: SEENMP and Peace Institute.

Koltsova, Olessia. 2006. *News Media and Power in Russia.* New York: Routledge.

Koltsova, Olessia. 2001. "News Production in Contemporary Russia Practices of Power." *European Journal of Communication* 16(3):315–335.

Kononczuk, Wojciech. 2013. "The Presidential 'Family' in Ukraine Is Developing its Business Base." *OSW Analyses.* Accessed December 28, 2015. http://www.osw.waw.pl/en/publikacje/analyses/2013-06-26/presidential-family-ukraine-developing-its-business-base.

Korrespondent. 2012. "Zanadto garni novyny." (Too Good News) *Korrespondent,* January, 31. Accessed August 16, 2016. http://ua.korrespondent.net/journal/1313733-korrespondent-zanadto-garni-novini-ukrayinske-telebachennya-vse-silnishe-padae-v-objmi-cenzuri.

Kramer, David, Robert Nurick, Oleksandr Sushko, Viktoria Syumar, Damon Wilson, and Matthew Schaaf. 2012. "Sounding the Alarm Round 2: Protecting Democracy in Ukraine. A Follow-up Freedom House Report." Retrieved October 20, 2015. https://www.freedomhouse.org/sites/default/files/Ukraine%202012%20English%20FINAL.pdf.

Kramer, David, Robert Nurick, Damon Wilson, and Evan Alterman. 2011. "Sounding the Alarm: Protecting Democracy in Ukraine: A Freedom House Report on the State of Democracy and Human Rights in Ukraine." Accessed August 16, 2016. https://www.wan-ifra.org/sites/default/files/field_article_file/Freedom%20House%20Report_0.pdf.

Krasnoboka, Natalya. 2009. "Beyond Democracy: Is There a Study of the Post-Soviet Russian Media Outside of the Democratic Theory?" Paper presented at the conference "Beyond East and West: Two Decades of Media Transformation after the Fall of Communism" at Central European University, Budapest, 25–27 June 2009.

Krasnoboka, Natalya, and Kees Brants. 2006. "Old and New Media, Old and New Politics? On- and Offline Reporting in the 2002 Ukrainian Election Campaign." In *Mass Media and Political Communication in New Democracies*, edited by Katrin Voltmer, 92–113. London: Routledge.

Krasnoboka, Natalya, and Holli A. Semetko. 2006. "Murder, Journalism and the Web: How the Gongadze Case Launched the Internet Era in Ukraine." In *The Internet and Politics: Citizens, Voters and Activists*, edited by Sarah Oates, Diana Owen, and Rachel K. Gibson, 164-184. New York: Routledge.

Kryshtanovskaya, Olga, and Stephen White. 1996. "From Soviet *Nomenklatura* to Russian Elite." *Europe-Asia Studies* 48(5):711–733.

Kudelia, Serhiy. 2014. "The House That Yanukovych Built." *Journal of Democracy*, 25(3) (July 2014):19–34.

Kudelia, Serhiy. 2013. "If Tomorrow Comes: Power Balance and Time Horizons in Ukraine's Constitutional Politics." *Demokratizatsiya* 21(2):151–178.

Kudelia, Serhiy. 2012. "The Sources of Continuity and Change of Ukraine's Incomplete State." *Communist and Post-Communist Studies*, 45(3):417–428.

Kudelia, Serhiy. 2011. "Politics and Democracy." In *Open Ukraine: Changing Course Towards a European Future*, edited by Taras Kuzio and Daniel S. Hamilton, 1–20. Washington, DC: Center for Transatlantic Relations.

Kudelia, Serhiy. 2010. "Explaining Elite Cooperation in Ukraine: From Kuchma to Yanukovych." Paper presented at International Summer School "Approaches to Post-Soviet Transformations," Dnipropetrovsk (Ukraine), 5–9 July 2010.

Kudelia, Serhiy, and Taras Kuzio. 2015. "Nothing Personal: Explaining the Rise and Decline of Political Machines in Ukraine." *Post-Soviet Affairs*, 31(3):250–278.

Kulyk, Volodymyr. 2014. "The Media at the Time of Unrest: A Report of a Maidan Participant." *Russian Journal of Communication* 6(2):181–185.

Kulyk, Volodymyr. 2013. "Language Policy in the Ukrainian Media: Authorities, Producers and Consumers." *Europe-Asia Studies*, 65(7):1417–1443.

Kulyk, Volodymyr. 2011. "The Media, History and Identity: Competing Narratives of the Past in the Ukrainian Popular Press." *National Identities*, 13(3):287–303.

Kulyk, Volodymyr. 2010. *Dyskurs ukraïnskykh mediï: identychnosti, ideolohiï, vladni stosunky.* (The Ukrainian Media Discourse: Ideologies, Identities, Power Relations) Kyiv: Krytyka.

Kuzio, Taras. 2012. "Democratic Revolutions from a Different Angle: Social Populism and National Identity in Ukraine's 2004 Orange Revolution." *Journal of Contemporary European Studies*, 20(1):41–54.

Kuzio, Taras. 2009. "Ukraine: Pluralistic Media Will Ensure Lively Campaign." *Oxford Analytica*, October 19. Accessed September 21, 2011. www.taraskuzio.net/media23_files/10.pdf.

Kuzio, Taras. 2005. "The Opposition's Road to Success." *Journal of Democracy*, 16(2):117–130.

Kyiv Post. 2005. "Jed Sunden Looks Back on 10 Years with Kyiv Post and KP Publications." *Kyiv Post*, October 19. Accessed September 21, 2011. www.kyivpost.com/news/business/bus_general/detail/23376/.

Lauk, Epp. 2015. "A View from the Inside: The Dawning of De-Westernization of CEE Media and Communication Research?" *Media and Communication*, 3(4):1–4.

Law of Ukraine on the Protection of Public Morality. 2004. In 14: Vidomosti of the Verhovna Rada of Ukraine.

Law of Ukraine on Television and Radio Broadcasting. 2006. In 18: Vidomosti of the Verhovna Rada of Ukraine.

Lauth, Hans-Joachim. 2000. "Informal Institutions and Democracy." *Democratization*, 7(4):21–50.

Ledeneva, Alena. 2009. "From Russia with Blat: Can Informal Networks Help Modernize Russia?" *Social Research*, 76(11):257–288.

Ledevena, Alena. 2006. *How Russia Really Works: The Informal Practices That Shaped Post-Soviet Politics and Business.* Ithaca, NY: Cornell University Press.

Ledeneva, Alena. 1998. *Russia's Economy of Favours: Blat, Networking and Informal Exchange.* Cambridge: Cambridge University Press.

Ledeneva, Alena, and Stanislav Shekshnia. 2011. "Doing Business in Russian Regions: Informal Practices and Anti-Corruption Strategies." Russie. Nei. Visions 58:4–24.

Legvold, Robert. 2009. "Corruption, the Criminalized State and Post-Soviet Transition." In *Corruption, Global Security and World Order*, edited by Robert I. Rotberg, 194–238. Brookings Institution Press.

Leshchenko, Serhiy. 2014. "Ukraine's Puppet Masters: A Typology of Oligarchs." *Eurozine*, May 15. Accessed August 16, 2016. http://www.eurozine.com/articles/2014-05-15-leshchenko-en.html

Leshchenko, Serhiy. 2006. "Orbity politychnykh media: sfera vplyvu Pinchuka, Akhmetova, Poroshenka, Yushchenka." (Political Media Orbits: The Sphere of Influence of Pinchuk, Akhmetov, Poroshenko, and Yushchenko) *Ukrainska Pravda*, December 6. Accessed August 14, 2013. www.pravda.com.ua/rus/articles/2006/12/6/4409790.

Levitsky, Steven, and Lucan A. Way. 2002. "The Rise of Competitive Authoritarianism." *Journal of Democracy* 13:51–63.

Ligachova, Natalia. 2015. "MediaOBOZ ili mediaAVANGARD?" (Media-baggage or Media-vanguard?) *Mediasapiens*, April 20. Accessed August 16, 2016. http://osvita.mediasapiens.ua/trends/1411978127/mediaoboz_ili_mediaavan gard/.

Ligachova, Natalia. 2014. "Shcho poperedu v tyh chii mrii zbuvaiutsia?" (Media-2014: What Is the Future of Those Whose Dreams Come True?) *MediaSapiens*, December 26. Accessed August 16, 2016. http://osvita.media sapiens.ua/trends/1411978127/media2014_scho_poperedu_v_tikh_chii_mrii _zbuvayutsya/.

Ligachova, Natalia. 2012. "Telenovyny rozpovidaiut pro inakshu, nizh ie, realnist." (Newscasts are Providing Coverage of Fictional Reality Instead of Actual One) *Telekrytyka*, January 3. Accessed August 16, 2016. http://www.telekriti ka.ua/expert/2012-01-03/68491.

Ligachova, Natalia. 2008a. "Nekotoryie voprosy dzinsovedeniia." (Some Issues of *Dzhynsa* Making) *Telekrytyka*, March 26. Accessed August 14, 2013. www.telekritika.ua/media-continent/authorcolumn/nl/2008-03-26/37372.

Ligachova, Natalia. 2008b. "Barbosizatsiia vsei strany." (Bamboozling of the Entire Country) *Telekrytyka*, August 4. Accessed September 5, 2015. http://ru.telek ritika.ua/nl/2008-08-04/39830.

Ligachova, Natalia. 2007a. "Rabovladel'cheskoe televideniie, ili neformat." (Slave TV or Out-of-Format) *Telekrytyka*, March 3. Accessed August 14, 2013. www.tele kritika.ua/nl/2007-03-20/8601.

Ligachova, Natalia. 2007b. "Teleshou na deribanie strany." (TV-show Which Accompanies "Plundering" the Country) *Ukrainska Pravda*, April 16. Accessed August 16, 2016. http://www.pravda.com.ua/articles/2007/04/16/3228971/?at tempt=1.

Ligachova, Natalia. 2007c. "Media Ukrainy: na pereputie." (Ukrainian Media at a Crossroad) *Otechestvennyie zapiski*, 2(35). Accessed August 16, 2016. http://www.strana-oz.ru/2007/2/media-ukrainy-na-perepute.

Ligachova, Natalia. 2006. "Dniu zhurnalista posviashchaetsia". (For Journalists' Day) *Telekrytyka*, June 7. Accessed August 14, 2013. www.telekritika.ua/nl/2006-06-07/7094.

Lindberg, Staffan I. 2003. "It's Our Time to Chop: Do Elections in Africa Feed Neo-patrimonialism Rather Than Counteract It?" *Democratization* 10(2):121–40.

Linde, Jonas, and Joakim Ekman. 2011. "Patterns of Stability and Performance in Post-Communist Hybrid Regimes." In *20 Years since the Fall of the Berlin Wall: Transitions, State-Breakup and Democratic Politics in Central Europe and Germany*, edited by Elisabeth Bakke and Ingo Peters, 97–115. Berlin: Berliner Wissenschafts-Verlag.

Maliukevicius, Nerijus. 2007. "Russia's Information Policy in Lithuania: The Spread of Soft Power or Information Geopolitics?" *Baltic Security & Defence Review* 9:150–170.

Malygina, Kateryna. 2010. "Ukraine as a Neo-Patrimonial State: Understanding Political Change in Ukraine in 2005–2010." *Southeast Europe Review for Labour and Social Affairs* 13(1):7–27.

Matuszak, Slawomir. 2012. *The Oligarchic Democracy: The Influence of Business Groups on Ukrainian Politics*. OSW Studies, Issue 42. Warsaw: Centre for Eastern Studies.

Mazzoleni, Gianpietro. 1991. "Media Moguls in Italy." In *Media Moguls*, edited by Jeremy Tunstall and Michael Palmer, 162–182. London: Routledge.

McCargo, Duncan. 2012. "Partisan Polyvalence: Characterizing the Political Role of Asian Media." In *Comparing Media Systems Beyond the Western World*, edited by Daniel Hallin and Paolo Mancini, 201–223. Cambridge: Cambridge University Press.

McFaul, Michael. 2005. "Transitions from Postcommunism." *Journal of Democracy*, 16(3):5–19.

McNair, Brian. 2000. "Power, Profit, Corruption, and Lies: The Russian Media in the 1990s." In *De-Westernizing Media Studies*, edited by James Curran and Myung-Jin Park, 79–94. London: Routledge.

McNair, Brian. 1996. "Television in Post-Soviet Russia: From Monolith to Mafia." *Media, Culture & Society*, 18:489–499.

Mediananny. 2012. "Boris Lozhkin: dokhody televideniia v proshlom godu sostavili $400 millionov." (Boris Lozhkin: TV Income Was $400 Million Last Year) *Mediananny*, April 7. Accessed August 14, 2013. http://mediananny.com/raznoe/18627.

Mediasapiens. 2015a. "Monitoring telenovyn: na fronti obslugovuvannia oligarkhiv bez zmin." (TV News Monitoring: All Quiet on the Front of Servicing Oligarchs' Interests) *Mediasapiens*, January 5. Accessed August 16, 2016. http://osvita.mediasapiens.ua/monitoring/monitoring_overview/monitoring_telenovin_na_fronti_obslugovuvannya_oligarkhiv_bez_zmin/.

Mediasapiens. 2015b. "Monitoring: golovni dzhinsovyky aktyvizuvalysya." (Monitoring: The Main *Dzynsa*-makers Became More Active) *Mediasapiens*, February 2. Accessed August 16, 2016. http://osvita.mediasapiens.ua/monitoring/monitoring_overview/monitoring_golovni_dzhinsoviki_aktivizuvalisya/.

Mediasapiens. 2012. "Vdaleke ot tsivilizatsii." (Away from Civilization) *Mediasapiens*, September 6. Accessed August 14, 2013. http://osvita.mediasapiens.ua/material/9967.

Melnykovska, Inna, and Rainer Schweickert. 2008. "Who You Gonna Call? Oligarchic Clans as a Bottom-Up Force of Neighborhood Europeanization in Ukraine." *Arbeitspapiere des Osteuropa-Instituts der Freien Universität Berlin* 67. Accessed August 14, 2013. www.econstor.eu/handle/10419/28882.

Meyer, Gerd, ed. 2008. *Formal Institutions and Informal Politics in Central and Eastern Europe: Hungary, Poland, Russia and Ukraine*. Opladen and Farmington Hills: Barbara Budrich Publishers.

Mickiewicz, Ellen. 2000. "Institutional Incapacity, the Attentive Public, and Media Pluralism in Russia." In *Democracy and the Media: A Comparative Perspective*, edited by Richard Gunther and Anthony Mughan, 85–121. Cambridge: Cambridge University Press.

Mirkadirov, Rauf. 2014. "Novyny z Feisbuka viyny oligarkhiv ta igry dobrochyntsiv." (News from the Facebook, Oligarchic Wars and Charity Plays) *Mediasapiens*, July 15. Accessed August 16, 2016. http://osvita.mediasapiens.ua/moni toring/daily_news/novini_z_feysbuka_viyni_oligarkhiv_ta_igri_dobrochintsiv/.

Mnich, Antonina. 2014. "Regionalna teledzhynsa u zhovtni kambek u chasy Yanukovycha." (Regional *Dzynsa* in October: A Comeback into Yanukovych Time?) *Mediasapiens*, November 15. Accessed August 16, 2016. http://osvi ta.mediasapiens.ua/monitoring/regional_news/regionalna_teledzhinsa_u_zhov tni_kambek_u_chasi_yanukovicha/.

Mommsen, Margareta. 2012. "Russias's Political Regime: Neo-Soviet Authoritarianism and Patronal Presidentalism." In *Presidents, Oligarchs and Bureaucrats: Forms of Rule in the Post-Soviet Space*, edited by Susan Stewart, Margarete Klein, Andrea Schmitz and Hans-Henning Schröder, 63–87. Farnham: Ashgate.

MSI-Ukraine. 2006/2007. 2008. 2009. 2010. 2011. 2012. 2013. 2014. 2015. IREX. "Media Sustainability Index (MSI), Europe and Eurasia: Ukraine." http://www.irex.org/projects/msi/europe-eurasia.

Müller, Jan Werner. 2012. "Europe's Perfect Storm: The Political and Economic Consequences of the Eurocrisis." *Dissent*, Fall:47–53.

Mungiu-Pippidi, Alina. 2012. "Freedom Without Impartiality: The Vicious Circle of Media Capture." In *Media Transformations in the Post-Communist World: Eastern Europe's Tortured Path to Change*, edited by Peter Gross and Karol Jakubowicz, 49–66. Lanham: Lexington Books.

Mungiu-Pippidi, Alina. 2008. "How Media and Politics Shape Each Other in the New Europe." In *Finding the Right Place on the Map: Central and Eastern European Media Change in a Global Perspective*, edited by Karol Jakubowicz and Miklós Sükösd, 87–100. Bristol, UK, and Chicago, IL: Intellect Ltd.

Mungiu-Pippidi, Alina. 2005. "Deconstructing Balkan Particularism: The Ambiguous Social Capital of Southeastern Europe." *Journal of Southeast European and Black Sea Studies*, 5(1):45–65.

myNews-in.net. 2011. "Marina Mirgorodskaia pokhvastalas svoim bogatstvom." (Marina Mirgorodskaia Bragged about Her Wealth) *myNews-in.net*, June 10. Accessed July 20, 2011. http://mynews-in.net/news/society/2011/06/10/25081 13.html.

National Security and Defence Magazine. 2009. "Topical Problems in Social Relations in the AR of Crimea." *National Security and Defence Magazine*, 5(109):53. Accessed December 29, 2015. http://www.uceps.org/eng/files/cate gory_journal/NSD109_eng.pdf

National Television and Radio Broadcasting Council. 2008. "Rekomendacii shcho do vyznachennia movy program i peredach." (Recommendations on the Choice of Language of Programs) March 26. Accessed September 27, 2011. http://nrada.gov.ua/ua/normativnydokumenty/rekomendacii.html

Nayem, Mustafa, and Serhiy Leshchenko. 2008. "Oliharkhichni viyny: yak prodavaly kanal *Inter.*" (Oligarch Wars: How the *Inter* Channel Was Sold) *Ukrainska Pravda*, July 29. Accessed August 14, 2013. www.pravda.com.ua/articles/2008/07/29/3503640.

Neef, Christian. 2012. "PR Disaster: A Bank, a TV Channel, and Four Yachts." *Spiegel Online*, May 8. Accessed August 14, 2013. www.spiegel.de/international/europe/tymoshenko-case-puts-yanukovych-on-defensive-a-831732-2.html.

Nikolayenko, Olena. 2004. "Press Freedom during the 1994 and 1999 Presidential Elections in Ukraine: A Reverse Wave?" *Europe-Asia Studies*, 56:661–686.

Oates, Sarah. 2013. *Revolution Stalled: The Political Limits of the Internet in the Post-Soviet Sphere*. Oxford: Oxford University Press.

Oates, Sarah. 2007. "The Neo-Soviet Model of the Media." *Europe-Asia Studies*, 59(8):1279–1297.

Obozrevatel. 2013. "Mediaprostir Ukrainy: sproba analizu." (An Attempt to Analyze the Ukrainian Media Space) *Obozrevatel*, February 18. Accessed August 14, 2013. http://obozrevatel.com/politics/83765-media-prostir-ukraini-sproba-analizu.htm.

O'Donnell, Guillermo A. 1998. "Horizontal Accountability in New Democracies." *Journal of Democracy*, 9(3):112–126.

O'Donnell, Gulliermo A. 1996. "Illusions about Consolidation." *Journal of Democracy* 7(2):34–51.

O'Donnell, Guillermo A. 1994. "Delegative Democracy." *Journal of Democracy*, 5(1):55–69.

Ogonek. 2011. "Bitva za Kuchmu." (The Battle for Kuchma) *Kommersant*, 5179(20), May 23. Accessed August 14, 2013. www.kommersant.ru/doc/1641854/print.

Olszanski, Tadeusz. 2010. "The Party of Regions Monopolises Power in Ukraine." *OSW Commentary*, 40.

Onuch, Olga. 2014. "Who Were the Protesters?" *Journal of Democracy* 25(3):44–51. http://muse.jhu.edu/journals/journal_of_democracy/v025/25.3.onuch.html.

Onufrienko, Anton, and Irina Mironova. 2008. "Televizionnyi rynok: komu prinadlezhit Ukraina." (Television Market: Who Owns Ukraine) *Kommersant*, December 22. Accessed August 14, 2013. www.kommersant.ua/doc/1098087.

Paneyakh, Ella. 2003. "Neformalnye instituly i ispolzovanie formal'nykh pravjl: zakon deistvuyushchii vs. zakon priinenyaemyi." (Informal Institutions and Use of Formal Rules: Real Law vs. Under Elaboration) *Poliiicheskaya nauka*, 1:33–52.

Papathanassopoulos, Stylianos. 1999. "The Effects of Media Commercialization on Journalism and Politics in Greece." *Communication Review*, 3(4):379–402.

Roudakova, Natalia. 2012. "Comparing Processes: Media, 'Transitions,' and Historical Change." In *Comparing Media Systems Beyond the Western World*, edited by Daniel Hallin and Paolo Mancini, 246–277. Cambridge: Cambridge University Press.

Roudakova, Natalia. 2008. "Media-Political Clientelism: Lessons from Anthropology." *Media, Culture & Society*, 30(1):41–59.

Rulyova, Natalia. 2007. "Domesticating the Western Format on Russian TV: Subversive Glocalization in the Game Show Pole Chudes (The Field of Miracles)." *Europe-Asia Studies* 59(8):1367–1386.

Rupnik, Jacques, and Jan Zielonka. 2013. "Introduction: The State of Democracy 20 Years on Domestic and External Factors." *East European Politics & Societies* 27(1):3–25.

Rupnik, Jacques. 2007. "From Democracy Fatigue to Populist Backlash." *Journal of Democracy* 18(4):17–25.

Ryabinska, Natalya. 2014. "Media Capture in Post-Communist Ukraine: Actors, Methods and Conditions." *Problems of Post-Communism* 61(2):46–60.

Ryabinska, Natalya. 2011. "The Media Market and Media Ownership in Post-Communist Ukraine." *Problems of Post-Communism* 58(6):3–20.

Salomon, Eve, and Karol Jakubowicz. 2007. "Analysis and Comments on Law of Ukraine Amending the Law of Ukraine on the National Television and Radio Broadcasting Council of Ukraine. Prepared for the Media Division of the Council of Europe at the Request of the Ukrainian Authorities." Accessed August 20, 2015. http://www.coe.int/t/dghl/standardsetting/media/news/ATCM(2007)002_en.pdf.

Salovaara-Moring, Inka. 2012. "Digital (R)Evolutions? Internet, New Media and Informed Citizenship in Central and Eastern Europe." In *Media Transformations in the Post-Communist World: Eastern Europe's Tortured Path to Change*, edited by Peter Gross and Karol Jakubowicz, 99–114. Lanham: Lexington Books.

Sandholtz, Wayne, and Rein Taagepera. 2005. "Corruption, Culture, and Communism." *International Review of Sociology*, 15(1):109–131.

Sharafutdinova, Gulnaz. 2010. *Political Consequences of Crony Capitalism inside Russia*. Notre Dame: University of Notre Dame Press.

Shcherbyna, Serhii. 2012. "Televiziina monopoliia." (TV Monopoly) *Ukrainska Pravda*, July 23. Accessed August 14, 2013. www.pravda.com.ua/articles/2012/07/23/6969348.

Sherr, James. 2007. "Ukraine's Security: The Interplay of Internal and External Factors." *European Security Forum*, Working Paper No. 24:17–22.

Shevchenko, Taras. 2004. "How to Guarantee the Independence of the National Council of Ukraine in Charge of TV and Radio Broadcasting in the New Version of the Law of Ukraine 'On the National Council of Ukraine in Charge of TV and Radio Broadcasting?'" *The Kharkiv Human Rights Protection group*, April 8. Accessed October 30 2015. http://www.khpg.org/en/index.php?id=1081416013.

Sirutavičius, Vladas. 2006. "Ukraine: The Orange Revolution and its Aftermath." *Lithuanian Annual Strategic Review 2005*. Vilnius: Lithuanian Military Academy.

Siumar, Viktoria, and Serhii Taran. 2005. "Bespredelnyi peredel: vladeltsy zavodov, gazet, parokhodov v bor'be za svoiu svobodu slova." (Unlimited Redistribution: The Owners of Factories, Newspapers, and Steamboats Fight for Their Freedom of Speech) *Dzerkalo Tyzhnia*, August 2. Accessed August 14, 2013. http://gazeta.zn.ua/POLITICS/bespredelnyy_peredel_vladeltsy_zavodov,_ga zet,_parokhodov_v_bor be_za_svoyu_svobodu_slova.html.

Sokolenko, Natalka. 2013. "Parketni novyny ta loialnist do vlady zamist standartiv." (Pro-government Articles and Loyalty to the Authorities Instead of Journalism Standards) *Mediasapiens*, April 3. Accessed April 4, 2015. http://osvita.me diasapiens.ua/monitoring/regional_news/parketni_novini_ta_loyalnist_do_vla di_zamist_standartiv/.

Sparks, Colin. 2000. "Media Theory After the Fall of European Communism: Why the Old Models from East and West Won't Do Any More." In *De-Westernizing Media Studies*, edited by James Curran and Myung-Jin Park, 35–49. London: Routledge.

Sparks, Colin, and Anna Reading. 1998. *Communism, Capitalism, and the Mass Media*. London: Sage Publications.

Splichal, Slavko. 2000. "Reproducing Political Capitalism in the Media of East-Central Europe." *Medijska istraživanja*, 6(1):5–17.

Splichal, Slavko. 1994. *Media Beyond Socialism: Theory and Practice in East-Central Europe*. Boulder: Westview Press.

Steinmo, Sven. 2008. "Historical Institutionalism." In *Approaches and Methodologies in the Social Sciences: A Pluralist Perspective*, edited by Donatella Della Porta and Michael Keating, 118–138. Cambridge: Cambridge University Press.

Stetka, Vaclav. 2015. "The Rise of Oligarchs as Media Owners." In *Media and Politics in New Democracies. Europe in a Comparative Perspective*, edited by Jan Zielonka, 85–98. Oxford: Oxford University Press.

Stetka, Vaclav. 2012. "From Multinationals to Business Tycoons: Media Ownership and Journalistic Autonomy in Central and Eastern Europe." *The International Journal of Press/Politics* 17(4):433–456.

Sükösd, Miklós. 2000. "Democratic Transformation and the Mass Media in Hungary: From Stalinism to Democratic Consolidation." In *Democracy and the Media: A Comparative Perspective*, edited by Richard Gunther and Anthony Mughan, 122–164. Cambridge: Cambridge University Press.

Sükösd, Miklós, and Péter Bajomi-Lázár. 2003. *Reinventing Media: Media Policy Reform in East–Central Europe*. Budapest: Central European University Press.

Szostek, Joanna. 2014a. "The Media Battles of Ukraine's EuroMaidan". *Digital Icons: Studies in Russian, Eurasian and Central European New Media*, 11:1–19.

Szostek, Joanna. 2014b. "Russia and the News Media in Ukraine: A Case of 'Soft Power?'" *East European Politics & Societies* 28(3):463–486.

Sztompka, Piotr. 2000. *Civilizational Competence: A Prerequisite of Post-Communist Transition*. Retrieved August 17, 2014. http://www.friendspartners.org/newfri ends/audem/audem92/Sztompka.html.

Telekrytyka. 2012. "Telekanaly nyni rozpovidaiut' pro inshu, nizh ie, realnist'." (TV Channels Today Speak About a Reality Which Does Not Exist) *Telekrytyka*, January 3. Accessed October 7, 2015. http://www.telekritika.ua/mediasuspilst vo/expert/2012-01-03/68491.

Telekrytyka. 2010. "Vid Kuchmy do Yushchenka: desiatylitnii marafon stoiannia na misti." (From Kuchma to Yushchenko: A Ten-years Long Marathon of Standstill) *Telekrytyka*, January 19. Accessed August 16, 2016. http://www.telekritika.ua/spec_tk/ukrainski_zmi/2010-01-19/50530.

Telekrytyka. 2009. "*1+1* pereoformyv licenziiu, de vporiadkuvav merezhu ta zminyv koncepciiju movlennia." (*1+1* TV Channel Renewed Its License, Where It Put in Order its Network and Changed the Channel's Broadcasting Conception) *Telekrytyka*, November 11. Accessed August 16, 2016. http://www.telekritika.u a/news/2009-11-11/49182.

Telekrytyka. 2008. "Aleksandr Chernenko: 'Komunalnye SMI—PR-sluzhba Chernovetskogo.'" (Alexander Chernenko: "The Municipal Media Are Chernovetskyi's PR Agencies") *Telekrytyka*, May 6. Accessed September 21, 2015. www.telekritika.ua/news/2008-05-06/38221.

Telekrytyka. 2007. "'NIS'—novyniarnia maibutniogo?" ("NIS"—A News Supplier of the Future?) *Telekrytyka*, May 30. Accessed December 28, 2015. http://www.telekritika.ua/process/2007-05-30/8961.

Telekrytyka. 2006. "Nakazano movchaty?" (Ordered to Remain Silent?) *Telekrytyka*, May 23. Accessed August 14, 2013. www.telekritika.ua/monitoring-archive/ 2006-05-23/7028.

Texty.org.ua. 2014. "Infografika: obsiahy rosijskoho kontentu na TB ne tilky ne zmenshuiutsia, a navit zrostaiut". (Infographics: The Amount of Russian Content on TV Does Not Decrease but Even Increases) http://texty.org.ua/p g/blog/krystofer/read/56126/Infografika_Obsagy_rosijskogo_kontentu_na_T B_ne.

Transparency International. 2009. "Corruption Perception Index (CPI)." Retrieved May 12, 2013. http://www.transparency.org/research/cpi/cpi_2009.

Trochev, Alexei. 2010. "Meddling with Justice: Competitive Politics, Impunity, and Distrusted Courts in Post-Orange Ukraine." *Demokratizatsiya* 18(2):122–147.

Tsai, Kellee. 2014. "China: Economic Liberalization, Adaptive Informal Institutions, and Party-State Resilience." In *Oxford Handbook of Transformations of the State*, edited by Stephan Leibfried, Frank Nullmeier, Evelyne Huber, Matthew Lange, Jonah Levy, and John Stephens, 654–670. New York: Oxford University Press.

Tsetsura, Katerina, and Anastasia Grynko. 2009. "An Exploratory Study of the Media Transparency in Ukraine." *Public Relations Journal*, 3(2). Accessed March 2, 2013. www.prsa.org/prjournal/Vol3No2/6D-030205.pdf

Tunstall, Jeremy, and Michael Palmer, eds. 1991. *Media Moguls*. London: Routledge.

Tyzhden. 2013. "V OBSE vvazhajut shcho proekt zakonu pro gromadske telebachennia treba dopraciuvaty." (OSCE Believes That the Law on Public Broadcasting Has To Be Refined) *Tyzhden*, September 10. Accessed August 16, 2016. http://tyzhden.ua/News/88939.

unian.ua. 2010. "Zakon, 'Pro zakhyst suspilnoii morali' potrebuye znachnoii korekciii." (The Law "On the Protection of Public Morality" Requires Significant Correction) *unian.ua*, March 24. Accessed April 2, 2015. http://unian.net/ukr/n ews/news-368994.html

Vakaliuk, Artem, and Maksym Lazebnik 2009. "Obyom reklamno-komunikatsionnogo rynka Ukrainy v 2009 godu i prognoz na 2010 god: ekspertnaia otsenka Vseukrainskoi reklamnoi koalitsyi." (The Size of Ukraine's Advertising-Communication Market in 2009 and the Market Forecast for 2010: Expert Evaluation from the All-Ukrainian Advertising Coalition) Accessed September 25, 2015. www.uapp.org/pub_analitics/8492.html.

van Zon, Hans. 2001. "Neo-patrimonialism as an Impediment to Economic Development: The Case of Ukraine." *Journal of Communist Studies and Transition Politics*, 17(3):71–95.

Vartanova, Elena. 2012. "The Russian Media Model in the Context of Post-Soviet Dynamics." In *Comparing Media Systems Beyond the Western World*, edited by Daniel Hallin and Paolo Mancini, 119–142. Cambridge: Cambridge University Press.

Vartanova, Elena. 2009. "Russian Media: Market and Technology as Driving Forces of Change." In *Perspectives to the Media in Russia: "Western" Interests and Russian Developments*, edited by Elena Vartanova, Hannu Nieminen, and Minna-Mari Salminen, 283–301. Helsinki: Aleksanteri Institute.

Vartanova, Elena. ed. 2007. *Media and Changes*. Moscow: MediaMir; Faculty of Journalism, Moscow State University.

Vartanova, Elena. 2002. "Media Structures: Changed and Unchanged." In *Russian Media Challenge*, edited by Kaarle Nordenstreng, Elena Vartanova, and Yassen Zassoursky, 21–72. Helsinki: Aleksanteri Institute.

Vartanova, Elena, Hanni Nieminen, and Minna-Mari Salminen, eds. 2009. *Perspectives to the Media in Russia: "Western" Interests and Russian Developments.* Helsinki: Aleksanteri Institute.

Voltmer, Katrin. 2013. *The Media in Transitional Democracies.* Cambridge: Polity.

Voltmer, Katrin. 2012. "How Far Can Media Systems Travel?" In *Comparing Media Systems Beyond the Western World,* edited by Daniel Hallin and Paolo Mancini, 119–142. Cambridge: Cambridge University Press.

Voltmer, Katrin. 2008. "Comparing Media Systems in New Democracies: East Meets South Meets West." *Central European Journal of Communication,* 1(1):23–40.

Voltmer, Katrin. 2000. "Constructing Political Reality in Russia. Izvestiya—Between Old and New Journalistic Practices." *European Journal of Communication* 15(4):469–500.

Voltmer, Katrin, and Rüdiger Schmitt-Beck. 2006. "New Democracies Without Citizens? Mass Media and Democratic Orientations: A Four Country Comparison." In *Mass Media and Political Communication in New Democracies,* edited by Katrin Voltmer, 228–245. London: Routledge.

Voltmer, Katrin, Alina Dobreva, and Fabro Boaz Steibel. 2013. "The Dark Side of Journalism: Corruption and the Media–Politics Nexus in Bulgaria and Brazil." Paper presented at IAMCR Conference in Dublin, 25–29 June 2013.

Vybory.mediasapiens. 2012. "Gazeti 'Ekspres' zaproponuvaly kil'ka milionov hryven' za vysvitlennia sotsialnykh initsiatyv prezydenta." (*Express* Newspaper Was Offered Several Million Hryvnas for Propagandizing President's Social Initiatives), August 31. Accessed September 15, 2012. http://vybory.media sapiens.ua/2012/08/31/holovnomu-redaktoru-hazety-ekspres-zaproponuvaly-kilka-miljoniv-hryven-za-vysvitlennya-sotsialnyh-initsiatyv-prezydenta/.

Wang, Hongying. 2000. "Informal Institutions and Foreign Investment in China." *Pacific Review* 13(4):525–556.

Way, Lucan A. 2004. "The Sources and Dynamics of Competitive Authoritarianism in Ukraine." *Journal of Communist Studies and Transition Politics* 20(1):143–161.

Weber, Max. 1978. *Economy and Society: An Outline of Interpretive Sociology.* Berkeley: University of California Press.

Wolowski, Pawel. 2008. "Ukrainian Politics After the Orange Revolution: How Far from Democratic Consolidation?" In *Ukraine: Quo Vadis?,* edited by Sabine Fischer, 25–53. Institute for Security Studies, European Union.

World Bank. 2011. *Trends in Corruption and Regulatory Burden in Eastern Europe and Central Asia: A World Bank Study.* Washington, DC: The World Bank.

World Bank. 2000. *Anticorruption in Transition: A Contribution to the Policy Debate.* Washington, DC: The World Bank.

Wyka, Angelika W. 2009. "On the Way to Dumbing Down... The Case of Central Europe." *Central European Journal of Communication,* 2(1):133–147.

Wyka, Angelika W. 2008. "In Search of the East Central European Media Model—the Italianization Model? A Comparative Perspective on the East Central European and South European Media Systems." In *Comparing Media Systems in Central Europe: Between Commercialization and Politicization*, edited by Bogusława Dobek-Ostrowska and Michał Głowacki, 55–69. Wrocław: University of Wrocław Press.

Yerevan Press Club/Eastern Partnership Civil Society Forum. 2011. *Media Landscapes of Eastern Partnership Countries.* http://www.isp.org.pl/uploads/filemanager/webmedialandscapeseng1.pdf

Zakusylo, Mariana. 2010. "Zavorozheni politreklamoiu." (Charmed by Political Advertising) *Telekrytyka*, January 15, 2010. Accessed September 23, 2015. http://www.telekritika.ua/vibor2009/2010-01-15/50439?theme_page=1550&.

Zakusylo, Mariana, Galyna Petrenko, Roman Golovenko, Roman Kabachii, and Iryna Chulivska. 2015. "Diievist' zakonu pro prozorist' mediavlasnosti." (Effectiveness of the Law of Transparency of Media Ownership) *Telekrytyka*. Accessed August 16, 2016. https://issuu.com/marynadorosh/docs/prozorist_mediavlasnosti_final#embed.

Zassoursky, Ivan. 2009. "Free to Get Rich and Fool Around." In *The Post-Soviet Russian Media: Conflicting Signals*, edited by Birgit Beumers, Stephen Hutchings, and Natalia Rulyova, 29–41. New York: Routledge.

Zassoursky, Ivan. 2004. *Media and Power in Post-Soviet Russia*. Armonk: M.E. Sharpe.

Zassoursky, Ivan. 2002. "Media and Power: Russia in the Nineties." In *Russian Media Challenge*, edited by Kaarle Nordenstreng, Elena Vartanova, and Yassen Zassoursky, 73–91. Helsinki: Aleksanteri Institute.

Zassoursky, Ivan. 2000. "Russian Media in the Nineties: Driving Factors of Change, Actors, Strategies and the Results." Paper written for the project "Transformation and Globalization: Driving Actors and Factors of Post-Soviet Change. A Study of Actors, Interests, Institutions, and Modes of Regulation." Accessed December 28, 2015. http://www.oocities.org/zassoursky/artic.htm.

Zielonka, Jan, ed. 2015a. *Media and Politics in New Democracies: Europe in a Comparative Perspective.* Oxford: Oxford University Press.

Zielonka, Jan. 2015b. "Introduction: Fragile Democracy, Volatile Politics, and the Quest for a Free Media." In *Media and Politics in New Democracies. Europe in a Comparative Perspective*, edited by Jan Zielonka, 1–21. Oxford: Oxford University Press.

Zielonka, Jan, and Paolo Mancini. 2011. "Executive Summary: A Media Map of Central and Eastern Europe." Report of the project "Media and Democracy in Central and Eastern Europe." Accessed 15 October 2015. http://mde.politics.ox.ac.uk.

Zimmer, Kerstin. 2008. "Formal Institutions and Informal Politics in Ukraine." In *Formal Institutions and Informal Politics in Central and Eastern Europe: Hungary, Poland, Russia and Ukraine*, edited by Gerd Meyer, 267–303. Opladen and Farmington Hills: Barbara Budrich.

Name index

A

Abramovich, Roman 118
Akhmetov, Rinat 62–65, 105 n 76, 107, 112, 121
Alterman, Evan 50
Åslund, Anders 12 n 3, 14, 39–41, 53, 58
Austin, Anne 96
Avădani, Ioana 70

B

Bagdikian, Ben 7
Bajomi-Lázár, Péter (Bajomi-Lazar, Peter) 57 n 27
Barnard, Jonathan 96
Becker, Jonathan 13 n 5, 15, 117
Belyakov, Alexander 13 n 5, 70, 80
Bennich-Björkman, Li 26
Berezovsky, Boris 118
Berglund, Sten 13, 13 n 4, 16, 17, 23
Besley, Timothy 57
Bezulyk, Anna 121
Bohutskyi, Oleksandr 111
Boone, Peter 39
Böröcz, József 33
Brants, Kees 13 n 5, 14
Bratton, Michael 43
Bulavka, Yevhen 100

C

Capello, Maja 13 n 5
Carothers, Thomas 18, 24

Chernovetskyi, Leonid 100
Chomsky, Noam 7
Chulivska, Iryna 136
Cohen, Sacha Baron 87
Collins, Kathleen 33
Coman, Ioana 14, 29
Corneo, Giacomo 57, 59
Curran, James 16, 56

D

D'Anieri, Paul 19, 26, 40 n 20, 42, 45 n 23, 46–48, 51, 53, 67
Dankova, Natalia 120
Danylov, Viktor 92
Darden, Keith A. 19, 26, 32 n 16, 45 n 23, 51–53, 76 n 48
de Smaele, Hedwig 13 n 5, 15, 86
Degtereva, Elena 13 n 5, 125
Derkach, Andrii 92
Diamond, Larry 18, 24
Dobek-Ostrowska, Bogusława 13 n 5, 17
Dobovšek, Bojan 57
Dovzhenko, Otar 7, 60, 64, 68 n 34, 71 n 37, 74 n 43, 76 n 47, 77, 81 n 52, 82, 84, 92, 111 n 83, 115, 118–122, 124, 133, 133 n 91, 134
Downey, John 13 n 5, 17, 113
Downing, John 14, 23, 56
Dragomir, Marius 82, 86, 102 n 72
Dunn, John 118
Dutsyk, Diana 7, 13 n 5, 60, 62–64, 66, 69, 114

Dyczok, Marta 7, 8, 13 n 5, 14, 16, 53, 60, 63, 64, 66, 68 n 35, 69, 99, 119, 120 n 88

E

Ekiert, Grzegorz 13, 16
Ekman, Joakim 13, 13 n 4, 16, 16 n 8, 17, 17 n 9, 23
Englund, Will 71

F

Firtash, Dmytro (Dmitry Firtash) 61, 63, 71, 103 n 74, 107, 119
Fisun, Oleksandr (Aleksandr Fisun) 19, 42–44, 47, 48, 66
Fritz, Verena 42, 43
Fuksman, Borys (Boris Fuksman) 111 n 83
Futey, Bohdan 79

G

Gallina, Nicole 32
Galli, Eleonora 96
Gaman-Golutvina, Oxana 16
Ganev, Venelin 34
Gel'man, Vladimir (Vladimir Gelman) 19, 29, 30, 30 n 15, 32, 32 n 16, 34–37, 57
Ghinea, Cristian 70
Głowacki, Michał 13 n 5, 17
Golovenko, Roman 136
Gongadze, Georgi (Georgy Gongadze, Heorhij Gongadze, Giorgi Gongadze) 46, 71
Gross, Peter 13 n 5, 14, 17, 29
Grynko, Anastasia 81
Grytsenko, Oksana 65
Grzymala-Busse, Anna 18, 19, 24, 26, 31–33, 35, 37, 80
Guasti, Petra 57

Guseva, Marina 80
Gusinsky, Vladimir 117

H

Hale, Henry 19, 32 n 16, 43, 44, 46, 48, 49, 67
Hallin, Daniel C. 15 n 6, 16, 18, 23 n 11, 24, 108
Havrylyshyn, Oleh 40 n 18
Hayoz, Nicolas 32
Hellman, Joel 26, 27
Helmke, Gretchen 18, 24, 32, 33, 34, 37, 52 n 25
Herman, Edward 7
Hombach, Bodo 104, 104 n 75
Holmes, Leslie 25, 42
Hrvatin, Sandra 109
Hutcheon, Nicola 96

I

Ieremenko, Svitlana 81 n 51
Inglehart, Ronald 29
Ivanov, Valerii 66, 85

J

Jakubowicz, Karol 13 n 5, 17, 83, 113, 119
Johnson, Dennis W. 98
Johnson, Simon 37
Julliard, Jean-François 80, 84, 92

K

Kabachii, Roman 116
Kalinina, Svetlana 95, 96
Karklins, Rasma 26–28, 33, 75
Kaspruk, Viktor 108
Katasonova, Dusia 73 n 42
Kaufmann, Daniel 26
Keane, John 111 n 84
Keith, Linda 51, 80

Khabyuk, Oleksii 13 n 5
Khaminich, Svitlana 108
Khoroshkovsky, Valeriy (Valeriy Khoroshkovskyi) 84
King, Charles M. 18, 24
Kiriya, Ilya 13 n 5, 125
Klimkiewicz, Beata 101
Klitschko, Vitali 61
Klymenko, Oleksandr 64 n 31
Kolomoisky, Ihor (Igor Kolomoisky, Ihor Kolomoyskyy) 62, 63–65, 103, 112, 115, 119
Koltsova, Olessia 16, 110
Konchalovsky, Andrei 71
Kononczuk, Wojciech 102
Kostenko, Natalia 66
Kramer, David 50, 85
Krasnoboka, Natalya 13 n 5, 14, 23
Kravchuk, Leonid 40 n 18, 68 n 35
Kryshtanovskaya, Olga 34
Kuchma, Leonid 11 n 2, 25, 30 n 14, 39, 40 n 18, 44, 45–48, 47 n 24, 50, 63, 64, 66, 66 n 32, 67–69, 68 n 25, 70, 71, 73, 77, 80, 89, 91, 92, 103, 111, 111 n 83, 119, 121, 133
Kudelia, Serhiy 19, 32 n 16, 35, 39, 42, 44–50, 68, 127
Kulyk, Volodymyr 13 n 5, 100
Kurchenko, Serhiy (Sergey Kurchenko, Sergei Kurchenko) 64 n 31, 65 69, 102, 115 n 86
Kuzio, Taras 44, 48, 50, 69, 105
Kuzovkin, Oleksandr 73
Kvurt, Kostiantyn 116

L

Lauk, Epp 16 n 7
Lauth, Hans-Joachim 33
Lazebnik, Maksym 65, 97 n 64
Ledeneva, Alena 32 n 16, 33, 34, 34 n 17, 36, 37
Legvold, Robert 34 n 17
Leshchenko, Serhiy 61–63, 69
Levitsky, Steven 18, 24, 32–34, 37, 52 n 25
Ligachova, Natalia 7, 66, 70, 71 n 37, 72, 73, 73 n 41, 74, 111 n 83, 119–122, 124, 133
Linde, Jonas 16 n 8
Liovochkin, Serhiy (Sergey Lyovochkin) 61, 63, 103 n 74, 107, 119
Lozhkin, Borys (Boris Lozhkin) 65, 102, 115 n 86
Luong, Pauline Jones 35

M

Maliukevicius, Nerijus 107 n 81
Malygina, Kateryna 43, 44, 47, 48, 50, 53, 57, 68
Mancini, Paolo 15 n 6, 16, 18, 23 n 11, 24, 108
Matuszak, Slawomir 12 n 3, 14, 39, 40 n 19, 20, 41, 42, 66
Mazzoleni, Gianpietro 108
McCargo, Duncan 32 n 16, 74
McChesney, Robert W. 7
McFaul, Michael 44
Medvedchuk, Viktor 69
Melnykovska, Inna 60, 76 n 46
Meyer, Gerd 19, 32 n 16, 33
Mickiewicz, Ellen 118
Mihelj, Sabina 13 n 5, 17
Mijatović, Dunja 92
Mironova, Irina 95, 97, 111
Mnich, Antonina 134
Mokridi, Tetiana 84
Mommsen, Margareta 12 n 3

Mungiu-Pippidi, Alina 18, 20, 24, 26–28, 55, 57, 59, 60, 66, 70, 75, 112

N

Nakaa, Mounira 80
Nayem, Mustafa 61, 62, 69
Nikolayenko, Olena 13 n 5
Nordenstreng, Kaarle 13 n 5
Novel, Anne Sophie 80

O

O'Donnell, Guillermo A. 18, 24, 33, 35, 53
Oates, Sarah 13 n 5, 15
Olszanski, Tadeusz 62, 79 n 49
Onuch, Olga 127
Onufrienko, Anton 95, 97, 111

P

Palmer, Michael 108
Paneyakh, Ella 32 n 16, 34, 36
Papathanassopoulos, Stylianos 108
Park, Myung-Jin 16, 56
Pasti, Svetlana 13 n 5
Pekkala, Kirsi 80
Peruško, Zrinjka 96 n 61, 113, 114
Petković, Brankica 109
Petrenko, Galyna 136
Pinchuk, Viktor 61, 63–65, 68, 70, 71, 103, 103 n 74, 112, 119
Pleines, Heiko 12 n 3, 13, 39, 40, 47
Pluzhnikov, Ihor 68
Poludenko, Anna 70
Popova, Maria 49, 50
Popović, Helena 96 n 61, 113, 114

Poroshenko, Petro 40, 99 n 67, 102, 115 n 86
Prat, Andrea 57
Price, Monroe 75
Prodaieva, Yevheniia 64
Prytula, Olena 65
Puglisi, Rosaria 12 n 3, 14, 39, 40, 42, 44, 48, 58, 60
Putin, Vladimir 21, 117, 118, 125, 127
Pylypenko, Ganna 108

R

Rachkevych, Mark 69
Reading, Anna 14, 16, 23
Rein, Taagepera 29
Riabchuk, Mykola 13 n 5
Richter, Andrei 75, 77, 88, 89
Robinson, Neil 35, 41 n 21
Rosenholm, Arja 13 n 5
Roudakova, Natalia 13 n 5
Rozkladai, Ihor 135, 136 n 92
Rupnik, Jacques 17 n 10, 32 n 16
Ryabinska, Natalya 13 n 5

S

Salomon, Eve 83
Salovaara-Moring, Inka 15
Sandholtz, Wayne 29
Schiller, Dan 7
Schweickert, Rainer 60, 76 n 46
Semenchenko, Mariia 70
Sharafutdinova, Gulnaz 32 n 16, 37
Shcherbyna, Serhii 69
Shekshnia, Stanislav 32 n 16, 34
Sherr, James 40
Shevchenko, Taras 83, 87, 100
Shuster, Savik 121, 121 n 89, 122

Sirutavičius, Vladas 39
Siumar, Viktoria 62, 69, 80
Sokolenko, Natalka 80
Souberou, Bachir 80
Sparks, Colin 14, 16, 23
Štětka, Václav (Vaclav Stetka) 12 n 3, 17 n 10, 57 n 27, 104 n 75, 108 n 82, 110
Stouli, Sami 80
Stromberg, David 57
Sükösd, Miklós (Miklos Sukosd) 13 n 5, 102, 102 n 72
Sunden, Jed 102, 102 n 73, 104, 115 n 86
Sych, Vitalii 115 n 86
Szostek, Joanna 13 n 5
Sztompka, Piotr 29

T

Taran, Serhii 69
Tkachenko, Oleksandr 133
Trochev, Alexei 48
Trubina, Elena 13 n 5
Tsetsura, Katerina 81
Tunstall, Jeremy 108
Tymoshenko, Yulia 50, 62, 71, 73

U

Ulianenko, Oles' 87

V

Vakaliuk, Artem 97 n 64
van de Walle, Nicholas 43
van Zon, Hans 44
Vartanova, Elena 13 n 5, 14, 29, 32 n 16, 86
Vidal, Elsa 80, 84, 92
Voltmer, Katrin 18, 24, 93, 112
Voorhoof, Dirk 87

W

Way, Lucan A. 18, 19, 24, 45 n 23, 46, 53, 67
Weber, Max 43
Wilson, Damon 50, 85
White, Stephen 34
Wolowski, Pawel 41, 41 n 21, 42, 48, 49, 60, 66, 67
Wyka, Angelika W. 102 n 72, 123

Y

Yanukovych, Oleksandr 69
Yanukovych, Viktor 11 n 2, 12, 25, 30 n 14, 44, 47 n 24, 49, 56, 58, 62, 63, 64 n 31, 66 n 33, 68, 68 n 34, 72, 73, 75, 77–82, 84, 87–89, 91, 92, 98, 100 n 69, 102, 112, 115 n 86, 117, 121, 122, 132, 133
Yatseniuk, Arseniy 61, 119
Yushchenko, Andriy 73
Yushchenko, Viktor 11 n 2, 25, 47–49, 58, 61, 66–69, 72–74, 77, 81, 84, 86, 89–91, 99, 120, 122, 133

Z

Zahoor, Mohammad 102 n 73
Zakusylo, Mariana 97 n 64, 136
Zassoursky, Ivan 114
Zhuravsky, Vitaly 91
Zielonka, Jan 13 n 5, 16 n 7, 17, 32 n 16
Zimmer, Kerstin 32 n 16, 35–37, 42–44, 51, 53

Subject index

C

Censorship
  in-house 77, 78, 131
  self- 78, 78, 93
  temnyky 66, 66 n 32, 67, 133
Clientelism 35, 75
Coercion (use of law-enforcement agencies for political purposes)
  as informal norm 44, 45
  in politics-media relationships 76, 77, 79, 80
Concentration
  of media ownership 58, 64, 112–114, 116–119, 132, 133
  editorial 114, 115

D

Depoliticization 121, 122, 133
Digitilization 69, 79, 85
Dzhynsa; see hidden advertising (*dzhynsa*)

F

Formal institutions
  and informal institutions 32–38, 43, 52, 53, 57, 93, 94
  as a means to enforce informal institutions 37, 52
  poor quality and self-interest of institution-builders 31, 32, 36, 37, 46
  poor quality in transitional societies 36, 52, 53

H

Hidden advertising (*dzhynsa*) 70, 81, 81 n 51, 82, 134
Horizontal accountability
  deficit 35, 49, 51
  and dominance of informal institutions 35
  institutions and private interests of institution-builders 35, 38, 51
See also: judiciary

I

Informal institutions (informality) 32–34, 38, 52
  and democratization 25, 33, 38, 43
  and horizontal accountability 35
  and practices in media-politics relationships 75–77, 80, 81, 134
  and state/institution building 35
  definition of 32
  dominance over formal institutions 33, 45, 46
  and communist legacies 33, 34
  and quality of newly built formal institutions 51, 52
  enforcement of 37, 52
  resilience of 34–37
See also: clientelism, coercion (use of law-enforcement agencies for political purposes), hidden advertising (*dzhynsa*), patronage
Internet (see new media)

J

Judiciary
 changes in independence, in 1994–2013 48, 50, 79
 independence and dominance of informal institutions 35, 38, 52, 53, 128
 misuse as a means of media control 79, 80

M

Media
 democratization and cultural/historical legacies 29–31
 democratization and newly built institutions and structures 128–130, 134
 evolution in post-communist countries, diverging paths of 18, 59
 freedom scores, and their correlation with corruption rates 26, 26 n 12
Media capture 18, 20, 27, 55, 57–59, 66, 70, 75, 91, 104, 128
 agents of 59, 60, 66
 and informal influence on the media 57, 67
 definition of 57
 implications for media content 58, 70–72, 74, 77, 80, 114, 118, 119, 122
Media market
 barriers for market entry 116, 117
 dominance of politicized ownership at 60–63, 108, 130
 'overpopulation' 97, 116, 130
Media ownership
 changes in 68, 69
 concentration of 112, 113
 foreign (Russian) 103, 103 n 74
 foreign (Western) 102–104
 oligarchic 60, 63, 108
 politicized 108–110, 130
 state/municipal 98, 99

Media-related laws and regulations
 anti-monopoly 114
 attempts to tighten 87, 88, 90, 91
 frequent change of 90
 governing the broadcasting licensing procedure and the activity National Television and Radio Broadcasting Council 83, 85
 liberalism of 88
 on public service broadcasting 91, 92, 135
 on transparency of media ownership 91, 114 n 85, 135
 poor quality of/deficiencies in, and political control over media 36, 83, 85–87, 91
 regulating the National Expert Commission for the Protection of Public Morality 86, 87
 selective enforcement of, as a means of media control 90, 93, 94
Media regulatory and supervisory bodies
 See: National Television and Radio Broadcasting Council, National Expert Commission for the Protection of Public Morality

N

National Expert Commission for the Protection of Public Morality 86–88
 attempts to use for control over media 87, 88
National Television and Radio Broadcasting Council 63, 76, 78, 82–85, 90, 136
 misuse as a means of media control 84, 85
New media
 attempts to control 87, 88
 freedom 65, 136
 ownership 65, 102, 113

O

Oligarchs (oligarchy)
  and media ownership 60, 108, 112, 117, 118
  as media captors 70, 104, 111, 132
  control over media, methods 77, 78
  control over media, effects 70, 71, 74, 131
  impact on state institutions and institution-building 39–42, 45
  rise of 39, 40

P

Partisan polyvalence 74, 131
Patrimonialism and neo-patrimonialism 44, 129
Patronage 33, 43, 45, 46, 48, 67

R

Russian media 29, 105–107, 118
  presence on Ukrainian media market 105, 106
  products in Ukrainian media 105, 106, 108
  Ukrainians' trust in 106, 106 n 78

S

State
  and control over the media, effects 71–73
  and control over the media, means 66–69, 75–77
  as an aggregate of competing (economic, political, and bureaucratic) interests 66, 67
  neo-patrimonial 44, 45
  See also: state capture
State capture
  agents of 27, 39, 40, 42, 43
  and cultural/historical legacies 28–30
  and formation of disabling surrounding for democratic reforms 31, 32
  and media capture 27
  and partial reform equilibrium 27, 28
  and state- and institution building 31, 32
  and the amendments to the Constitution of Ukraine (2004 and 2010) 67, 68, 78
  definition of 26, 27

U

Ukraine
  impact of private interests 39–42
  institutional changes, in 1994–2013 45–50
  and changes in media freedom 45–50
  and dominance of informal institutions 50, 51
  and the amendments to the Constitution of Ukraine (2004 and 2010) 47–50
  main agents of 41, 42

Ukrainian media
  as a business, profitability of 65, 66
  commercialization 97, 108, 120, 121, 123, 124, 132, 133
  competition from Russian media 42
  concentration 58, 64, 113, 114, 120, 123, 132
  freedom, changes in, 1994–2013 30, 30 n 14, 46–50, 67, 68
  tabloidization 97, 120, 121, 123, 124, 133
See also: media capture, media market, media ownership, media-related laws and regulations, media regulatory and supervisory bodies

SOVIET AND POST-SOVIET POLITICS AND SOCIETY

Edited by Dr. Andreas Umland

ISSN 1614-3515

1   Андреас Умланд (ред.)
    Воплощение Европейской
    конвенции по правам человека в
    России
    Философские, юридические и
    эмпирические исследования
    ISBN 3-89821-387-0

2   Christian Wipperfürth
    Russland – ein vertrauenswürdiger
    Partner?
    Grundlagen, Hintergründe und Praxis
    gegenwärtiger russischer Außenpolitik
    Mit einem Vorwort von Heinz Timmermann
    ISBN 3-89821-401-X

3   Manja Hussner
    Die Übernahme internationalen Rechts
    in die russische und deutsche
    Rechtsordnung
    Eine vergleichende Analyse zur
    Völkerrechtsfreundlichkeit der Verfassungen
    der Russländischen Föderation und der
    Bundesrepublik Deutschland
    Mit einem Vorwort von Rainer Arnold
    ISBN 3-89821-438-9

4   Matthew Tejada
    Bulgaria's Democratic Consolidation
    and the Kozloduy Nuclear Power Plant
    (KNPP)
    The Unattainability of Closure
    With a foreword by Richard J. Crampton
    ISBN 3-89821-439-7

5   Марк Григорьевич Меерович
    Квадратные метры, определяющие
    сознание
    Государственная жилищная политика в
    СССР. 1921 – 1941 гг
    ISBN 3-89821-474-5

6   Andrei P. Tsygankov, Pavel
    A.Tsygankov (Eds.)
    New Directions in Russian
    International Studies
    ISBN 3-89821-422-2

7   Марк Григорьевич Меерович
    Как власть народ к труду приучала
    Жилище в СССР – средство управления
    людьми. 1917 – 1941 гг.
    С предисловием Елены Осокиной
    ISBN 3-89821-495-8

8   David J. Galbreath
    Nation-Building and Minority Politics
    in Post-Socialist States
    Interests, Influence and Identities in Estonia
    and Latvia
    With a foreword by David J. Smith
    ISBN 3-89821-467-2

9   Алексей Юрьевич Безугольный
    Народы Кавказа в Вооруженных
    силах СССР в годы Великой
    Отечественной войны 1941-1945 гг.
    С предисловием Николая Бугая
    ISBN 3-89821-475-3

10 Вячеслав Лихачев и Владимир
    Прибыловский (ред.)
    Русское Национальное Единство,
    1990-2000. В 2-х томах
    ISBN 3-89821-523-7

11 Николай Бугай (ред.)
    Народы стран Балтии в условиях
    сталинизма (1940-е – 1950-е годы)
    Документированная история
    ISBN 3-89821-525-3

12 Ingmar Bredies (Hrsg.)
    Zur Anatomie der Orange Revolution
    in der Ukraine
    Wechsel des Elitenregimes oder Triumph des
    Parlamentarismus?
    ISBN 3-89821-524-5

13 Anastasia V. Mitrofanova
    The Politicization of Russian
    Orthodoxy
    Actors and Ideas
    With a foreword by William C. Gay
    ISBN 3-89821-481-8

14 *Nathan D. Larson*
    Alexander Solzhenitsyn and the
    Russo-Jewish Question
    ISBN 3-89821-483-4

15 *Guido Houben*
    Kulturpolitik und Ethnizität
    Staatliche Kunstförderung im Russland der neunziger Jahre
    Mit einem Vorwort von Gert Weisskirchen
    ISBN 3-89821-542-3

16 *Leonid Luks*
    Der russische „Sonderweg"?
    Aufsätze zur neuesten Geschichte Russlands im europäischen Kontext
    ISBN 3-89821-496-6

17 *Евгений Мороз*
    История «Мёртвой воды» – от страшной сказки к большой политике
    Политическое неоязычество в постсоветской России
    ISBN 3-89821-551-2

18 *Александр Верховский и Галина Кожевникова (ред.)*
    Этническая и религиозная интолерантность в российских СМИ
    Результаты мониторинга 2001-2004 гг.
    ISBN 3-89821-569-5

19 *Christian Ganzer*
    Sowjetisches Erbe und ukrainische Nation
    Das Museum der Geschichte des Zaporoger Kosakentums auf der Insel Chortycja
    Mit einem Vorwort von Frank Golczewski
    ISBN 3-89821-504-0

20 *Эльза-Баир Гучинова*
    Помнить нельзя забыть
    Антропология депортационной травмы калмыков
    С предисловием Кэролайн Хамфри
    ISBN 3-89821-506-7

21 *Юлия Лидерман*
    Мотивы «проверки» и «испытания» в постсоветской культуре
    Советское прошлое в российском кинематографе 1990-х годов
    С предисловием Евгения Марголита
    ISBN 3-89821-511-3

22 *Tanya Lokshina, Ray Thomas, Mary Mayer (Eds.)*
    The Imposition of a Fake Political Settlement in the Northern Caucasus
    The 2003 Chechen Presidential Election
    ISBN 3-89821-436-2

23 *Timothy McCajor Hall, Rosie Read (Eds.)*
    Changes in the Heart of Europe
    Recent Ethnographies of Czechs, Slovaks, Roma, and Sorbs
    With an afterword by Zdeněk Salzmann
    ISBN 3-89821-606-3

24 *Christian Autengruber*
    Die politischen Parteien in Bulgarien und Rumänien
    Eine vergleichende Analyse seit Beginn der 90er Jahre
    Mit einem Vorwort von Dorothée de Nève
    ISBN 3-89821-476-1

25 *Annette Freyberg-Inan with Radu Cristescu*
    The Ghosts in Our Classrooms, or: John Dewey Meets Ceauşescu
    The Promise and the Failures of Civic Education in Romania
    ISBN 3-89821-416-8

26 *John B. Dunlop*
    The 2002 Dubrovka and 2004 Beslan Hostage Crises
    A Critique of Russian Counter-Terrorism
    With a foreword by Donald N. Jensen
    ISBN 3-89821-608-X

27 *Peter Koller*
    Das touristische Potenzial von Kam''janec'–Podil's'kyj
    Eine fremdenverkehrsgeographische Untersuchung der Zukunftsperspektiven und Maßnahmenplanung zur Destinationsentwicklung des „ukrainischen Rothenburg"
    Mit einem Vorwort von Kristiane Klemm
    ISBN 3-89821-640-3

28 *Françoise Daucé, Elisabeth Sieca-Kozlowski (Eds.)*
    Dedovshchina in the Post-Soviet Military
    Hazing of Russian Army Conscripts in a Comparative Perspective
    With a foreword by Dale Herspring
    ISBN 3-89821-616-0

29　*Florian Strasser*
Zivilgesellschaftliche Einflüsse auf die
Orange Revolution
Die gewaltlose Massenbewegung und die
ukrainische Wahlkrise 2004
Mit einem Vorwort von Egbert Jahn
ISBN 3-89821-648-9

30　*Rebecca S. Katz*
The Georgian Regime Crisis of 2003-
2004
A Case Study in Post-Soviet Media
Representation of Politics, Crime and
Corruption
ISBN 3-89821-413-3

31　*Vladimir Kantor*
Willkür oder Freiheit
Beiträge zur russischen Geschichtsphilosophie
Ediert von Dagmar Herrmann sowie mit
einem Vorwort versehen von Leonid Luks
ISBN 3-89821-589-X

32　*Laura A. Victoir*
The Russian Land Estate Today
A Case Study of Cultural Politics in Post-
Soviet Russia
With a foreword by Priscilla Roosevelt
ISBN 3-89821-426-5

33　*Ivan Katchanovski*
Cleft Countries
Regional Political Divisions and Cultures in
Post-Soviet Ukraine and Moldova
With a foreword by Francis Fukuyama
ISBN 3-89821-558-X

34　*Florian Mühlfried*
Postsowjetische Feiern
Das Georgische Bankett im Wandel
Mit einem Vorwort von Kevin Tuite
ISBN 3-89821-601-2

35　*Roger Griffin, Werner Loh, Andreas Umland (Eds.)*
Fascism Past and Present, West and East
An International Debate on Concepts and
Cases in the Comparative Study of the
Extreme Right
With an afterword by Walter Laqueur
ISBN 3-89821-674-8

36　*Sebastian Schlegel*
Der „Weiße Archipel"
Sowjetische Atomstädte 1945-1991
Mit einem Geleitwort von Thomas Bohn
ISBN 3-89821-679-9

37　*Vyacheslav Likhachev*
Political Anti-Semitism in Post-Soviet
Russia
Actors and Ideas in 1991-2003
Edited and translated from Russian by Eugene
Veklerov
ISBN 3-89821-529-6

38　*Josette Baer (Ed.)*
Preparing Liberty in Central Europe
Political Texts from the Spring of Nations
1848 to the Spring of Prague 1968
With a foreword by Zdeněk V. David
ISBN 3-89821-546-6

39　*Михаил Лукьянов*
Российский консерватизм и
реформа, 1907-1914
С предисловием Марка Д. Стейнберга
ISBN 3-89821-503-2

40　*Nicola Melloni*
Market Without Economy
The 1998 Russian Financial Crisis
With a foreword by Eiji Furukawa
ISBN 3-89821-407-9

41　*Dmitrij Chmelnizki*
Die Architektur Stalins
Bd. 1: Studien zu Ideologie und Stil
Bd. 2: Bilddokumentation
Mit einem Vorwort von Bruno Flierl
ISBN 3-89821-515-6

42　*Katja Yafimava*
Post-Soviet Russian-Belarussian
Relationships
The Role of Gas Transit Pipelines
With a foreword by Jonathan P. Stern
ISBN 3-89821-655-1

43　*Boris Chavkin*
Verflechtungen der deutschen und
russischen Zeitgeschichte
Aufsätze und Archivfunde zu den
Beziehungen Deutschlands und der
Sowjetunion von 1917 bis 1991
Ediert von Markus Edlinger sowie mit einem
Vorwort versehen von Leonid Luks
ISBN 3-89821-756-6

44 *Anastasija Grynenko in Zusammenarbeit mit Claudia Dathe*
    Die Terminologie des Gerichtswesens der Ukraine und Deutschlands im Vergleich
    Eine übersetzungswissenschaftliche Analyse juristischer Fachbegriffe im Deutschen, Ukrainischen und Russischen
    Mit einem Vorwort von Ulrich Hartmann
    ISBN 3-89821-691-8

45 *Anton Burkov*
    The Impact of the European Convention on Human Rights on Russian Law
    Legislation and Application in 1996-2006
    With a foreword by Françoise Hampson
    ISBN 978-3-89821-639-5

46 *Stina Torjesen, Indra Overland (Eds.)*
    International Election Observers in Post-Soviet Azerbaijan
    Geopolitical Pawns or Agents of Change?
    ISBN 978-3-89821-743-9

47 *Taras Kuzio*
    Ukraine – Crimea – Russia
    Triangle of Conflict
    ISBN 978-3-89821-761-3

48 *Claudia Šabić*
    "Ich erinnere mich nicht, aber L'viv!"
    Zur Funktion kultureller Faktoren für die Institutionalisierung und Entwicklung einer ukrainischen Region
    Mit einem Vorwort von Melanie Tatur
    ISBN 978-3-89821-752-1

49 *Marlies Bilz*
    Tatarstan in der Transformation
    Nationaler Diskurs und Politische Praxis 1988-1994
    Mit einem Vorwort von Frank Golczewski
    ISBN 978-3-89821-722-4

50 *Марлен Ларюэль (ред.)*
    Современные интерпретации русского национализма
    ISBN 978-3-89821-795-8

51 *Sonja Schüler*
    Die ethnische Dimension der Armut
    Roma im postsozialistischen Rumänien
    Mit einem Vorwort von Anton Sterbling
    ISBN 978-3-89821-776-7

52 *Галина Кожевникова*
    Радикальный национализм в России и противодействие ему
    Сборник докладов Центра «Сова» за 2004-2007 гг.
    С предисловием Александра Верховского
    ISBN 978-3-89821-721-7

53 *Галина Кожевникова и Владимир Прибыловский*
    Российская власть в биографиях I
    Высшие должностные лица РФ в 2004 г.
    ISBN 978-3-89821-796-5

54 *Галина Кожевникова и Владимир Прибыловский*
    Российская власть в биографиях II
    Члены Правительства РФ в 2004 г.
    ISBN 978-3-89821-797-2

55 *Галина Кожевникова и Владимир Прибыловский*
    Российская власть в биографиях III
    Руководители федеральных служб и агентств РФ в 2004 г.
    ISBN 978-3-89821-798-9

56 *Ileana Petroniu*
    Privatisierung in Transformationsökonomien
    Determinanten der Restrukturierungs-Bereitschaft am Beispiel Polens, Rumäniens und der Ukraine
    Mit einem Vorwort von Rainer W. Schäfer
    ISBN 978-3-89821-790-3

57 *Christian Wipperfürth*
    Russland und seine GUS-Nachbarn
    Hintergründe, aktuelle Entwicklungen und Konflikte in einer ressourcenreichen Region
    ISBN 978-3-89821-801-6

58 *Togzhan Kassenova*
    From Antagonism to Partnership
    The Uneasy Path of the U.S.-Russian Cooperative Threat Reduction
    With a foreword by Christoph Bluth
    ISBN 978-3-89821-707-1

59 *Alexander Höllwerth*
    Das sakrale eurasische Imperium des Aleksandr Dugin
    Eine Diskursanalyse zum postsowjetischen russischen Rechtsextremismus
    Mit einem Vorwort von Dirk Uffelmann
    ISBN 978-3-89821-813-9

60 Олег Рябов
    «Россия-Матушка»
    Национализм, гендер и война в России XX века
    С предисловием Елены Гощило
    ISBN 978-3-89821-487-2

61 Ivan Maistrenko
    Borot'bism
    A Chapter in the History of the Ukrainian Revolution
    With a new introduction by Chris Ford
    Translated by George S. N. Luckyj with the assistance of Ivan L. Rudnytsky
    ISBN 978-3-89821-697-5

62 Maryna Romanets
    Anamorphosic Texts and Reconfigured Visions
    Improvised Traditions in Contemporary Ukrainian and Irish Literature
    ISBN 978-3-89821-576-3

63 Paul D'Anieri and Taras Kuzio (Eds.)
    Aspects of the Orange Revolution I
    Democratization and Elections in Post-Communist Ukraine
    ISBN 978-3-89821-698-2

64 Bohdan Harasymiw in collaboration with Oleh S. Ilnytzkyj (Eds.)
    Aspects of the Orange Revolution II
    Information and Manipulation Strategies in the 2004 Ukrainian Presidential Elections
    ISBN 978-3-89821-699-9

65 Ingmar Bredies, Andreas Umland and Valentin Yakushik (Eds.)
    Aspects of the Orange Revolution III
    The Context and Dynamics of the 2004 Ukrainian Presidential Elections
    ISBN 978-3-89821-803-0

66 Ingmar Bredies, Andreas Umland and Valentin Yakushik (Eds.)
    Aspects of the Orange Revolution IV
    Foreign Assistance and Civic Action in the 2004 Ukrainian Presidential Elections
    ISBN 978-3-89821-808-5

67 Ingmar Bredies, Andreas Umland and Valentin Yakushik (Eds.)
    Aspects of the Orange Revolution V
    Institutional Observation Reports on the 2004 Ukrainian Presidential Elections
    ISBN 978-3-89821-809-2

68 Taras Kuzio (Ed.)
    Aspects of the Orange Revolution VI
    Post-Communist Democratic Revolutions in Comparative Perspective
    ISBN 978-3-89821-820-7

69 Tim Bohse
    Autoritarismus statt Selbstverwaltung
    Die Transformation der kommunalen Politik in der Stadt Kaliningrad 1990-2005
    Mit einem Geleitwort von Stefan Troebst
    ISBN 978-3-89821-782-8

70 David Rupp
    Die Rußländische Föderation und die russischsprachige Minderheit in Lettland
    Eine Fallstudie zur Anwaltspolitik Moskaus gegenüber den russophonen Minderheiten im „Nahen Ausland" von 1991 bis 2002
    Mit einem Vorwort von Helmut Wagner
    ISBN 978-3-89821-778-1

71 Taras Kuzio
    Theoretical and Comparative Perspectives on Nationalism
    New Directions in Cross-Cultural and Post-Communist Studies
    With a foreword by Paul Robert Magocsi
    ISBN 978-3-89821-815-3

72 Christine Teichmann
    Die Hochschultransformation im heutigen Osteuropa
    Kontinuität und Wandel bei der Entwicklung des postkommunistischen Universitätswesens
    Mit einem Vorwort von Oskar Anweiler
    ISBN 978-3-89821-842-9

73 Julia Kusznir
    Der politische Einfluss von Wirtschaftseliten in russischen Regionen
    Eine Analyse am Beispiel der Erdöl- und Erdgasindustrie, 1992-2005
    Mit einem Vorwort von Wolfgang Eichwede
    ISBN 978-3-89821-821-4

74 Alena Vysotskaya
    Russland, Belarus und die EU-Osterweiterung
    Zur Minderheitenfrage und zum Problem der Freizügigkeit des Personenverkehrs
    Mit einem Vorwort von Katlijn Malfliet
    ISBN 978-3-89821-822-1

75   Heiko Pleines (Hrsg.)
     Corporate Governance in post-
     sozialistischen Volkswirtschaften
     ISBN 978-3-89821-766-8

76   Stefan Ihrig
     Wer sind die Moldawier?
     Rumänismus versus Moldowanismus in
     Historiographie und Schulbüchern der
     Republik Moldova, 1991-2006
     Mit einem Vorwort von Holm Sundhaussen
     ISBN 978-3-89821-466-7

77   Galina Kozhevnikova in collaboration
     with Alexander Verkhovsky and
     Eugene Veklerov
     Ultra-Nationalism and Hate Crimes in
     Contemporary Russia
     The 2004-2006 Annual Reports of Moscow's
     SOVA Center
     With a foreword by Stephen D. Shenfield
     ISBN 978-3-89821-868-9

78   Florian Küchler
     The Role of the European Union in
     Moldova's Transnistria Conflict
     With a foreword by Christopher Hill
     ISBN 978-3-89821-850-4

79   Bernd Rechel
     The Long Way Back to Europe
     Minority Protection in Bulgaria
     With a foreword by Richard Crampton
     ISBN 978-3-89821-863-4

80   Peter W. Rodgers
     Nation, Region and History in Post-
     Communist Transitions
     Identity Politics in Ukraine, 1991-2006
     With a foreword by Vera Tolz
     ISBN 978-3-89821-903-7

81   Stephanie Solywoda
     The Life and Work of
     Semen L. Frank
     A Study of Russian Religious Philosophy
     With a foreword by Philip Walters
     ISBN 978-3-89821-457-5

82   Vera Sokolova
     Cultural Politics of Ethnicity
     Discourses on Roma in Communist
     Czechoslovakia
     ISBN 978-3-89821-864-1

83   Natalya Shevchik Ketenci
     Kazakhstani Enterprises in Transition
     The Role of Historical Regional Development
     in Kazakhstan's Post-Soviet Economic
     Transformation
     ISBN 978-3-89821-831-3

84   Martin Malek, Anna Schor-
     Tschudnowskaja (Hrsg.)
     Europa im Tschetschenienkrieg
     Zwischen politischer Ohnmacht und
     Gleichgültigkeit
     Mit einem Vorwort von Lipchan Basajewa
     ISBN 978-3-89821-676-0

85   Stefan Meister
     Das postsowjetische Universitätswesen
     zwischen nationalem und
     internationalem Wandel
     Die Entwicklung der regionalen Hochschule
     in Russland als Gradmesser der
     Systemtransformation
     Mit einem Vorwort von Joan DeBardeleben
     ISBN 978-3-89821-891-7

86   Konstantin Sheiko in collaboration
     with Stephen Brown
     Nationalist Imaginings of the
     Russian Past
     Anatolii Fomenko and the Rise of Alternative
     History in Post-Communist Russia
     With a foreword by Donald Ostrowski
     ISBN 978-3-89821-915-0

87   Sabine Jenni
     Wie stark ist das „Einige Russland"?
     Zur Parteibindung der Eliten und zum
     Wahlerfolg der Machtpartei
     im Dezember 2007
     Mit einem Vorwort von Klaus Armingeon
     ISBN 978-3-89821-961-7

88   Thomas Borén
     Meeting-Places of Transformation
     Urban Identity, Spatial Representations and
     Local Politics in Post-Soviet St Petersburg
     ISBN 978-3-89821-739-2

89   Aygul Ashirova
     Stalinismus und Stalin-Kult in
     Zentralasien
     Turkmenistan 1924-1953
     Mit einem Vorwort von Leonid Luks
     ISBN 978-3-89821-987-7

90 Leonid Luks
Freiheit oder imperiale Größe?
Essays zu einem russischen Dilemma
ISBN 978-3-8382-0011-8

91 Christopher Gilley
The 'Change of Signposts' in the
Ukrainian Emigration
A Contribution to the History of
Sovietophilism in the 1920s
With a foreword by Frank Golczewski
ISBN 978-3-89821-965-5

92 Philipp Casula, Jeronim Perovic
(Eds.)
Identities and Politics
During the Putin Presidency
The Discursive Foundations of Russia's
Stability
With a foreword by Heiko Haumann
ISBN 978-3-8382-0015-6

93 Marcel Viëtor
Europa und die Frage
nach seinen Grenzen im Osten
Zur Konstruktion ‚europäischer Identität' in
Geschichte und Gegenwart
Mit einem Vorwort von Albrecht Lehmann
ISBN 978-3-8382-0045-3

94 Ben Hellman, Andrei Rogachevskii
Filming the Unfilmable
Casper Wrede's 'One Day in the Life
of Ivan Denisovich'
Second, Revised and Expanded Edition
ISBN 978-3-8382-0044-6

95 Eva Fuchslocher
Vaterland, Sprache, Glaube
Orthodoxie und Nationenbildung
am Beispiel Georgiens
Mit einem Vorwort von Christina von Braun
ISBN 978-3-89821-884-9

96 Vladimir Kantor
Das Westlertum und der Weg
Russlands
Zur Entwicklung der russischen Literatur und
Philosophie
Ediert von Dagmar Herrmann
Mit einem Beitrag von Nikolaus Lobkowicz
ISBN 978-3-8382-0102-3

97 Kamran Musayev
Die postsowjetische Transformation
im Baltikum und Südkaukasus
Eine vergleichende Untersuchung der
politischen Entwicklung Lettlands und
Aserbaidschans 1985-2009
Mit einem Vorwort von Leonid Luks
Ediert von Sandro Henschel
ISBN 978-3-8382-0103-0

98 Tatiana Zhurzhenko
Borderlands into Bordered Lands
Geopolitics of Identity in Post-Soviet Ukraine
With a foreword by Dieter Segert
ISBN 978-3-8382-0042-2

99 Кирилл Галушко, Лидия Смола
(ред.)
Пределы падения – варианты
украинского будущего
Аналитико-прогностические исследования
ISBN 978-3-8382-0148-1

100 Michael Minkenberg (ed.)
Historical Legacies and the Radical
Right in Post-Cold War Central and
Eastern Europe
With an afterword by Sabrina P. Ramet
ISBN 978-3-8382-0124-5

101 David-Emil Wickström
Rocking St. Petersburg
Transcultural Flows and Identity Politics in
the St. Petersburg Popular Music Scene
With a foreword by Yngvar B. Steinholt
Second, Revised and Expanded Edition
ISBN 978-3-8382-0100-9

102 Eva Zabka
Eine neue „Zeit der Wirren"?
Der spät- und postsowjetische Systemwandel
1985-2000 im Spiegel russischer
gesellschaftspolitischer Diskurse
Mit einem Vorwort von Margareta Mommsen
ISBN 978-3-8382-0161-0

103 Ulrike Ziemer
Ethnic Belonging, Gender and
Cultural Practices
Youth Identitites in Contemporary Russia
With a foreword by Anoop Nayak
ISBN 978-3-8382-0152-8

104 Ksenia Chepikova
'Einiges Russland' - eine zweite
KPdSU?
Aspekte der Identitätskonstruktion einer
postsowjetischen „Partei der Macht"
Mit einem Vorwort von Torsten Oppelland
ISBN 978-3-8382-0311-9

105 Леонид Люкс
Западничество или евразийство?
Демократия или идеократия?
Сборник статей об исторических дилеммах
России
С предисловием Владимира Кантора
ISBN 978-3-8382-0211-2

106 Anna Dost
Das russische Verfassungsrecht auf dem
Weg zum Föderalismus und zurück
Zum Konflikt von Rechtsnormen und
-wirklichkeit in der Russländischen Föderation
von 1991 bis 2009
Mit einem Vorwort von Alexander Blankenagel
ISBN 978-3-8382-0292-1

107 Philipp Herzog
Sozialistische Völkerfreundschaft,
nationaler Widerstand oder harmloser
Zeitvertreib?
Zur politischen Funktion der Volkskunst
im sowjetischen Estland
Mit einem Vorwort von Andreas Kappeler
ISBN 978-3-8382-0216-7

108 Marlène Laruelle (ed.)
Russian Nationalism, Foreign Policy,
and Identity Debates in Putin's Russia
New Ideological Patterns after the Orange
Revolution
ISBN 978-3-8382-0325-6

109 Michail Logvinov
Russlands Kampf gegen den
internationalen Terrorismus
Eine kritische Bestandsaufnahme des
Bekämpfungsansatzes
Mit einem Geleitwort von
Hans-Henning Schröder
und einem Vorwort von Eckhard Jesse
ISBN 978-3-8382-0329-4

110 John B. Dunlop
The Moscow Bombings
of September 1999
Examinations of Russian Terrorist Attacks
at the Onset of Vladimir Putin's Rule
Second, Revised and Expanded Edition
ISBN 978-3-8382-0388-1

111 Андрей А. Ковалёв
Свидетельство из-за кулис
российской политики I
Можно ли делать добро из зла?
(Воспоминания и размышления о
последних советских и первых
постсоветских годах)
With a foreword by Peter Reddaway
ISBN 978-3-8382-0302-7

112 Андрей А. Ковалёв
Свидетельство из-за кулис
российской политики II
Угроза для себя и окружающих
(Наблюдения и предостережения
относительно происходящего после 2000 г.)
ISBN 978-3-8382-0303-4

113 Bernd Kappenberg
Zeichen setzen für Europa
Der Gebrauch europäischer lateinischer
Sonderzeichen in der deutschen Öffentlichkeit
Mit einem Vorwort von Peter Schlobinski
ISBN 978-3-89821-749-1

114 Ivo Mijnssen
The Quest for an Ideal Youth in
Putin's Russia I
Back to Our Future! History, Modernity, and
Patriotism according to Nashi, 2005-2013
With a foreword by Jeronim Perović
Second, Revised and Expanded Edition
ISBN 978-3-8382-0368-3

115 Jussi Lassila
The Quest for an Ideal Youth in
Putin's Russia II
The Search for Distinctive Conformism in the
Political Communication of Nashi, 2005-2009
With a foreword by Kirill Postoutenko
Second, Revised and Expanded Edition
ISBN 978-3-8382-0415-4

116 Valerio Trabandt
Neue Nachbarn, gute Nachbarschaft?
Die EU als internationaler Akteur am Beispiel
ihrer Demokratieförderung in Belarus und der
Ukraine 2004-2009
Mit einem Vorwort von Jutta Joachim
ISBN 978-3-8382-0437-6

117 *Fabian Pfeiffer*
Estlands Außen- und Sicherheitspolitik I
Der estnische Atlantizismus nach der
wiedererlangten Unabhängigkeit 1991-2004
Mit einem Vorwort von Helmut Hubel
ISBN 978-3-8382-0127-6

118 *Jana Podßuweit*
Estlands Außen- und Sicherheitspolitik II
Handlungsoptionen eines Kleinstaates im
Rahmen seiner EU-Mitgliedschaft (2004-2008)
Mit einem Vorwort von Helmut Hubel
ISBN 978-3-8382-0440-6

119 *Karin Pointner*
Estlands Außen- und Sicherheitspolitik III
Eine gedächtnispolitische Analyse estnischer
Entwicklungskooperation 2006-2010
Mit einem Vorwort von Karin Liebhart
ISBN 978-3-8382-0435-2

120 *Ruslana Vovk*
Die Offenheit der ukrainischen
Verfassung für das Völkerrecht und
die europäische Integration
Mit einem Vorwort von Alexander
Blankenagel
ISBN 978-3-8382-0481-9

121 *Mykhaylo Banakh*
Die Relevanz der Zivilgesellschaft
bei den postkommunistischen
Transformationsprozessen in mittel-
und osteuropäischen Ländern
Das Beispiel der spät- und postsowjetischen
Ukraine 1986-2009
Mit einem Vorwort von Gerhard Simon
ISBN 978-3-8382-0499-4

122 *Michael Moser*
Language Policy and the Discourse on
Languages in Ukraine under President
Viktor Yanukovych (25 February
2010–28 October 2012)
ISBN 978-3-8382-0497-0 (Paperback edition)
ISBN 978-3-8382-0507-6 (Hardcover edition)

123 *Nicole Krome*
Russischer Netzwerkkapitalismus
Restrukturierungsprozesse in der
Russischen Föderation am Beispiel des
Luftfahrtunternehmens "Aviastar"
Mit einem Vorwort von Petra Stykow
ISBN 978-3-8382-0534-2

124 *David R. Marples*
'Our Glorious Past'
Lukashenka's Belarus and
the Great Patriotic War
ISBN 978-3-8382-0574-8 (Paperback edition)
ISBN 978-3-8382-0675-2 (Hardcover edition)

125 *Ulf Walther*
Russlands "neuer Adel"
Die Macht des Geheimdienstes von
Gorbatschow bis Putin
Mit einem Vorwort von Hans-Georg Wieck
ISBN 978-3-8382-0584-7

126 *Simon Geissbühler (Hrsg.)*
Kiew – Revolution 3.0
Der Euromaidan 2013/14 und die
Zukunftsperspektiven der Ukraine
ISBN 978-3-8382-0581-6 (Paperback edition)
ISBN 978-3-8382-0681-3 (Hardcover edition)

127 *Andrey Makarychev*
Russia and the EU
in a Multipolar World
Discourses, Identities, Norms
With a foreword by Klaus Segbers
ISBN 978-3-8382-0629-5

128 *Roland Scharff*
Kasachstan als postsowjetischer
Wohlfahrtsstaat
Die Transformation des sozialen
Schutzsystems
Mit einem Vorwort von Joachim Ahrens
ISBN 978-3-8382-0622-6

129 *Katja Grupp*
Bild Lücke Deutschland
Kaliningrader Studierende sprechen über
Deutschland
Mit einem Vorwort von Martin Schulz
ISBN 978-3-8382-0552-6

130 *Konstantin Sheiko, Stephen Brown*
History as Therapy
Alternative History and Nationalist
Imaginings in Russia, 1991-2014
ISBN 978-3-8382-0665-3

131 *Elisa Kriza*
Alexander Solzhenitsyn: Cold War
Icon, Gulag Author, Russian
Nationalist?
A Study of the Western Reception of his
Literary Writings, Historical Interpretations,
and Political Ideas
With a foreword by Andrei Rogatchevski
ISBN 978-3-8382-0589-2 (Paperback edition)
ISBN 978-3-8382-0690-5 (Hardcover edition)

132 Serghei Golunov
     The Elephant in the Room
     Corruption and Cheating in Russian
     Universities
     ISBN 978-3-8382-0570-0

133 Manja Hussner, Rainer Arnold (Hgg.)
     Verfassungsgerichtsbarkeit in
     Zentralasien I
     Sammlung von Verfassungstexten
     ISBN 978-3-8382-0595-3

134 Nikolay Mitrokhin
     Die "Russische Partei"
     Die Bewegung der russischen Nationalisten in
     der UdSSR 1953-1985
     Aus dem Russischen übertragen von einem
     Übersetzerteam unter der Leitung von Larisa Schippel
     ISBN 978-3-8382-0024-8

135 Manja Hussner, Rainer Arnold (Hgg.)
     Verfassungsgerichtsbarkeit in
     Zentralasien II
     Sammlung von Verfassungstexten
     ISBN 978-3-8382-0597-7

136 Manfred Zeller
     Das sowjetische Fieber
     Fußballfans im poststalinistischen
     Vielvölkerreich
     Mit einem Vorwort von Nikolaus Katzer
     ISBN 978-3-8382-0757-5

137 Kristin Schreiter
     Stellung und Entwicklungspotential
     zivilgesellschaftlicher Gruppen in
     Russland
     Menschenrechtsorganisationen im Vergleich
     ISBN 978-3-8382-0673-8

138 David R. Marples, Frederick V. Mills
     (eds.)
     Ukraine's Euromaidan
     Analyses of a Civil Revolution
     ISBN 978-3-8382-0660-8

139 Bernd Kappenberg
     Setting Signs for Europe
     Why Diacritics Matter for
     European Integration
     With a foreword by Peter Schlobinski
     ISBN 978-3-8382-0663-9

140 René Lenz
     Internationalisierung, Kooperation
     und Transfer
     Externe bildungspolitische Akteure in der
     Russischen Föderation
     Mit einem Vorwort von Frank Ettrich
     ISBN 978-3-8382-0751-3

141 Juri Plusnin, Yana Zausaeva, Natalia
     Zhidkevich, Artemy Pozanenko
     Wandering Workers
     Mores, Behavior, Way of Life, and Political
     Status of Domestic Russian Labor Migrants
     Translated by Julia Kazantseva
     ISBN 978-3-8382-0653-0

142 Matthew Kott, David J. Smith (eds.)
     Latvia – A Work in Progress?
     100 Years of State- and Nation-building
     ISBN 978-3-8382-0648-6

143 Инна Чувычкина (ред.)
     Экспортные нефте- и газопроводы
     на постсоветском пространстве
     Анализ трубопроводной политики в свете
     теории международных отношений
     ISBN 978-3-8382-0822-0

144 Johann Zajaczkowski
     Russland – eine pragmatische
     Großmacht?
     Eine rollentheoretische Untersuchung
     russischer Außenpolitik am Beispiel der
     Zusammenarbeit mit den USA nach 9/11 und
     des Georgienkrieges von 2008
     Mit einem Vorwort von Siegfried Schieder
     ISBN 978-3-8382-0837-4

145 Boris Popivanov
     Changing Images of the Left in
     Bulgaria
     The Challenge of Post-Communism in the
     Early 21st Century
     ISBN 978-3-8382-0667-7

146 Lenka Krátká
     A History of the Czechoslovak Ocean
     Shipping Company 1948-1989
     How a Small, Landlocked Country Ran
     Maritime Business During the Cold War
     ISBN 978-3-8382-0666-0

147 Alexander Sergunin
     Explaining Russian Foreign Policy
     Behavior
     Theory and Practice
     ISBN 978-3-8382-0752-0

148 Darya Malyutina
     Migrant Friendships in
     a Super-Diverse City
     Russian-Speakers and their Social
     Relationships in London in the 21st Century
     With a foreword by Claire Dwyer
     ISBN 978-3-8382-0652-3

149 Alexander Sergunin, Valery Konyshev
     Russia in the Arctic
     Hard or Soft Power?
     ISBN 978-3-8382-0753-7

150 John J. Maresca
     Helsinki Revisited
     A Key U.S. Negotiator's Memoirs
     on the Development of the CSCE into the OSCE
     With a foreword by Hafiz Pashayev
     ISBN 978-3-8382-0852-7

151 Jardar Østbø
     The New Third Rome
     Readings of a Russian Nationalist Myth
     With a foreword by Pål Kolstø
     ISBN 978-3-8382-0870-1

152 Simon Kordonsky
     Socio-Economic Foundations of the
     Russian Post-Soviet Regime
     The Resource-Based Economy and Estate-
     Based Social Structure of Contemporary
     Russia
     With a foreword by Svetlana Barsukova
     ISBN 978-3-8382-0775-9

153 Duncan Leitch
     Assisting Reform in Post-Communist
     Ukraine 2000–2012
     The Illusions of Donors and the Disillusion of
     Beneficiaries
     With a foreword by Kataryna Wolczuk
     ISBN 978-3-8382-0844-2

154 Abel Polese
     Limits of a Post-Soviet State
     How Informality Replaces, Renegotiates, and
     Reshapes Governance in Contemporary
     Ukraine
     With a foreword by Colin Williams
     ISBN 978-3-8382-0845-9

155 Mikhail Suslov (ed.)
     Digital Orthodoxy in the Post-Soviet
     World
     The Russian Orthodox Church and Web 2.0
     With a foreword by Father Cyril Hovorun
     ISBN 978-3-8382-0871-8

156 Leonid Luks
     Zwei „Sonderwege"? Russisch-
     deutsche Parallelen und Kontraste
     (1917-2014)
     Vergleichende Essays
     ISBN 978-3-8382-0823-7

157 Vladimir V. Karacharovskiy, Ovsey I.
     Shkaratan, Gordey A. Yastrebov
     Towards a New Russian Work Culture
     Can Western Companies and Expatriates
     Change Russian Society?
     With a foreword by Elena N. Danilova
     Translated by Julia Kazantseva
     ISBN 978-3-8382-0902-9

158 Edmund Griffiths
     Aleksandr Prokhanov and Post-Soviet
     Esotericism
     ISBN 978-3-8382-0903-6

159 Timm Beichelt, Susann Worschech
     (eds.)
     Transnational Ukraine?
     Networks and Ties that Influence(d)
     Contemporary Ukraine
     ISBN 978-3-8382-0944-9

160 Mieste Hotopp-Riecke
     Die Tataren der Krim zwischen
     Assimilation und Selbstbehauptung
     Der Aufbau des krimtatarischen
     Bildungswesens nach Deportation und
     Heimkehr (1990-2005)
     Mit einem Vorwort von Swetlana
     Czerwonnaja
     ISBN 978-3-89821-940-2

161 Olga Bertelsen (ed.)
     Revolution and War in
     Contemporary Ukraine
     The Challenge of Change
     ISBN 978-3-8382-1016-2

162 Natalya Ryabinska
     Ukraine's Post-Communist
     Mass Media
     Between Capture and Commercialization
     With a foreword by Marta Dyczok
     ISBN 978-3-8382-1011-7

ibidem.eu